DISKI 320

W0040507

DISKI
Dissertationen zur Künstlichen Intelligenz

Mit Unterstützung des Fachbereichs 1 „Künstliche Intelligenz" der
Gesellschaft für Informatik e.V. herausgegeben von

Editor-in-Chief: Wolfgang Bibel

K.-D. Althoff, Hildesheim	W. Kropatsch, Wien
F. Baader, Dresden	R. Kruse, Magdeburg
C. Beierle, Hagen	E. Lehmann, Stuttgart
W. Bibel, Darmstadt	K. Mainzer, Augsburg
W. Brauer, München	B. Mertsching, Paderborn
G. Brewka, Leipzig	C. Möbus, Oldenburg
H. Bunke, Bern	K. Morik, Dortmund
H.-D. Burkhard, Berlin	H.-H. Nagel, Karlsruhe
Th. Christaller, Sankt Augustin	B. Nebel, Freiburg
W. Coy, Berlin	B. Neumann, Hamburg
A. B. Cremers, Bonn	H. Niemann, Erlangen
P. Deussen, Karlsruhe	F. Puppe, Würzburg
W. Dilger, Chemnitz	B. Radig, München
R. Dillmann, Karlsruhe	L. De Raedt, Leuven
L. Dreschler-Fischer, Hamburg	M. M. Richter, Kaiserslautern
Chr. Freksa, Bremen	H. Ritter, Bielefeld
U. Furbach, Koblenz	C. Rollinger, Osnabrück
J. Fürnkranz, Darmstadt	G. Sagerer, Bielefeld
U. Geske, Berlin	T. Schaub, Potsdam
T. Gordon, Berlin	M. Schmidt-Schauss, Frankfurt/M
G. Görz, Erlangen	J. H. Siekmann, Saarbrücken
G. Gottlob, Oxford	G. Smolka, Saarbrücken
Chr. Habel, Hamburg	H. S. Stiehl, Hamburg
W. von Hahn, Hamburg	H. Stoyan, Erlangen
K. Harbusch, Koblenz	G. Strube, Freiburg
J. Hertzberg, Osnabrück	R. Studer, Karlsruhe
O. Herzog, Bremen	P. Struss, München
W. Hoeppner, Duisburg	M. Thielscher, Dresden
S. Hölldobler, Dresden	R. Trappl, Wien
H.H. Hoos, Vancouver	I. Wachsmuth, Bielefeld
K. P. Jantke, Leipzig	W. Wahlster, Saarbrücken
M. Jarke, Aachen	Chr. Walther, Darmstadt
A. Kobsa, Irvine	R. Wiehagen, Kaiserslautern
M. Kohlhase, Bremen	S. Wrobel, Bonn
C. Kreitz, Potsdam	

An Agent Control Perspective on Qualitative Spatial Reasoning

Towards More Intuitive Spatial Agent Development

Frank Dylla

Frank Dylla
SFB/TR 8 – Spatial Cognition
Universität Bremen
Enrique-Schmidt-Straße 5
28359 Bremen
Germany

Dissertation zur Erlangung des Grades eines
Doktors der Ingenieurwissenschaften (Dr.-Ing.)
Vorgelegt im Fachbereich 3 (Mathematik und Informatik)
der Universität Bremen im Januar 2008

Gutachter: Prof. Christian Freksa, Ph.D. (Universität Bremen)
                 Prof. Gerhard Lakemeyer, Ph.D. (RWTH Aachen)

Datum des Promotionskolloquiums: 29.02.2008

SFB/TR 8 Monographs Volume 5
Monograph Series of the Transregional Collaborative Research Center SFB/TR 8
Thomas Barkowsky, Christian Freksa, Christoph Hölscher, Bernd
Krieg-Brückner, Bernhard Nebel (series editors).

Bibliographic information published by *Die Deutsche Bibliothek*
Die Deutsche Bibliothek lists this publication in the *Deutsche Nationalbibliografie*;
Detailed bibliographic data is available on the Internet at http://dnb.ddb.de.

© 2008, Akademische Verlagsgesellschaft Aka GmbH, Heidelberg

Akademische Verlagsgesellschaft Aka GmbH

Postfach 103305
69023 Heidelberg
Tel.: 06221 21881
Fax: 06221 167355
info@aka-verlag.de

All rights reserved. No part of this publication may be reproduced, stored in a retrieval
system, or transmitted, in any form or by any means, electronic, mechanical,
photocopying, recording, or otherwise, without prior permission from the publisher.

Reproduced from PDF supplied by the author
Printed in the Netherlands

ISSN 0941-5769
ISBN 978-3-89838-320-2 (Aka)
ISBN 978-1-58603-914-1 (IOS Press)

Zusammenfassung

Ein großer Teil der Interaktionen im täglichen Leben von Menschen wird von Regeln und Konventionen bestimmt. Dies beinhaltet zum Beispiel wie man sich im Strassenverkehr oder an Bushaltestellen verhalten muss, bzw. soll. Eine gemeinsame Eigenschaft solcher Regeln ist, dass sie normalerweise in natürlicher Sprache formuliert sind und daher viele qualitative Begriffe, wie "von links", "rechts abbiegen", oder "in Kollisionsgefahr", verwenden, um räumliche Situationen zu beschreiben. Welches Verhalten als korrekt bzw. sinnvoll erachtet wird, wird nicht unbedingt nur durch die räumliche Beziehung der Objekte untereinander, sondern auch durch andere Eigenschaften der Objekte bestimmt. Zum Beispiel wird im Strassenverkehr von Fußgängern anderes Verhalten erwartet als von Personen in Fahrzeugen.

Agenten, die sich in solchen Umfeldern bewegen, müssen sich solcher Regeln bewusst sein und sich entsprechend verhalten können. In dieser Arbeit beschäftigen wir uns mit der Frage, wie man solche Regelsysteme mit Methoden des *qualitativen räumlichen Schließens* (QSR) formalisieren kann und diese Formalisierung zur regelkonformen Steuerung von Agenten einsetzen kann.

Da die relative Orientierung zwischen Objekten aus unserer Sicht der wichtigste räumliche Aspekt zur Steuerung von Agenten ist, entwickeln wir ein allgemeines Kalkül zur Darstellung solcher Informationen. Wir zeigen, dass das auf orientierten Punkten basierende Kalkül $\mathcal{OPRA}_m$ das zur Zeit ausdrucksstärkste relative Orientierungskalkül ist. Wir zeigen dies, indem wir andere Orientierungskalküle, wie z.B. das FlipFlop Kalkül oder das Doppelkreuz Kalkül, auf Mengen von $\mathcal{OPRA}_m$-Relationen abbilden und mit Hilfe dieser Abbildungen Relationen zwischen verschiedenen Kalkülen übersetzen, die Kompositionstabelle des Ursprungskalküls bestimmen, sowie dessen konzeptuelle Nachbarschaftsstruktur ableiten. Dafür entwickeln wir einen Kompositionsalgorithmus für $\mathcal{OPRA}_m$-Relationen und untersuchen die Eigenschaften dieser Komposition. Wir zeigen, dass mit Hilfe der Komposition nicht alle inkonsistenten Teilkonfigurationen erkannt werden können (closure under constraints). Daher führen wir zusätzliche Operationen ein, damit diese Inkonsistenzen effektiv erkannt werden können.

Mit $\mathcal{OPRA}_m$ und anderen relativen Orientierungskalkülen ist es nur in eingeschränkter Art und Weise möglich zu repräsentieren, ob sich zwei Objekte in die gleiche oder entgegengesetzte Richtung bewegen, sich voneinander weg bewegen, oder sich aufeinander zu bewegen (*alignment knowledge*). Dieses Wissen ist in vielen Situationen der Agentenkontrolle sehr wichtig. Daher entwickeln wir ein spezielles Kalkül ($\mathcal{AC}$) und vereinigen es mit $\mathcal{OPRA}_m$ zu $\mathcal{OPRA}_m^\star$. Da die Komposition basierend auf den individuellen Kompositionstabellen nicht die beste Komposition ergibt, optimieren wir diese mit Hilfe von Ungleichungssystemen, die bestimmte geometrische Eigenschaften der Relationen formalisieren.

Um Agenten steuern zu können, erweitern wir das Modell der konzeptuellen Nachbarschaft, da es in seiner ursprünglichen Form zu unspezifische Informationen über mögliche Veränderungen in der Welt enthält. Wir untersuchen den Einfluss verschiedener Aspekte, zum Beispiel die Bewegungsmöglichkeiten von Agenten, auf die Nachbarschaftsrelationen und reichern den konzeptuellen Nachbarschaftsgraphen mit diesen Informationen an (action-augmented conceptual neighborhood graph).

Des Weiteren können fehlerhafte Sensorwahrnehmungen zu Widersprüchen mit bereits vorhandenem Wissen führen, d.h. das qualitative Weltmodell ist inkonsistent. Dadurch wird das Modell unbrauchbar, da man nicht bestimmen kann, welche Teile die Inkonsistenz verursachen. Wir stellen ein Verfahren zur Auflösung solcher Inkonsistenzen vor, das in Bezug auf verschiedene Nachbarschaftsdistanzen nur eine minimale Anzahl von Veränderungen in dem Weltmodell vornimmt (minimal constraint network relaxation).

Wir benutzen den erweiterten konzeptuellen Nachbarschaftsgraphen, um Kollisionsvermeidungsregeln in sogenannten Regel-Transitionssystemen (rule transition systems) zu formalisieren. Wenn mehrere Agenten aufeinander treffen, werden mögliche Aktionen und ihre Effekte auf Basis dieser Transitionssysteme bestimmt und in einem Abhängigkeitsgraphen zusammengefasst. Wir zeigen, dass im Falle eines konsistenten Graphen regelkonforme Aktionen für alle Agenten generiert werden können. Sonst widersprechen sich die angewendeten Regeln und es können keine Aktionen generiert werden, die allen Regeln genügen. Wir demonstrieren die Eignung unseres Ansatzes zur Steuerung von Agenten in einem Simulator im Rahmen von Kollisionsvermeidungsregeln in der Schifffahrt (SailAway).

Abstract

A considerable part of everyday human interaction is guided by regulations and constraints, for example, regulations on how to behave in traffic scenarios or how to behave at bus stops. These rules have in common that they are usually formulated in natural language and, hence, extensively use *qualitative terms*, such as 'to the left', 'turn right' or 'in danger of collision', to describe spatial situations and actions. In addition, which behavior is considered to be correct for a certain agent may not only depend on the spatial situation at hand, but also on the current role of an agent in a particular situation. For example, what an agent is allowed to do may depend on whether she is a pedestrian or whether she is using a vehicle.

Agents acting in such environments must not only be aware of these rules, but also must be able to process them correctly. In this thesis we deal with the question how rule systems can be formalized by means of methods from qualitative spatial reasoning (QSR), and how these formalizations can be applied to control agents.

From our point of view relative orientation between objects is the most important aspect for agent control. We develop a general calculus for representing relative orientation. We show that the calculus $\mathcal{OPRA}_m$ based on oriented points is the most expressive calculus currently defined. We do this by mapping other orientation calculi, for example, the FlipFlop Calculus or the Double Cross Calculus, to sets of $\mathcal{OPRA}_m$ relations, so that we can apply these mappings to mediate between different calculi, to derive the composition table of the original calculus, and to determine the conceptual neighborhood structure. To this end, we develop a composition algorithm for $\mathcal{OPRA}_m$ relations and investigate reasoning properties of the composition. As the composition is not "closed under constraints", we introduce additional operations to be able to identify inconsistent configurations effectively.

$\mathcal{OPRA}_m$ and other relative orientation calculi only have a limited expressiveness to represent whether two objects move in the same direction, move in the opposite direction, move away from each other, or move towards each other (*alignment knowledge*). This kind of knowledge is very important in terms of agent control in many situations. Hence, we develop a specialized calculus ($\mathcal{AC}$) and combine it with $\mathcal{OPRA}_m$ to $\mathcal{OPRA}_m^\star$. As the composition based on the individual composition operations is not optimal, we optimize it by means of sets of inequalities representing certain geometric properties.

We extend the concept of conceptual neighborhood for controlling agents, because currently the concept does not contain information specific enough regarding how the world might evolve. We investigate the impact of different aspects, for example, the motion capabilities of agents, on neighborhood relations and augment the conceptual neighborhood graph with this information (action-augmented conceptual neighborhood graph).

Furthermore, inaccurate sensor perceptions might lead to inconsistencies with information gathered previously, i.e. the qualitative world model is inconsistent. This turns the complete world model useless for further applications, because it is not possible to derive which fragments caused the inconsistency. We present a method for dissolving such inconsistencies with a minimal number of modifications regarding different neighborhood distance measures (minimal constraint network relaxation).

We utilize the action-augmented conceptual neighborhood graph to formalize collision regulations in so-called *rule transition systems*. If multiple agents meet, potential actions and their effects are determined on the basis of these rule transition systems and combined in a constraint network. We show that, if the constraint network is consistent, we can generate rule-compliant actions for all agents. Otherwise, some of the applied rules conflict, and we cannot generate actions that are in compliance with all rules. We demonstrate the applicability of our approach to navigating agents in a simulated environment in accordance to collision regulations in vessel navigation (SailAway).

Acknowledgement — Danksagung

Writing this thesis took considerable time and effort. During this time, there have been many people that helped me in one way or another. Several of them deserve my special thanks.

First, many sincere thanks to Christian Freksa, my advisor, for his ongoing encouragement and support. I deeply enjoyed the openminded, interdisciplinary research environment that he created. He has given me great freedom in pursuing new ideas and directions, and has always been there if I needed advice. Our discussions and his comments helped me very much in sharpening and focusing my ideas.

Also, many thanks to Gerhard Lakemeyer, who already believed in me when I was an undergraduate student, and helped me with my first steps in science.

I like to express my gratitude to all people who influenced my work during the last years, gave me insights in discussions, and thus, brought me into the position that I was able to write this thesis. Parts of this work have been presented at conferences and workshops. Several colleagues world-wide provided feedback on these occasions either as reviewers or in discussions at these events.

Thanks to all colleagues and friends at the Cognitive Systems department at Universität Bremen for the excellent and inspiring working conditions. A very special thanks to my colleagues Diedrich Wolter, Jan Oliver Wallgrün, and Lutz Frommberger from the R3 project for their cooperation and inspiring ideas concerning my research. In addition, I thank Reinhard Moratz for introducing oriented points and developing $\mathcal{OPRA}_m$. I address further thanks for collaboration and interesting discussions to Alexander Ferrein, Stefan Schiffer, Nico van de Weghe, Stefan Wölfl, and Bernhard Nebel.

For digging through my thesis and deskewing my cumbersome English with great effort I like to thank the proof readers Kai-Florian Richter, Holger Schultheis, and Wim Holtmann for their excellent work.

Financial support for my research by the Deutsche Forschungsgesellschaft in the R3-[Q-Shape] project of the SFB/TR 8 Spatial Cognition (2003-2008) and in a project of the SPP 1125 (2002-2003) is gratefully acknowledged.

In addition, I want to thank my parents for giving me the opportunity to attend university, and supporting me at all times.

Finally, I owe much to my partner Berit. It is hard to express how much I appreciate her support. I am deeply in debt to her for all her emotional support, her belief in me, for tolerating my moods, and her love. I dedicate my thesis to her.

To Berit

Contents

List of Figures

List of Tables

Chapter 1

Introduction

In this chapter we give the motivation for the work presented in this thesis. Heaving the long-term goal of integrating techniques from qualitative spatial reasoning (QSR) and reasoning about action and change (RAC) in mind, the goal of this thesis is to investigate QSR techniques with respect to actions and their effects. We present the cornerstones and problems on our way to an effective qualitative approach to control agents. We end the chapter with an outline of the organization of the remainder of this thesis.

1.1 Motivation

A considerable part of everyday human interaction is guided by regulations, for example regulations on how to behave in traffic scenarios, recommendations on how to use escalators, rules on how to enter subways and buses, rules of politeness at bottlenecks in traffic situations, in sports, in games, in expert recommendation systems, and so on. Generally speaking, behavior is restricted by conditions and constraints. Nowadays, we find more and more robotic systems in everyday life. Robotic systems are also known as autonomous agent systems.

Representatives of autonomous agent systems are, for example, robots supporting elderly people care or house keeping, toys for playing with children, and driver assistance systems in traffic vehicles. A general task that all these systems need to cope with is interacting with the environment, including other agents. This especially includes acting in space and communicating about space. Agents that have to solve navigational tasks need to consider aspects that go far beyond single-agent goal-directed deliberation: what an agent does in a specific situation often interferes with what other agents do at the same time. In order to avoid conflicts or even collisions, agents must be aware that situations in space are governed by laws, rules, and agreements between the involved agents. Therefore, artificial agents interacting with humans need not only to be aware of these regulations, but also must be able to process them.

Examples of such sets of rules are traffic regulations, e.g. if two cars meet at an intersection, the car from the right having the right of way and the car from the left having to obey this right of way. Another example: collision regulations in vessel navigation, e.g. if two motor boats are in head-on or nearly head-on position, one navigational rule prescribes that both boats need to turn starboard[1] and pass on the port side of the other.

These rules have in common that they are usually formulated in natural language and hence extensively use *qualitative terms* like 'to the left', 'turn right' or 'in danger of collision', to describe spatial situations and actions. For example, in traffic laws qualitative concepts are used to describe relevant situations and also the "correct" behavior of agents in these situations. In a right of way road traffic scenario the correct behavior of the vehicle giving way is partially given by 'taking clear action to show that she will be waiting, especially by moderate speed'. In addition, which behavior is considered to be correct for a certain agent may not only depend on the spatial situation at hand, but also on the current *role* of an agent in a particular situation. What an agent is allowed to do may depend on whether she is a pedestrian or whether she is using a vehicle, and if so, which kind of vehicle.

In contrast, quantitative data are values measured in quantities, e.g. $90°$, turn $270°$, or 250 meters. Although robot systems rely on metric data concerning sensory input and motor control, implementing such rule sets in agent systems based on pure metric data is in most cases a complicated and error-prone undertaking. Providing agent developers with auxiliary methods and tools for making such tasks less complicated and thus, less error-prone, is an expedient objective.

The problem of formalizing agent behavior regarding a specific set of regulations must be considered from two different standpoints. First, what are adequate qualitative spatial representations for the formalization and how can we reason with these representations. Second, what actions should the agent perform to achieve behavior which is in compliance with the regulations? Answers to the first aspect can be found in the area of *Qualitative Spatial Representation and Reasoning*, and to the second in the area of *Reasoning about Action and Change*.

Qualitative Spatial Reasoning[2]   is an established field of research investigating qualitative representations of space that abstract from the details of the physical world together with reasoning techniques that allow predictions about spatial relations, even when precise quantitative information is not available (Cohn, 1997). QSR includes investigations of human understanding of space, qualitative representations of different spatial aspects (e.g. orientation, topology, size), and mathematical properties of operations for manipulating and combining the represented knowledge. A qualitative description is one that captures distinctions that make an important, qualitative

---

[1]*Starboard* is the nautical term that refers to the right side of a vessel with respect to its *bow* (front); *port* refers to the left hand side, *stern* to the back.

[2]As reasoning is not possible without representation we will not distinguish between them generally in the remainder of this thesis. That is, we shall refer to qualitative spatial representation or qualitative spatial reasoning only.

difference, and ignores others. Cohn & Hazarika (2001b) summarize the essence of qualitative spatial reasoning as finding ways to represent continuous properties of the world by discrete systems of symbols, i.e. with a limited set of vocabulary. These symbols describe the relationships between objects in a specific domain. Therefore, such a symbol is called a *relation*. A complete model for a certain domain is called a *qualitative calculus*. It consists of the set of relations between objects from this domain and the operations defined on these relations. Examples for operations are union, converse, and composition. The relations of a spatial calculus are often used to formulate constraints about the spatial configuration of objects from the domain of the calculus.

Reasoning about Action and Change Within the RAC community several high-level frameworks have been presented for supporting agent development. Physical agents interacting with their environment are expected to show reasonable behavior in order to solve a given task. In order to do so any given physical agent has to make plans and monitor changes in the world caused by the agents itself or by the other agents present in that world, meanwhile executing its plans and possibly anticipating plans of other agents. Agents' plans are formulated on the basis of actions of agents or events in the world which change certain properties of the world. That is, complex behavior modeling can be abstracted from low-level control. The term 'low-level control' refers to all processes which deal with the underlying system, e.g. motor control, self-localization or object perception. High-level control coordinates the low-level processes, i.e. it derives a plan to achieve the robot's overall goals. Although it is possible to use metrical (quantitative) data within these frameworks, high-level control is based on abstract symbols. It describes properties of the world and actions within the world, which frequently only can be described on a qualitative level. A property of the world is, for example, the location of an object, e.g. 'inside the house' or 'north of the tree'.

A collection of properties known to the robot, regardless whether described quantitatively or qualitatively, is called world model. Currently, qualitative spatial world models within autonomous agent systems, if used at all, are rather ad hoc – at least from a logical perspective (Bennett, 1997). In these ad hoc models abstract symbols are often derived from an introspective point of view of the system developer to represent certain properties of the world which are important for solving a specific task the developer has on her mind. Because of their vaguely defined semantics, in most cases naive abstract symbols cannot usually be used directly for checking whether all spatial information is consistent or for deriving reasonable action sequences such that agents can be controlled in space. Instantiating quantitative prototypes of the qualitative symbols and deriving results algebraically and, in the end, transferring it back to the qualitative representation seems expedient but is unsatisfying. Intuitively, such ad hoc representations are sufficient from a representational view, but not from a reasoning perspective, because implications cannot be drawn directly from the qualitative representation itself.

To summarize, a spatial abstraction for representing dynamics on a high level of abstraction is a good method for developers of artificial agents. The representation made should be suitable a) for reasoning about spatial configurations and b) for deriving reasonable actions from within the chosen representation for acting in these configurations. Investigating qualitative spatial representations with the consideration of how actions may affect and change an agent's world model is a promising starting point for doing so.

1.2   Problem, Goal, and Approach

The desire for a single qualitative framework for representation and reasoning in the context of dynamic agents raises the idea to integrate approaches from qualitative spatial reasoning and from reasoning about action and change. The aim of this thesis is to make a step in the direction of this long term goal by developing an effective approach to agent control based on QSR methods in combination with the concept that actions affect properties of the world in a specific way. For example, standing in front of a door and moving forward results in passing the door, while turning right results in the door being to the left instead of in front. So, the dynamics of the objects involved must be represented in context of the relations of the underlying calculus. Throughout the thesis we apply a set of collision regulations for vessel navigation as our example domain to clarify our approaches. The set of regulations contains rules like:

> When two power-driven vessels are crossing so as to involve risk of collision, the vessel which has the other on her own starboard side shall keep out of the way and shall, if the circumstances of the case admit, avoid crossing ahead of the other vessel.

In general, dynamic process knowledge in qualitative representations can be represented by the concept of *conceptual neighborhood* (Freksa, 1992a). Two spatial relations of a qualitative spatial calculus are conceptually neighboring if they can be continuously transformed into each other without resulting in a third relation in between. Intuitively, when standing in front of an object, it is not possible to move behind that object without passing to the left or right of it. Therefore, *left* and *right* are conceptual neighbors of *front*. In contrast, *front* and *behind* are not conceptual neighboring. The complete relational structure between conceptual neighbors can be represented as a *conceptual neighborhood graph* with a vertex for each relation and edges for each pair of neighboring relations. In its current variant conceptual neighborhood expresses the theoretical existence of an action that leads from one relation to a neighboring one. For agent control it is necessary to know which action has to be performed to achieve the desired goal.

In the context of agent control task-specific properties of the agents and objects involved need to be considered. The most important properties are founded in the mobility, i.e. in the degrees of freedom in motion, of the objects involved, for example, whether the represented entity is a stable object or a dynamic agent, and in the latter

case, how the agent is able to move. For some agents it is only possible to turn while
they are moving forward, as for example cars or vessels. Others can move in more
or less arbitrary direction. In addition, if we deal with several dynamic agents we
also need to take into account the interplay of their actions. So, to represent how
specific actions change the relation between the objects we must extend the conceptual
neighborhood structure: given a binary calculus where two objects are related, each
edge between two relations is augmented by a tuple of actions which lead from one
relation to the other. We refer to this resulting extended graph structure as an *action-
augmented conceptual neighborhood graph* ($\mathcal{ACNG}$). From a physical standpoint, an
infinite variety of actions are possible, for example regarding speed and turning angle.
We restrict our considerations to only very coarse actions in this thesis, in general
forward/backward motion and left/right turning. because our aim is merely to show
that our approach is workable.

The individual regulations from a rule set can be modeled as a partial graph of the
$\mathcal{ACNG}$, which we call a *rule transition system*. Many rules are formulated for two
agents only and do not consider situations with a larger number of participants. Once
a rule set has been formalized, we can deliberate on alternative actions within a single
rule, and also consider whether rule-compliant actions are available regarding situations with more than two agents. By encoding the knowledge in terms of a constraint
network and checking whether the network is inconsistent, one can determine whether
conflicting knowledge in qualitative representations exists. If this is the case, rules are
contradictory with each other, otherwise, the rules are consistent with each other. For
example, the soundness of a rule set can be investigated by checking for conflicting
rules with respect to $n > 2$ agents. Similarly, completeness can be investigated by
checking whether all potential configurations are covered.

We need to obtain an adequate representation of the information necessary for formalizing navigation constraints before the neighborhood structure can be augmented
thereby. That additional information permits the formalization of navigation constraints. For our first investigation we restrict our examination to abstractions of objects to points. Although we are dealing with extended objects we are interested in the
general connections between formal qualitative abstractions and their potential with
respect to spatial agent control. Looking at several rules or regulations on navigation
revealed that relative orientation between two objects regarding the intrinsic fronts of
objects or the direction of motion is the most prominent spatial aspect. Looking at an
example rule from the domain of collision regulations for vessel navigation "When two
power-driven vessels are crossing so as to involve risk of collision, the vessel which has
the other on her own starboard side shall keep out of the way and shall, if the circumstances of the case admit, avoid crossing ahead of the other vessel." underlines this.
The terms 'crossing', 'starboard', and 'ahead' describe relative orientation. Although
'risk of collision' contains additional speed and distance aspects it can be captured by
orientation change over time as well. Because we abstract from aspects like distance
and speed we cannot expect to gain rule-compliant behavior that is optimal regarding

the distance travelled or the time consumed.

There exist a large number of relative orientation calculi based on points or oriented line segments. Thus, system developers cannot be expected to be experts in the large variety of orientation calculi. Consequently, we aim at developing an *umbrella calculus* for orientation knowledge, which is as universal as possible. We show that the Oriented Point Relation Algebra ($\mathcal{OPRA}_m$) is a good candidate for such an umbrella calculus. In contrast to calculi previously presented, the basic objects of $\mathcal{OPRA}_m$ are oriented points. Oriented points are ordinary points with an additional orientation attribute; angular resolution can be chosen by the granularity parameter m. The composition of $\mathcal{OPRA}_m$ was only roughly sketched in the literature. So, we need to give a detailed algorithmic method for affiliating compositions of $\mathcal{OPRA}_m$ relations. To show the expressivity of $\mathcal{OPRA}_m$ we present transformations of different orientation calculi into $\mathcal{OPRA}_m$ relations and explain how composition of the other calculi can be derived on the basis of $\mathcal{OPRA}_m$.

In many situations we need to know whether distance between the objects increases, decreases, or stays unchanged over time, i.e. whether the objects point away from each other, towards each other, or are parallel. Such knowledge is essential, for example, to direct robots in a hallway or for preventing collisions between two agents. Providing we can assume straight motion in the direction of the objects' intrinsic fronts, one can derive changes in distance on the basis of relative orientation information. Such knowledge can be represented, roughly, by considering whether or not the lines in the direction of the objects' current motion are parallel. We call this aspect *spatial alignment*, or simply *alignment*.

Unfortunately, no existing calculus, including $\mathcal{OPRA}_m$, that deals with relative orientation is capable of representing alignment. Therefore, we define an independent calculus, called *Alignment Calculus* ($\mathcal{AC}$), and derive composition and neighborhood structure. To gain a single representation $\mathcal{OPRA}_m$ and the Alignment Calculus must be combined. The combined calculus is called $\mathcal{OPRA}_m^\star$. The combination of two calculi, especially the composition operation, is not trivial. Due to interdependencies between the representations the operations cannot be regarded separately. Instead, similarities and connections must be found and represented accordingly. In case of $\mathcal{OPRA}_m$ and $\mathcal{AC}$ we define the compound composition operation based on the original $\mathcal{OPRA}_m$ composition and geometric properties of the $\mathcal{AC}$ relations with respect to each potential composition result.

Additionally, if qualitative representations are used for agent control it may happen that information perceived currently conflicts with information gathered previously, e.g. due to sensory failure, or if several robots exchange their qualitative world models. The qualitative knowledge can be represented in terms of a constraint network. The problem is: if the network was found to be inconsistent we cannot derive which knowledge fragments caused the inconsistency. So, the complete world model is useless for further application. In this thesis we elaborate the idea of using conceptual neighborhood to resolve conflicting information. The idea was first elicited by Moratz & Freksa (1998). The distance between two relations in the neighborhood graph can be used to formulate appropriate distance measures between constraint networks. This allows searching for a consistent representation with minimal changes regarding the inconsistent knowledge.

Based on the considerations above on qualitative spatial reasoning and agent control we develop an effective qualitative approach to steer vessels in a simulated environment according to collision avoidance rules.

1.3 Hypotheses and Contributions of this Thesis

The main hypothesis of this work is:

- Qualitative spatial representations and reasoning techniques are suitable for agent control. Explicit metric knowledge is not required.

We can specify further:

- We can develop a calculus for spatial orientation that comprises a great number of specialized calculi.

- Orientation knowledge is sufficient for representing collision avoidance regulations.

- Conceptual neighborhood is an adequate means for resolving conflicting information.

Based on these hypotheses we pursue the following goals in this thesis:

- We develop an *umbrella calculus* for representing a wide range of relative orientation information including alignment.

- We show how composition and neighborhood structure for other relative orientation calculi can be extracted by expressing them in terms of this umbrella calculus.

- We extend the idea of conceptual neighborhood with task-specific properties to *action-augmented conceptual neighborhood* such that it can be applied for agent control purposes.

- We describe an approach to deduce consistent representations from an inconsistent model regarding minimal change with respect to constraint relaxation.

- We demonstrate the applicability of a qualitative orientation calculus to navigate mobile agents.

1.4   Outline of this Thesis

The remainder of this thesis is organized as follows. We will first introduce relevant aspects of qualitative spatial representation and reasoning in detail. Within Chapter 2 we review different aspects of spatial representations and introduce reasoning strategies connected to qualitative representations. Afterwards we introduce specific orientation representations.

In Chapter 3 we apply $\mathcal{OPRA}_m$ as a general approach to representing orientation information. We derive the composition of $\mathcal{OPRA}_m$ and discuss some reasoning properties before the neighborhood structure is given. Subsequently, we show how several well known orientation calculi, based on points or oriented line segments, can be expressed with a set of $\mathcal{OPRA}_m$ relations. We demonstrate how composition and neighborhood structure of the encoded calculi are extracted.

Alignment knowledge is essential for controlling agents. In Chapter 4 we define the Alignment Calculus and combine it with $\mathcal{OPRA}_m$ to $\mathcal{OPRA}_m^\star$. To derive a correct composition we apply the composition algorithm for $\mathcal{OPRA}_m$ and additional inequalities to represent constraints given by the Alignment Calculus. In addition, we refine the neighborhood structure of $\mathcal{OPRA}_m$ to the structure for $\mathcal{OPRA}_m^\star$ and give an iconic representation of $\mathcal{OPRA}_m^\star$ relations.

In Chapter 5 we explain how qualitative orientation calculi can be applied to agent control. We augment the well known concept of conceptual neighborhood for relations by explicit actions such that action patterns can be generated in order to achieve agent's goals. Additionally, we consider inconsistent world models and how knowledge is restored by defining how a consistent world model is derived with a minimal distance to the original one.

In Chapter 6 we apply our results to the domain of collision regulations in vessel navigation in order to achieve rule-compliant agent behavior, i.e. in our case vessel navigation based on collision regulations, and in the end, we discuss our experiences made with this approach.

We end with a conclusion of the contributions in this thesis and an outlook on future work.

Chapter 2

Qualitative Spatial Representation and Reasoning

In this chapter we introduce the relevant aspects of qualitative spatial reasoning. We start with an overview and informal introduction to the domain of qualitative reasoning, especially qualitative spatial reasoning. Afterwards, a selection of spatial aspects, namely orientation, distance, and motion are contemplated and how they are treated in qualitative representations. Based on qualitative representations different reasoning methods can be pursued, namely constraint-based reasoning and neighborhood-based reasoning; these methods are detailed in this chapter. Since we are mainly concerned with orientation information in our approach, we introduce several orientation calculi at the end of this chapter.

2.1 Overview

Although the world is infinitely complex and our knowledge of the world is limited, i.e. incomplete, biological systems, especially humans, function quite well within this world without understanding it completely (Kuipers, 1994). Humans understand physical mechanisms such as bathtubs, indoor or outdoor navigation, bicycling, microwave ovens, and so on. Qualitative Reasoning (QR) is concerned with capturing such everyday commonsense knowledge of the physical world with a limited set of symbols and allows for dealing with the knowledge without numerical values (Cohn & Hazarika, 2001b). In addition, qualitative approaches are considered to be closer to how humans deal with commonsense knowledge compared to quantitative approaches (Renz, 2002).

Even though processes, as for example physiology or power plants, are more complex and a lot of expert knowledge is needed to understand them, they are also covered by the term commonsense knowledge. Therefore, QR is also concerned with the myriad of equations used by engineers and scientists to explain complex physical phenomena while creating quantitative models (Vilain et al., 1990). Although, knowledge about the world is always incomplete, by providing appropriate qualitative representations making relevant knowledge explicit in combination with corresponding reasoning methods, computers can be enabled to monitor, diagnose, predict, plan, or explain the behavior of physical systems in a qualitative manner. If applying quantitative models to describe complex commonsense knowledge it might be intracable or even unavailable. One reason for intractability of a quantitative model is that an infinite number of potential states or configurations are given. With qualitative representations conclusions and inferences can still be drawn even in the absence of complete knowledge, without applying any probabilistic or fuzzy-based techniques. In this work we will concentrate on the spatial aspects of qualitative reasoning. Space itself is a fundamental concept for humans to navigate in familiar or unfamiliar environments or to reason about properties of object configurations within such an environment. The subfield of qualitative reasoning that is concerned with representations of space is called Qualitative Spatial Reasoning (QSR).

In the remainder of this section we introduce the essence of qualitative spatial descriptions and how the representations are applied to formulate constraints on spatial configurations. We also show how we can deal with spatial change.

2.1.1 Qualitative Spatial Descriptions

A qualitative spatial description captures distinctions between objects that make an important qualitative difference but ignores others. In general, objects are abstracted to geometric primitives e.g. points, lines, or regions. The ability to focus on the important distinctions and ignore the unimportant ones is an excellent way to cope with incomplete knowledge (Kuipers, 1994). Cohn & Hazarika (2001b) summarize that the essence of qualitative spatial reasoning is to find ways to represent continuous properties of the world, also called continuities, by discrete systems of symbols, i.e. a finite vocabulary. These symbols describe the relationships between objects in a specific domain. Therefore, they are called *relations*. The domain is given by the set of objects considered, e.g. points, lines, or regions in the Euclidian plane.

Quantization is the process of summarizing indistinguishable perceptions or values into an equivalence class. The result of quantization is a (generally finite) set of quantities, called quantity space. Continuities can always be quantized, but it is the question whether the properties chosen are reasonable with respect to the given problem and the applied reasoning techniques. This means not all quantizations are equally useful regarding a certain problem. Forbus (1984) summarizes this in the principle of relevance. Forbus says that distinctions made by a quantization must be relevant to the kind of reasoning performed. Relations may describe different aspects of space as topology (e.g. 'outside' or 'inside'), orientation (e.g. 'right', 'left', 'ahead' or 'behind'), distance (e.g. 'close' or 'distant'), size (e.g. 'small' or 'large'), or shape (e.g. 'cube', 'circle', etc.). However, an important characteristic of perceptual precision is that a series of small changes, each imperceptible, may combine to form a perceptible change. Then the indistinguishability relation though reflexive and symmetric, is not transitive, which can lead to a paradox of perception (Cohn & Hazarika, 2001b).

In general, quantity spaces possess an inherent ordering which may be partial or total. Implications can be drawn by exploiting the transitivity of this ordering information. Two of these implications are for example a shift in perspective (converse operation) and the integration of local knowledge of two overlapping sets of objects into survey knowledge (the composition operation). For example, if we know that object B is right of A a change in perspective from A to B reveals that A is left of B (the converse operation). From knowing that B is left of A and C is left of B we can infer that C is also left of A (composition).

A complete model for a certain domain is called a *qualitative calculus*. It consists of the set of relations between objects from this domain and the operations defined on these relations. *Binary* calculi define relations between pairs of objects, *ternary* calculi define relations between triples of objects, and n-*ary* calculi define relations between n-tuples of objects. In general, operations defined for binary spatial calculi are union, intersection, converse, and composition. In case of higher-order relations operations may need to be refined, e.g. for ternary relations the converse operation must be refined, as six permutations of the related objects exist.

The first prominent calculus presented in the temporal domain was Allen's Temporal Interval Algebra (Allen, 1983). Further calculi based in the temporal domain are, for example, the Point Calculus (Vilain et al., 1990; Vilain & Kautz, 1986), the Point- and Interval Calculus (Dechter et al., 1991), the Generalized Interval Calculus (Ligozat, 1991), and the INDU (interval and duration) Calculus (Pujari & Sattar, 1999).

Temporal calculi can be interpreted in the spatial domain as well. This lead to the development of, for example, the cardinal direction calculus (Ligozat, 1998), a member of the group of n-point calculi (Balbiani & Condotta, 2002), or the Rectangle Calculus (Balbiani et al., 1998, 1999a), which is a special case of the n-Blocks Calculus (Balbiani et al., 1999b), or the Directed Interval Calculus (Renz, 2001).

Freksa & Röhrig (1993) classify approaches to qualitative spatial reasoning. Roughly, spatial calculi can be classified into two groups: topological and positional calculi. Topological calculi are for example the region-based calculi RCC-5 or RCC-8 (Randell et al., 1992) or the Cyclic Interval Calculus (Balbiani & Osmani, 2000). Positional calculi, i.e. calculi dealing with orientation or distance information, are for example the Double Cross Calculus (Freksa, 1992b), the FlipFlop Calculus (Ligozat, 1993), the Dipole Calculus (Schlieder, 1995) which has later been extended to the Dipole Relation Algebra (Moratz et al., 2000), the Ternary Point Configuration Calculus (Moratz et al., 2002), or the Star Calculus (Renz & Mitra, 2004).

2.1.2 Constraint Satisfaction

Relations of a spatial calculus are often used to formulate constraints about the spatial configuration of objects from the domain of the calculus. This results in the specification of a spatial *constraint satisfaction problem* (CSP) which can be solved with specific reasoning techniques, e.g. by applying composition and intersection operations on the incorporated relations. A prerequisite for applying constraint-based reasoning techniques is a set of *base relations* $\mathcal{BR}$, also called primitive relations, which are *jointly exhaustive and pairwise disjoint* (JEPD). In the case of binary relations JEPD means that for any pair of entities exactly one base relation holds. For arbitrary n-ary calculi this must hold for any n-tuple. Every relation of a calculus is a union of a subset of base relations. The set of all possible relations is then the powerset of the base relations ($2^{\mathcal{BR}}$), i.e. all feasible unions of primitive relations. If a relation contains more than one base relation, we will call this a *complex relation*. In many cases reasoning is done using the composition operation. As shown in the composition example above, potential relative positions between A and C can be constrained by combining the relations between AB and BC. In many cases, if the number of base relations is not too high, the composition results can be precomputed and stored in so-called *composition tables* (CT). However, storing such a table for calculi with a large number of base relations is not efficient. Composition can also be partly precomputed, with an algorithm supplied to calculate the rest, i.e. the requested composition result. This was done, for example, by van de Weghe (2004). Namely, van de Weghe (2004) gave a *composition rules table*, which was extracted by exploiting symmetries in the complete CT, with an additional simple algorithm to derive the requested composition result.

2.1.3   A Simple Example: Boat Race

For a more vivid comprehension of the concept of what qualitative calculi are and how they can be used to formulate constraints, we give a simple example based on a boat race scenario. This example is borrowed from Ligozat (2005). The underlying representation is the spatial version of the Point Algebra (PA) (Vilain et al., 1990). Primitive entities are 1D points on an oriented line, with pairs of points taking one of the relations: *behind, ahead*, or *same*.

Imagine, a friend tells us on a phone about a boat race on a river. We can try to understand the story by modeling the river as an oriented line and the boats of the five participants A, B, C, D, E as points moving along the line (see Fig. 2.1). Thus, our domain is the set of all 1D points on the oriented line.

According to the relations from the Point Algebra we can now distinguish for each pair of boats, whether one boat is *ahead* of the other boat, *behind* it, or on the *same* level. Using these relations to formulate the current situation in the race might lead to the following description of the scene:

1. A is *behind* B
2. E is *ahead* of B
3. A is *behind* C
4. D is on the *same* level as C
5. A is *ahead* of D

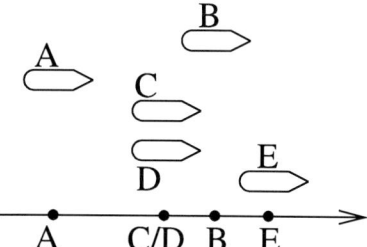

Figure 2.1: A possible situation in a boat race which can be modeled by 1D points on an oriented line and can be described by qualitative relations from the Point Algebra.

From this information we are able to conclude that our friend must have made an error, probably confusing the names of the participants:
We know that A is *behind* C (sentence 3) and D is *behind* A (conversion of sentence 5). From composing these two facts it follows that C and D cannot be on the *same* level which contradicts sentence 4.

On the other hand, only taking the first three sentences into account, we can conclude that E is also *ahead* of A by composing the facts A is *behind* B (sentence 1) and B is *behind* E (conversion of sentence 2). However, this information is not sufficient to derive the exact relation between C and E, as C can either be *ahead*, *behind* or on the *same* level as E.

2.1.4 Spatial Change

Space and time have always been considered to be important parts of commonsense reasoning. The physical world has a spatial extent and all objects which are dealt with are located in space relative to other objects. Spatial change appears whenever objects possess different spatial attributes at different times (Galton, 2000b), e.g. if objects change their locations over time. Therefore, it is a major goal of Qualitative Spatial Reasoning to develop effective and reasonable representations for dealing with spatial and temporal information.

Time is a scalar entity and thus, is very well suited for a qualitative approach. Temporal expressions mainly describe order and duration, e.g. 'after' or 'while', or more general categories, e.g. 'afternoon' or 'in time'. Due to inherent multi-dimensionality space is much more complex to deal with. This multi-dimensionality leads to a higher degree of freedom and manifold possibilities to describe entities and the relationships between them (Renz, 2002). Nevertheless, dealing with spatial change always incorporates knowledge about time, but not necessarily at an explicit level, i.e. using terms like *before* or *during*. *Conceptual Neighborhood* is a general abstraction of change with respect to entities represented in a calculus and was introduced by Freksa (1992a). We introduce this concept in more detail in Section 2.3.3.

2.2 Qualitative Spatial Representations

Before developing spatial representations several aspects of space must be regarded. First, some ontological questions must be considered, e.g. what do the primitive entities look like or the nature of the embedding space. Second, we need to examine what relationships must be considered, e.g. topology, orientation, or shape, so that it is possible to solve specific problems with the calculus.

One of the most important ontological questions is which spatial primitive to use. Some approaches developed in the QSR community take regions as primitive entities (Cohn & Hazarika, 2001b). Using regions often has advantages compared to using lower dimension entities as points or lines. Namely, if the spatial model is intended for reasoning about physical objects, the objects themselves have a spatial extent. "Regionalism", so to speak, may also predominate because of borrowing from or applying knowledge from the field of Geographical Information Systems (GIS). In GIS the representation of regions is fundamental. However, reasoning with extended objects is more complicated than reasoning with points or lines. Since point-based reasoning is a more tractable problem many calculi dealing with points or lines have been presented in recent years.

Additionally, the nature of the embedding space must be clarified. Typically, continuous space $\mathbb{R}^n$ is chosen for some dimensionality n. Most spatial representations were presented within this category for $n = 2$. For some applications it has been shown beneficial using different space, e.g. discrete space (Egenhofer & Sharma, 1993). In (Galton, 1999) a preliminary attempt is made to bridge the gap between abstract qualitative approaches and quantitative data driven low-level models in real-world applications by developing a high-level qualitative spatial theory presuming a discrete model of space.

Finally, we must consider what kinds of relations between primitive entities need to be represented. For example, entities can be related regarding their shape, orientation, distance, size, or topology. Hence, spatial representations are manifold regarding potential relations between their primitive entities. As topology and mereology are very natural qualitative aspects of space we will introduce them briefly below. As we are concerned with qualitative representations regarding autonomous agent control, the aspects of orientation, distance, and motion are of specific interest. Therefore, we will introduce them in more detail afterwards.

Topology is perhaps the most fundamental aspect of space because in topology only qualitative distinctions can be made (Cohn & Hazarika, 2001b). Roughly, topology considers relations between sets. The best known representations are the *Region Connection Calculi* (RCC), especially RCC-8. RCC-8 uses eight atomic relations describing the connectivity between two regions. For details see Randell et al. (1992) and Renz (2002). Mereology describes relationships between parts and the whole of entities. Mereology and topology are strongly connected because one can be expressed in terms of the other (Cohn & Hazarika, 2001b). Topology and mereology are useful abstractions for solving several problems. Nevertheless, they are not sufficient representations in many other cases, e.g. if navigational problems need to be solved.

2.2.1 Qualitative Orientation

Orientation is an important qualitative concept because communication about and dealing with orientation information plays a major role in everyday life. Orientation describes the position or alignment relative to other specific directions. These directions may be defined relative to one or more other objects (e.g. left of the road), or absolute, i.e. independent of specific entities in the domain (e.g. the cardinal directions north, east, south, and west). While we deal with binary relations in topology, orientation is a ternary relation. Orientation relationships are formed from the *object*, also called primary object or located object, a *reference object*, and a *frame of reference* (cf. the excursus on frames of reference below). If the frame of reference (FoR) is given, orientation can be represented as a binary relationship with respect to the FoR (Renz, 2002).

Excursus: Frames of Reference (FoR)

Frames of Reference (FoR) define the context in which spatial statements, e.g. spatial utterances or object configurations, are to be understood. Thus, they define a framework how objects have to be embedded in space, so that position and direction of incorporated objects can be resolved unambiguously.

Different categorizations of frames of reference have been proposed over recent years, sometimes with respect to certain disciplines. In this work we will follow the unifying categorization of FoR's first presented by Levinson (1996) and revised in (Levinson, 2003). Levinson reveals several conflicts and confusions of terminology with previous classifications. He proposes his own classification and redefines terms to overcome shortcomings of previous approaches where diverse concepts could not be expressed by employing opposite classes as 'egocentric' vs. 'allocentric' (psychological terminology, e.g. in (Zimbardo, 1988) or (Klatzky, 1998)), or 'deictic' vs. 'intrinsic' (cf. (Clementini et al., 1997; Retz-Schmidt, 1988)). Instead, he introduces the terms *origin*, *relatum*, and *referent*. In brief, the origin defines the center of the reference system, the relatum is the reference or ground object with respect to which the referent (another object) is to be located.

Levinson asks how to describe where something (the *referent*) is located with respect to something else (the *relatum*). If external features are used to determine the orientation of the reference object, it is called an *extrinsic* FoR, e.g. "The ball is north of the tree.". If inherent features of the relatum are used to constitute the FoR orientation it is called an *intrinsic* FoR, e.g. "The ball is in front of the house." (the inherent front of the house). If orientation is determined by regarding the viewpoint from which the reference object is seen, it is called a *deictic* FoR, e.g. "The ball is in front of the tree." or "The ball is in front of the goal."

A *relative* FoR relies on a viewpoint (*origin*) different from the relatum, e.g. "The ball is in front of the tree". In contrast, an *absolute* FoR, also called global FoR, is based on an (arbitrary) fixed direction or bearing, e.g. cardinal directions: "The ball is north of the tree.".

From a different perspective, intrinsic Frames of Reference are based on binary relations between the relatum (which is identical with the origin) and the referent. Relative Frames of Reference are based on ternary relations between origin, relatum, and referent. An absolute FoR is based on binary relations between relatum and referent regarding a fixed orientation.

Many approaches dealing with orientation are based on relationships between points in $\mathbb{R}^2$. Frank (1991), for example, introduced two approaches on modeling cardinal directions. He partitions the given Euclidean plane $\mathcal{P}$ into regions with respect to a reference point R and an absolute[1] *west-east/south-north* reference frame. Any point $P \in \mathcal{P}$ belongs to one of the nine basic relations: **North, NorthEast, East, SouthEast, South, SouthWest, West, NorthWest,** or **Equal.**

In (Frank, 1991, 1992) two different partition schemas are introduced: the cone-shaped and the projection-based approach. The models are depicted in Figure 2.2. In the cone-based model all relations, except **Eq,** represent planar cones. The linear borders are no individual relations and are assigned to one of the neighboring cones. In the projection-based model **NE, SE, SW,** and **NW** form planar cones. The linear borders between these four relations are relations themselves and are denoted by **N, E, S,** and **W.** The author argues that the projection-based approach is cognitively more adequate than the cone-based approach. For discussions on cognitive adequacy we refer to (Freksa, 1992b) and (Freksa & Zimmermann, 1993). The projection-based approach is also called the Cardinal (Direction) Algebra whose properties were further investigated in (Ligozat, 1998).

Based on previous work by Ligozat[2], Balbiani & Condotta (2002) show that the cardinal direction framework is the special case of the n-Point Calculus, where $n = 2$. The directions in any dimension can take one of the values $\{<, =, >\}$ with a result of

---

[1]Originally a psychological perspective was taken. Thus, the reference frame was called allocentric.

[2]Ligozat (1998) orders the base relations in an n-dimensional point lattice, which also defines a neighboring order, and thus, defines a so-called n-dimensional point topology.

3^n atomic relations. Because of the general structure they also show that the results already drawn for the Cardinal Direction Calculus in Euclidian plane, can be transferred to higher dimensions directly.

The orientation ranges in the Cardinal Algebra are fixed. The Star Calculus extends the projection-based approach to representing absolute orientation in such a way that the segmentation of the orientation ranges can be chosen arbitrarily (Renz & Mitra, 2004).

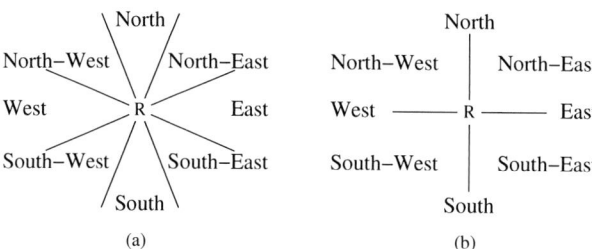

(a)   (b)

Figure 2.2: The cone-based relation model for points (a) and the projection-based variant (b).

Freksa (1992b) presents two ternary point calculi for representing relative orientation, the Single Cross Calculus and the Double Cross Calculus. Other calculi based on similar ideas are the FlipFlop Calculus (Ligozat, 1993), the Qualitative Trajectory Calculus (van de Weghe, 2004), or the Ego Calculus (Krieg-Brückner & Shi, 2006). We will go into detail on some of these calculi in Section 2.4.

Schlieder (1993) developed a calculus based on cyclic ordering information for representing relative orientation. He classifies ternary point configurations into one of the three categories clockwise, anti-clockwise, or collinear. Based on this classification Schlieder (1995) developed the Dipole Calculus for reasoning about pairs of oriented line segments (dipoles). Each line segment is defined by a start point and an end point. In the original approach no points are allowed to be equal and additionally, no three points were allowed on a line. By weakening this restriction such that points from different dipoles are allowed to be equal (points in general position), the Dipole Relation Algebra ($\mathcal{DRA}$) was developed (Moratz et al., 2000). In this paper also suggestions were made how problems with arbitrary configurations may be resolved. Compared to Schlieder's cyclic ordering the $\mathcal{DRA}$ can also be interpreted as a logical conjunction of four FlipFlop relations. Based on the early ideas of Schlieder, Röhrig (1994) developed a ternary representation where triples of points are classified on the basis of the $CYCORD(x, y, z)$ function. This function evaluates true if x, y, and z are in clockwise orientation. He also showed how other (not only orientation) calculi can be translated into $CYCORD$ terms.

Developing orientation calculi for extended objects is much more complex. Orientation information for extended objects is much more uncertain and ambiguous compared to dealing with points, e.g. due to complex shapes. For avoiding most of the problems arising due to dealing with extended objects, a popular approach is approximating, respectively prototyping, the incorporated objects, for example, to circles or to rectangles whose sides are aligned to the reference frame axis. Such approaches were for example considered in (Guesgen, 1989), (Papadias & Theodoridis, 1997), and (Balbiani et al., 1998). But even if such uniformly shaped objects are given there may exist several reasonable linguistic propositions for describing the configuration sufficiently (Renz, 2002). A prominent example is the Rectangle Algebra (in $\mathbb{R}^2$) where each dimension is considered separately with respect to the 13 Allen relations which leads to 13×13 base relations (Balbiani et al., 1998, 1999a). The Rectangle Algebra does not only capture the orientation between rectangles, but also their topological relation. Therefore this approach can be regarded as a unifying approach of orientation and topology (Renz, 2002). Goyal & Egenhofer (2001) take a less expressive approach by applying a 3×3 grid. The center of the grid completely encloses the spatial object, i.e. it forms the minimal bounding rectangle. Within the eight remaining cells we can now encode whether parts of the referent are contained or not. An extended version of this approach can quantitatively encode how much of the referent is contained in the specific area. Unfortunately, no formal semantics were given. Therefore, the correctness of reasoning operations on complex relations, i.e. a union of two or more base relations, remains unclear.

From the point of improving qualitative spatial data queries Billen & Clementini (2004) present a model for ternary relations between regions. The model is based on the collinearity invariant of three points under projective geometry. By exploiting these projective properties of two extended reference objects the plane is divided into five zones. Overall, 34 base relations can be distinguished by considering the intersections of an object with respect to these five zones. In (Clementini & Billen, 2006) the model is refined and algorithms for computing the relations are given.

A calculus combining cardinal direction relations and relative orientation relations is presented in (Isli et al., 2001). Because of disadvantageous computational properties of the Double Cross Calculus[3] a coarsened variant of Freksa's Double Cross Calculus is used. It turns out that this variant is equal to the FlipFlop Calculus (Ligozat, 1993), the $\mathcal{LR}$ refinement (Scivos & Nebel, 2005) respectively, which has been shown to have much better reasoning properties. Isli et al. (2001) presents an example where the configuration is considered consistent if evaluated with each calculus separately, but in case of the combined calculus is found to be inconsistent. In sum, the algorithm presented calculates: 1) path-consistency for the cardinal relations, 2) strong 4-consistency for FlipFlop relations, and 3) the interconnection between the two calculi. The interconnection is established within the composition table used, because

---

[3]The determination of satisfiability of constraint systems over Double Cross relations is NP-hard (Scivos & Nebel, 2001)

the composition result between two binary cardinal relations is also mapped to a set of relative relations.

2.2.2 Qualitative Distance

Distance is also a fundamental concept in everyday life. Contrary to topology and orientation, distance is a scalar entity. In most approaches for representing distance points are chosen as basic entities. Generally, two main categories can be distinguished: absolute and relative distance.

Absolute distance represents direct comparison between two entities and can be represented quantitatively as well as qualitatively. Absolute quantitative measurements are for example 100 meters and 200 kilometers, which may be represented qualitatively by 'close' and 'far'. Relative distance compares the distance between two spatial entities with regard to the distance to some third object. Representing relative distance is generally qualitative. Categories might be 'closer' or 'further'.

Reasoning with distance comprises problems. In (Renz, 2002) two general problems are sketched. First, assume a set of n points $p_1, \ldots, p_n$ on a line. Each pair (p_i, p_{i+1}) of points is regarded 'close'. Now, the question to ask is: for which number n p_n is far from p_1? This is a variant of the indistinguishability problem stated earlier, which describes that several imperceptible changes may sum up to a perceptible one. In addition, combining distance information between objects $dist(A, B)$ and $dist(B, C)$ (composition) is problematic as well. The overall distance is not only dependent on distance itself, but also on the orientation between the two legs. If both distances are 'far' and the angle between the legs are close to π the result might be something like 'very far', but if the angle is small, i.e. close to zero, the resulting relation might be 'close'. Therefore, it is reasonable to regard distance in conjunction with orientation. Calculi dealing with orientation and distance conjoined are called *positional calculi*.

2.2.3 Representing Positional Information

Frank (1992) uses a method which combines cardinal directions and relative distance measures. Based on an algebra of paths and distance classes he derived the composition and converse operation, demonstrating the limitations of separating distance and direction reasoning compared to combined reasoning. A qualitative framework for combining relative orientation and relative distance was presented in (Freksa, 1992b; Zimmermann & Freksa, 1993) by determining relative position of a point with respect to an oriented line segment between two other points[4]. This was further investigated in (Zimmermann & Freksa, 1996). Due to the distance information represented in the enriched representation, composition results might be less uncertain than without distance. A more sophisticated approach was taken in (Zimmermann, 1993) by combin-

---

[4]The basic idea was that the oriented line segment was determined by the start and end points of the motion of a single object.

ing orientation with the Δ-Calculus (Zimmermann, 1995). The Δ-Calculus is based on a ternary relation $x(>, d, y)$ denoting that x is larger than y by an amount of d. Clementini et al. (1997) propose a cone-based positional calculus with absolute distance measure regarding different variants of composition. They present algorithms for deriving the composition between relations with same, orthogonal, and opposite orientation. They also suggest an algorithm for composition of relations with arbitrary orientation. For calculi with finer granularity, i.e. making finer distinctions than *same*, *opposite*, and orthogonal (*left*/*right*), the composition is approximated by combining the results of the algorithms for these three prototypes. A similar approach to combining orientation and distance was taken in (Escrig & Toledo, 1998).

Liu (1998) presents a qualitative abstraction of orientation and distance and derives a set of inference rules for combining the two sources of knowledge. The approach is called qualitative trigonometry and qualitative arithmetic.

In (Isli & Moratz, 1999) the combination of different orientation and relative distance approaches on different levels of granularity were investigated. Based on these results the projection-based Ternary Point Configuration Calculus (TPCC) with two distance categories and 12 orientation categories is developed (Moratz et al., 2003). Together with special relations, i.e. if points coincide, it results in 27 base relations. A composition table was derived and applied in a route graph example. Investigating complexity issues revealed that reasoning with TPCC relations is in PSPACE. TPCC was further investigated and extended in (Dylla & Moratz, 2004; Moratz, 2007; Moratz & Ragni, 2008).

2.2.4   Qualitative Change and Qualitative Motion

Muller (1998b) emphasizes that change is a central concept in spatio-temporal domains, as very often the configuration of the represented entities change over time. According to Galton (2000b) change and time are two sides of the same coin as one cannot have one without the other[5]. The concept of change can be regarded from different viewpoints. Worboys (2001) distinguishes between the action of change and the results or effects of the change. Thus, two different definitions of change arise:

- **process of change**: an object o changes if and only if there exists a property P of o and distinct times t and t' such that o has property P at t and o does not have property P at t'. (Greek philosophy, e.g. Aristotle)

- **effect of change**: a change occurs if and only if there exists a proposition Π and distinct times t and t' such that Π is true at t but false at t' (Russell, 1903).

Several classifications discriminating various kinds of change have been proposed. For example, Johnson (1987) classifies change in terms of forces. Categories are for

---

[5]Galton remarks that some philosophers have the standpoint that time is in principle possible without change.

example diversion[6] or counterforce[7]. Worboys (2001) associates change with the term of production, i.e. one or more objects contribute to the creation of a new set of objects or transmit properties to an existing collection of objects. Galton (2000b) enumerates different types of change regarding the represented aspect of space, e.g. change in connectivity, orientation, distance, size, or location.

Several communities stress the distinction between continuous and discrete (discontinuous) change, e.g. (Pinto, 1998), (Moreira et al., 1999), and (Galton, 2000b). Intuitively, discontinuous change describes change that happens from one moment to the other, i.e. instantaneous change of property values. Continuous change on the other hand describes change that appears over time, i.e. property values vary continuously with time. For example, the position of a moving object changes continuously over time, but the property to be at the final position is discrete.

One abstraction of change is the approach of *conceptual neighborhood* (Freksa, 1991, 1992b) of relations of a qualitative calculus. Intuitively, conceptual neighborhood is a model for how the world could evolve in terms of transitions between qualitative relations. We will go into more details on conceptual neighborhood in Sec. 2.3.3 in the context of qualitative reasoning.

Regarding change in spatial environments leads to the crucial concept of motion. Even though an object is perceived at two different locations at different time points, i.e. two discrete perceptions, it is clear that due to object persistence some sort of continuous motion must have taken place (Galton, 2000b). Generally, motion is represented in trajectories. A *trajectory* is the path a moving body is following through space. Eschenbach et al. (1999) extracted the spatial properties of a trajectory as being connected, having a shape, being non-branching, and being a directed structure, or in other words a trajectory is a directed line. Because of the continuity between any two points of a trajectory, there is always a point in between.

Although, moving objects have been studied from multiple perspectives we will concentrate on a perspective concerning spatio-temporal reasoning and agent control. For an overview from other disciplines as database modeling, or video analysis we refer to (van de Weghe, 2004) as a starting point for further investigations.

Spatio-Temporal Reasoning

Renz (2002) summarizes the early history of spatio-temporal reasoning. Inspired by early work on reasoning about spatial commonsense knowledge the subfield of qualitative physics arose (Forbus, 1990; Weld & de Kleer, 1990). In addition, Hayes abetted the subfield by presenting the Naive Physics Manifesto (Hayes, 1978, 1985a,b; Israel, 1985), where space and time are represented by four-dimensional histories. Based on these histories Forbus (1980) presented a system for reasoning about motion through free space[8]. Within this approach qualitative and quantitative information was used.

---

[6]e.g. transformation and split
[7]e.g. disappearance
[8]Free space is meant to be $\mathbb{R}^3$ here.

Thereafter, more effort was taken in developing pure qualitative frameworks. Two important subfields of qualitative physics are qualitative dynamics and qualitative kinematics. The main focus on *qualitative dynamics* is in the forces, which cause the change of systems over time. This work is strongly influenced by research on how to represent *quantity spaces* qualitatively (Forbus, 1981), e.g. by utilizing the transitivity of the underlying order of the representation. *Qualitative kinematics* is the subfield of spatial reasoning concerned with the geometry of motion. Forbus et al. (1990) claims "There is no purely qualitative general-purpose kinematics" (*poverty conjecture*). Research in the following years has weakened this pessimistic proposition.

Rajagopalan (1994) investigates the extension to qualitative physics to cope with relative object positions in 2D. Although, qualitative abstractions are used, the method relies on position projections to the axis. Unfortunately, no sufficient calculus description with JEPD relations was given.

Muller (1998a) proposed an expressive framework for defining complex motion classes with close connection to natural language expressions, e.g. 'leave' or 'cross'. The representation shown is strongly connected to regions and topological relations. A similar approach is taken in (Cohn & Hazarika, 2001a).

In (Hornsby & Egenhofer, 2000) a model based on the explicit description of change with respect to states of existence and non-existence for identifiable objects was presented. Tracing changes is built upon the concept of identity – different from object properties, values, or structure – which is the unique characteristic that distinguishes one object from another. Additionally, Hornsby & Egenhofer (2002) present a framework for modeling the movement of objects over multiple granularities. Motion is represented by so-called geo-spatial lifelines, time-stamped records of the locations that an individual has occupied over a period of time.

Autonomous Agents

In the last decades great advances have been made in the area of autonomous robots. Reliable algorithms have been developed for dealing with low-level problems as collision avoidance and localization, e.g. (Fox et al., 2001) and (Montemerlo et al., 2003). Thus, it is reasonable to think about symbolic high-level approaches, i.e. systems for coordinating these low-level behaviors. Bennett (1997) remarks that spatial processing in robot control systems rely on algorithms which are rather ad-hoc from a logical point of view. The examples below integrate qualitative abstractions of spatial aspects, e.g. direction and velocity, but do not make use of qualitative reasoning approaches and techniques. This means, that most qualitative spatial representations are designed for representation purposes and not for qualitative reasoning about the knowledge represented. A prerequisite for the application of standard qualitative reasoning techniques is that the primitive relations used are jointly exhaustive and pairwise disjoint, i.e. exactly one relation holds at a time. This prerequisite is not met in many cases.

Stolzenburg et al. (2002) claim that in many approaches for qualitative spatial reasoning, navigation of an agent in a more or less static environment is considered. To accomplish the needs for dynamic scenarios, where the agent and other objects may move, they provide a framework incorporating not only orientation and distance, but also qualitative velocity, for intercepting moving objects.

ROBOCUP is an international joint project to promote AI, robotics, and related fields. Different soccer environments, i.e. several simulation or hardware leagues, were chosen as standard testbeds. The domain can be considered to be highly dynamic. For further details we refer to http://www.robocup.org. Riedel (2003) applies different qualitative positional models for comparing the similarity of spatial configurations in a ROBOCUP scenario, but no further reasoning was considered. In (Miene et al., 2003) work on rule-based motion interpretation in ROBOCUP is presented. It is based on spatio-temporal relations presented earlier (Miene & Visser, 2002) with which they were able to interpret situations over time during the game. They extended the approach such that they are able to interpret and predict complex situations. Qualitative relations applied are for example *no motion* or *close*. Rules are incorporated as background knowledge in form of first-order formulae. They are able to identify offside positions successfully and can also predict if a player risks running into an offside trap. The method is usable in real-time and is, in general, domain independent. Beetz et al. (2005) analyze ROBOCUP and real football games. The grounding of symbols, for example, *player under pressure* or *scoring opportunity*, rely heavily on quantitative data.

Fraser et al. (2004) investigate qualitative reasoning aspects regarding knowledge representation in robotics. They argue that qualitative approaches are especially appropriate for building robust control systems. They rely on a hybrid architecture, i.e. the combination of a reactive control part and a planning part. For details on control architectures we refer to Murphy (2000). Symbols are derived by hysteresis functions on the basis of sensor data. Nevertheless, the qualitative symbols used are rather domain dependent. In (Steinbauer et al., 2005) the importance of hysteresis for symbol grounding is strengthened. The authors propose the method of predicate hysteresis for dealing with unstable knowledge.

In (Dylla et al., 2005) a top-down approach to model dynamics of soccer knowledge as it can be found in soccer theory books is presented. The goal is to model soccer strategies and tactics in a way that they are usable for multiple ROBOCUP soccer leagues, i.e. for different hardware platforms. It is investigated if and how soccer theory can be formalized such that specification and execution is possible aiming at abstraction from hardware and from specific situations in leagues. Basic primitives compliant with the terminology known in soccer theory are introduced and examples are given regarding different leagues. As a basic method for deriving certain primitives, e.g. whether a passway is blocked, Voronoi diagrams were applied. Although, the authors emphasize that these primitives can be derived in different ways, this specific method inhibits the application of standard qualitative reasoning techniques.

In (Ferrein et al., 2005) the high-level action language GOLOG based on the *Situation Calculus* (McCarthy & Hayes, 1969) is chosen for intelligent decision making in the context of ROBOCUP. The Situation Calculus is a logical formalism designed for representing and reasoning about dynamical domains. The formalism consists of three types: *situations*, *actions* that can be performed in the world, and *fluents* describing properties of the world. The combination of facts in situations and general laws on effects of actions, enables inference of knowledge about future situations. Ferrein et al. (2005) rely on a hybrid architecture as well. For improving the underlying world model for the planning part qualitative spatial relations are introduced (Schiffer, 2005; Schiffer et al., 2006). Reasoning with the representation is achieved by calculating with quantitative prototypes and mapping the result back into the qualitative representation.

In (Worboys, 2005) a starting point for developing spatio-temporal extended process calculi is presented, i.e. the introduction of temporal capability into geographic information systems. Four different stages of spatio-temporal knowledge are defined: static state of the world, temporal snapshots, object change, and finally, the stage of events, actions, and processes. The approach concentrates on geographical phenomena with respect to topological connectivity of regions in space. Motion of objects is modeled as transitions between regions. Transition between regions is not further specified.

2.2.5 Spatial Semantic Hierarchy

Kuipers & Byun (1991) introduced the *Spatial Semantic Hierarchy* (SSH) of representations. The model is based on characteristics of human cognitive maps. The SSH is a model of knowledge of large-scale space consisting of multiple interacting representations, each qualitative and quantitative (Kuipers, 2000).

The structure of the SSH can be classified as a two-dimensional lattice. In the first dimension qualitative and quantitative representations are distinguished. In the second dimension five different layers are categorized: *sensory layer, control layer, causal layer, topological layer*, and *geometrical layer*.

The *sensory layer* deals with low-level sensors providing sensor names and values. The *control layer* takes the sensory data as input and provides reactive behaviors (sensori-motor patterns) and local geometric maps based on the agents' intrinsic frame of reference. Sometimes sensory and control layer are combined into a single layer. On the *causal layer* continuous behaviors (actions) linking distinctive states (views) assuming successful action execution are defined, i.e. a discrete model of states linked by actions is specified. On the *topological layer* an ontology of places, paths, and regions, with connectivity and containment relations are defined. In addition, so-called patchwork maps can be generated from local maps connected by causal and topological links. On the highest layer, the *geometrical layer*, these patchwork maps can be integrated into a single map with an absolute frame of reference.

2.3 Qualitative Spatial Reasoning

Based on qualitative representation and corresponding reasoning methods computers can be enabled to monitor, diagnose, predict, plan, or explain the behavior of physical systems. In general, two categories of reasoning based on qualitative spatial representations can be distinguished: *constraint-based reasoning* and *neighborhood-based reasoning*. In case of constraint-based reasoning, relations of a spatial calculus are used to formulate constraints about the spatial configuration. This results in the specification of a spatial *constraint satisfaction problem* (CSP) which can be solved with specific reasoning techniques. If neighborhood-based reasoning is performed the inherent connectivity structure of the relations of a calculus is exploited. This method is based on the assumption of persistent, continuously moving objects.

We will introduce these two approaches below after defining the structure of calculi and their operations on relations.

2.3.1 Qualitative Spatial Calculi and Operations

A qualitative spatial calculus defines operations on a finite set $\mathcal{R}$ of spatial relations, like *left-of*, *north-of*, *overlap*, etc. The spatial relations are defined over a usually infinite set of spatial objects, the domain D. The entities represented by D might be points, regions, or other spatial primitives (cf. Sec. 2.2).

For a start we consider *binary calculi*, in which $\mathcal{R}$ consists of binary relations $R \subseteq D \times D = D^2$. If necessary, we will give definitions for ternary or n-ary relations as well ($R \subseteq D \times ... \times D = D^n$).

The set of relations $\mathcal{R}$ of a spatial calculus is typically derived from a jointly exhaustive and pairwise disjoint (JEPD) set of *base relations* ($\mathcal{BR}$). Every relation in $\mathcal{R}$ is a union of a subset of the base relations. Since spatial calculi are typically used for constraint reasoning and unions of relations correspond to disjunctions of relational constraints, it is common to speak of disjunctions of relations as well and write them as sets $\{B_1, ..., B_n\}$ of base relations with $B_i \in \mathcal{BR}$. Using this convention, $\mathcal{R}$ is then either taken to be the powerset $2^{\mathcal{BR}}$ of the base relations (all unions of base relations) or a subset of the powerset. In order to be usable for constraint reasoning, $\mathcal{R}$ should contain at least the base relations B_i ($\forall i = 1, ..., n$), the empty relation $\emptyset$, the universal relation $U = D \times D$, and the identity relation $Id = \{(x, x) | x \in D\}$. $\mathcal{R}$ also needs to be closed under the operations defined in the following.

As the relations are subsets of tuples from the same Cartesian product, the set operations union, intersection, and complement can be applied directly:

Union:	$R_1 \cup R_2$	$=$	$\{\, r \mid r \in R_1 \vee r \in R_2 \,\}$
Intersection:	$R_1 \cap R_2$	$=$	$\{\, r \mid r \in R_1 \wedge r \in R_2 \,\}$
Complement:	$\overline{R} = U \setminus R$	$=$	$\{\, r \mid r \in U \wedge r \notin R \,\}$,

where R_1 and R_2 are n-ary relations from $\mathcal{R}$ and r is an n-tuple over the domain D, e.g. $r = (x, y)$ with $x, y \in D$ in the binary case.

In addition, two more operations are defined which allow derivation of new facts from given information, *conversion* and *composition*. In contrast to the set operations above, these two operations are dependent on the relation's arity. We will give explicit definitions for the binary and ternary case, and relate to the general case afterwards.

Conversion can be interpreted as shifting perspective from one entity to another. Regarding the Point Algebra in the boat race example (cf. Sec. 2.1.3), the converse of A is *behind* B yields B is *ahead* of A. The composition operation is especially important for constraint reasoning. Two relations can be integrated, i.e. they are composable, if they share one common entity (in the case of binary relations). The composition of two relations may result in additional knowledge. From knowing that E is *ahead* of B and B is *ahead* of A we can derive that also E is *ahead* of A. The composition operation is often given in form of look-up tables called *composition tables*. We give formal definitions of the converse and the composition operation for binary relations below:

Converse: $\qquad\qquad R^\smile \;=\; \{\, (y,x) \mid (x,y) \in R \,\}$

Composition: $\qquad R \circ S \;=\; \{\, (x,z) \mid \exists y \in D : ((x,y) \in R \wedge (y,z) \in S) \,\}.$

The definition of composition as presented above is also called *strong composition*. In contrast, for some calculi no finite set of relations exists that includes the base relations and is closed under composition as defined above. In this case, a *weak composition* is defined instead. Weak composition takes the union of all base relations that have a non-empty intersection with the result of the strong composition:

Weak composition: $\quad R_1 \circ_{weak} R_2 \;=\; \{\, r \mid r \in \mathcal{BR} \wedge r \cap (R_1 \circ R_2) \neq \emptyset \,\}$

While there is only one possibility to permute the two objects of a binary relation (ignoring the identical permutation) which corresponds to the converse operation, there exist five such permutations for the three objects of a ternary relation. The following operations were introduced in (Zimmermann & Freksa, 1996):

Inverse: $\qquad\qquad\quad \mathrm{Inv}(R) \;=\; \{\, (y,x,z) \mid (x,y,z) \in R \,\}$

Short cut: $\qquad\qquad\;\; \mathrm{Sc}(R) \;=\; \{\, (x,z,y) \mid (x,y,z) \in R \,\}$

Inverse short cut: $\qquad \mathrm{Sci}(R) \;=\; \{\, (z,x,y) \mid (x,y,z) \in R \,\}$

Homing: $\qquad\qquad\quad\;\; \mathrm{Hm}(R) \;=\; \{\, (y,z,x) \mid (x,y,z) \in R \,\}$

Inverse homing: $\qquad\;\; \mathrm{Hmi}(R) \;=\; \{\, (z,y,x) \mid (x,y,z) \in R \,\}$

Composition for ternary calculi is adapted from the binary definition as follows:

(Strong) composition: $\quad R_1 \circ R_2 \;=\; \{\, (w,x,z) \mid \exists y \in D :$
$$((w,x,y) \in R_1 \wedge (x,y,z) \in R_2) \,\}$$

We especially note that two entities must be shared by both relations, e.g. $x, y \in D$ as in the definition above, and not only one as in the binary case. Other ways of composing two ternary relations can be expressed by composing two permutations of relations (Scivos & Nebel, 2001). The definition of weak composition is identical to the binary case.

Condotta et al. (2006) state that not necessarily all permutations have to be defined individually. They define a permutation operation[9] and a rotation operation which are sufficient to generate all permutations for n-ary calculi. Nevertheless, all permutations must be specified as primitives if only weak composition is available as the resulting relations may depend on the order of applying the operations. This dependence influences the precision of the result so that not the most specific relation may result.

2.3.2 Constrained-Based Reasoning and Consistency

The relations $\mathcal{R}$ of a spatial calculus are often used to formulate constraints about the spatial configuration of objects from the domain of the calculus. The resulting spatial *constraint satisfaction problem* (CSP) then consists of a set of variables $V = \{v_1, ..., v_n\}$ (one for each spatial object considered) and a set of constraints $C_1, ..., C_m$ with $C_i \in \mathcal{R}$. Each variable v_i can take values from the domain of the utilized calculus. CSPs are often described as constraint networks (CN) which are completely labeled graphs $CN = < V, l >$ where the node set is the set of variables of the CSP and the labeling function $l : V \times V \rightarrow \mathcal{R}$ labels each edge with the constraining relation from the calculus. A CSP is called atomic if all edges are labeled with base relations.

Fig. 2.3 shows a constraint network for the boat race example based on the Point Algebra (cf. Sec. 2.1.3). The labels a, b, and s abbreviate the relations $ahead$, $behind$, and $same$. The variables v_i take the individual boats A to E abstracted as points. The edges not shown correspond to the universal relation U and thus are unconstrained.

A CSP is called *consistent* if an assignment for all variables to objects of the domain can be found, that satisfies all the constraints. Relations in quantitative CSPs are finite relations, and thus these sets of tuples can be manipulated explicitly. However, spatial CSPs usually have infinite domains and thus backtracking over the domains cannot be used to determine consistency. Therefore, special techniques for CSPs with relational constraints have been developed (Ladkin & Reinefeld, 1992).

Besides (global) consistency, weaker forms of consistency called *local consistencies* are of interest in QSR, as they can be used to decide or approximate consistency under specific conditions. Roughly, they can be employed as a forward checking technique reducing the CSP to a smaller equivalent one with the same set of solutions. Furthermore, in some cases they can be proven to be not only necessary but also sufficient for global consistency for the set $\mathcal{R}$ of relations of a given calculus. If this is only the case for a certain subset $\mathcal{S}$ of $\mathcal{R}$ and this subset exhaustively splits $\mathcal{R}$ (which means

---

[9]The permutation R' of a relation R in (Condotta et al., 2006) is defined by the interchange of the last two elements of an n-ary relation: $R' = \{(x_1, ..., x_{n-2}, x_n, x_{n-1}) | (x_1, ..., x_n) \in \mathcal{R}\}$.

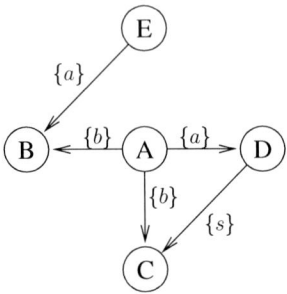

Figure 2.3: A constraint network over Point Algebra relations regarding the boat race example in Sec. 2.1. The direction of the arrows denotes how to read specific relations, e.g. E is *ahead* of B. The edges not shown correspond to the universal relation U and thus are unconstrained.

that every relation from $\mathcal{R}$ can be expressed as a disjunction of relations from $\mathcal{S}$), this at least allows to formulate a backtracking algorithm to determine global consistency by recursively splitting the constraints and using the local consistency as a decision procedure for the resulting CSPs with constraints from $\mathcal{S}$ (Ladkin & Reinefeld, 1992).

One important form of local consistency is *path-consistency* which means that for every triple (in binary CSPs) of variables each consistent evaluation of the first two variables can be extended to the third variable so that all constraints are satisfied. Path-consistency can be enforced syntactically based on the composition operation and the intersection operation, for instance with the algorithm by van Beek (1992) in $O(n^3)$ for binary relations, where n is the number of variables. As the transitivity of the underlying relations is exploited they are also called transitive closure algorithms. Thus, the algorithm is also called *algebraic-closure algorithm*. In Wallgrün et al. (2006) the term *scenario-consistency* is introduced to describe a path-consistent atomic constraint network. For ternary calculi several algorithms were investigated in Dylla & Moratz (2004) and Moratz & Ragni (2008) and resulted in a path-consistency algorithm with complexity $O(n^4)$.

Within the binary algorithm for determining path-consistency successively two constraining relations over three variables are composed and intersected with the relation already known for the resulting two variables until a fix point is reached. For example, one step is to compose the constraining relations for AB and BC and to intersect the result with the constraining relations for AC. If R_{ik} denotes the label of the edge between the nodes v_i and v_k the operation for each step can be defined as follows: $R_{ik} = R_{ik} \cap R_{ij} \circ R_{jk}$. If the empty relation is deduced by this operation the given configuration is definitely inconsistent. In Fig. 2.4 we determine the inconsistency of the boat race example.

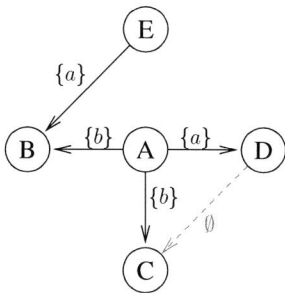

Figure 2.4: The constraint network representing the boat race example (cf. Fig. 2.3) after applying $R_{DC} = R_{DC} \cap R_{DA} \circ R_{AC}$. Because $R_{DC} = \emptyset$ the CSP is inconsistent.

However, this syntactic procedure does not necessarily yield the correct result with respect to path-consistency as defined above, e.g. if only weak composition is available. The same holds for syntactic procedures that compute other kinds of consistency. Whether syntactic consistency coincides with semantic consistency with respect to the domain needs to be investigated for each calculus individually. For an in-depth discussion we refer to Renz & Ligozat (2005) and Ligozat & Renz (2004).

Recently, the term *closure under constraints* has been introduced (Renz & Ligozat, 2005). The authors found evidence that this property is much more important for deciding global consistency based on path-consistency than the fact whether strong or weak composition is given for a calculus. If a calculus is found not to be closed under constraints path-consistency does not decide global consistency. A calculus is not closed under constraints if it is possible to *refine* a relation with an additional relation so that the intersection of both relations is empty. Formally, refinement to a subatomic relation is defined as:

Let Θ be a consistent atomic CSP over a set $\mathcal{A} \subseteq \mathcal{BR}$ and $xRy \in \Theta$ a constraint. Let R' be the union of all tuples $(u, v) \in R$ that can be instantiated to x and y as part of a solution of Θ. If $R' \subset R$, then Θ refines R to the subatomic relation R'.

Based on this refinement closure under constraints is defined as:

Let $\mathcal{A}$ be a set of atomic relations. $\mathcal{A}$ is closed under constraints if no relation $R \in \mathcal{A}$ can be refined to non-overlapping subatomic relation, i.e. , if for each $R \in \mathcal{A}$ all subatomic relations $R' \subset R$ to which R can be refined have a non-empty intersection.

2.3.3 Neighborhood-Based Reasoning

The notion of conceptual neighborhood has been introduced by Freksa (1991). Conceptual neighborhood extends static qualitative representations by interrelating the dis-

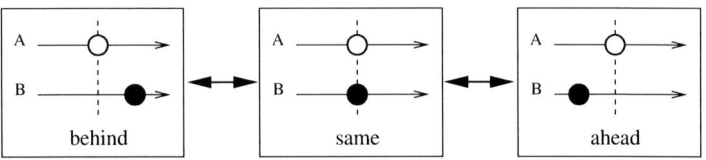

Figure 2.5: The relations of the Point Calculus arranged as a conceptual neighborhood graph $\mathcal{CNG}$.

crete set of base relations by the temporal aspect of transformation of the basic entities.

Two spatial relations of a qualitative spatial calculus are conceptually neighbored, if they can be continuously transformed into each other without resulting in a third relation in between.

The definition of conceptual neighborhood originates from work on time intervals and thus only continuous transformations on intervals (shortening, lengthening, and shifting) were considered. Later, the definition was also interpreted spatially. For moving objects we can say two relations are conceptual neighbors if continuous motion of the objects can cause an immediate transition between these two relations.

For instance, imagine two of the boats in the boat race example. The possible relations in our representation are *behind*, *same*, and *ahead*. The vessels are able to move forward with changing speed. In the configuration shown in Fig. 2.1 vessel A is *behind* B. Observing the scene a few minutes later shows that now A is *ahead* of B. But this is not the whole story. Assuming continuous motion it is not possible for A to overtake B without passing B at some time, i.e. being at the *same* level. Therefore, *ahead* and *behind* cannot be conceptually neighbored within our representation. In contrast, it is possible to get from *same* to either *ahead* or *behind*, and therefore, *ahead* and *behind* are conceptual neighbors of *same*.

The conceptual neighborhood relation, denoted by $\sim$, between the base relations $\mathcal{BR}$ of a qualitative calculus is often described in form of a *conceptual neighborhood graph* $\mathcal{CNG} =< \mathcal{BR}, \sim>$ as illustrated in Fig. 2.5 for the Point Algebra. Alternative names used in the literature are *conceptual neighborhood diagram* and *conceptual neighborhood structure*. A set of base relations which is connected in the $\mathcal{CNG}$ is called a *conceptual neighborhood*.

For convenience, we introduce a function cn : $\mathcal{BR} \rightarrow 2^{\mathcal{BR}}$ which yields all conceptual neighbors for a given base relation $b \in \mathcal{BR}$:

$$\text{cn}(b) = \{b'|(b, b') \in \sim\}$$

Later in this work, we utilize a function that takes a relation given in form of a set S of base relations and yields a coarser relation in which all conceptual neighbors of the base relations have been added. This function, called relax, is defined as follows:

$$\texttt{relax}(S) \;=\; \left(\bigcup_{b \in S} \texttt{cn}(b) \right) \cup S$$

The term *continuous transformation* is a central concept in the definition of conceptual neighborhood. Detailed investigations on different aspects of continuity have been presented in (Bennett & Galton, 2004; Davis, 2001; Galton, 2000a,b; Muller, 1998a). Conceptual neighborhood on the qualitative level corresponds to continuity on the geometric or physical level: continuous processes map onto identical or neighboring classes of descriptions (Freksa, 2004). Spatial neighborhoods are very natural perceptual and cognitive entities. However, the term *continuous* with regard to transformations needs a grounding in spatial change over time. Different kinds of transformations are considered as locomotion, growing or shrinking, or deformation will result in different neighborhood structures.

In the scope of this thesis continuous transformation is the continuous motion of a moving agent, e.g. a robot r. This can be described by the function $pos(r) : T \rightarrow P$, where T is a set of times and P is a set of possible positions of r. Now assuming T and P being topological spaces, the motion of r is continuous, if the function $pos(r)$ is continuous (Galton, 2000a).

Besides Freksa other researchers investigated conceptual neighborhood and its structure. Ligozat (1993) remarks that natural neighborhood relations between spatial relations should be reflected in qualitative spatial reasoning, having in mind the topology of the relations itself. It is considered that the partition of a plane is defined by the relations of a given calculus. He defines neighborhood by means of homeomorphic regions[10] and their dimensionality. Galton (2000b) ascribes conceptual neighborhood to the concept of dominance. It is based on the temporal nature of transitions between qualitative relations connected with the dimensionality of the relations. Intuitively, in case of the Point Calculus the relation *same* dominates *behind* and *ahead*, because *same* only might hold for an instant traversing from *behind* to *ahead* or vice versa. *Ahead* or *behind* cannot only hold for an instant of time as there is always another point between the current state and the state when *same* holds.

2.4 Qualitative Calculi Representing Relative Orientation

In this section we introduce several calculi representing relative orientation information between point objects. We describe the FlipFlop Calculus (Ligozat, 1993), the Single Cross Calculus and the Double Cross Calculus (Freksa, 1992b), the Dipole Relation Algebra (Moratz et al., 2000; Schlieder, 1995), the Qualitative Trajectory Calculus (van de Weghe, 2004; van de Weghe et al., 2005), and the Oriented Point Relation

---

[10]Two objects are homeomorphic if they can be deformed into each other by a continuous, invertible mapping.

Algebra (Moratz, 2006; Moratz et al., 2005). In the end we summarize the major connections between these calculi.

2.4.1   The FlipFlop Calculus (FFC) and the $\mathcal{LR}$ Refinement

The FlipFlop calculus (FFC) proposed in (Ligozat, 1993) describes the position of a point C (the referent) in the plane with respect to two other points A (the origin) and B (the relatum) as illustrated in Fig. 2.6. It can, for instance, be used to describe the spatial relation of C to B as seen from A. For configurations with $A \neq B$ the following base relations are distinguished: C can be to the **left** or to the **right** of the oriented line going through A and B, or C can be placed on the line resulting in one of the five relations **inside**, **front**, **back**, **start** ($C = A$) or **end** ($C = B$) (cf. Fig. 2.7). Relations for the case where A and B coincide were not included in Ligozat's original definition. This was done with the $\mathcal{LR}$ refinement (Scivos & Nebel, 2005) that introduces the relations **dou** ($A = B \neq C$) and **tri** ($A = B = C$)[11] as additional relations, resulting in a total of 9 base relations. A $\mathcal{LR}$ relation $rel_{\mathcal{LR}}$ is written as $A, B \; rel_{\mathcal{LR}} \; C$. The reference frame of the FlipFlop Calculus, respectively of $\mathcal{LR}$, is shown in Fig. 2.6. The seven base relations of the FFC are depicted in Fig. 2.7. In the following we will not distinguish between FFC and $\mathcal{LR}$ and refer to the $\mathcal{LR}$ set of base relations by FFC as well.

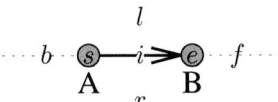

Figure 2.6: The reference frame for the $\mathcal{LR}$ calculus spanned by A and B. $\mathcal{LR}$ is a refined version of the FlipFlop Calculus.

2.4.2   Single Cross Calculus (SCC)

The Single Cross Calculus is a ternary calculus that describes the direction of a point C (the referent) with respect to a point B (the relatum) as seen from a third point A (the origin). It was proposed by Freksa (1992b). The plane is partitioned into regions by the line going through A and B and the perpendicular line through B. This results in eight distinct orientations as illustrated in Fig. 2.8(a). Throughout this thesis we denote these base relations by numbers from **0** to **7** instead of using linguistic

---

[11]In (Scivos & Nebel, 2005) the relations where originally named e_{12} (**dou**) and eq (**tri**). We use the terms dou and tri throughout the paper for referring to the two different cases in ternary calculi where origin and relatum coincide.

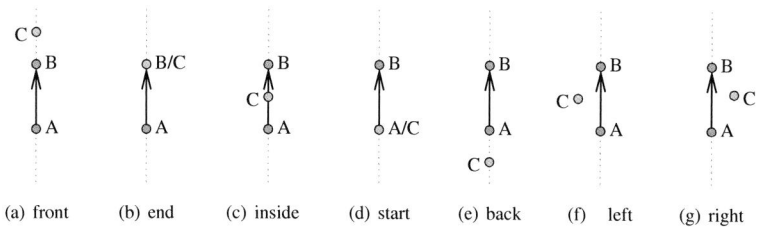

| (a) front | (b) end | (c) inside | (d) start | (e) back | (f) left | (g) right |

Figure 2.7: Pictorial representations of the seven FlipFlop relations (excluding *dou* and *tri*)

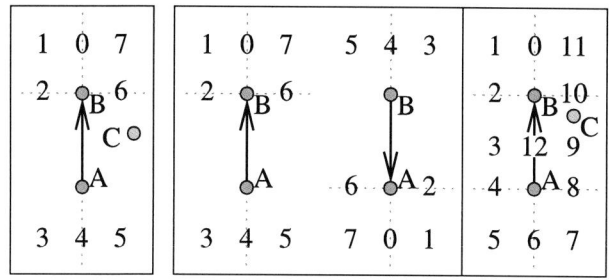

(a) Single Cross Calculus reference frame. (b) The two Single Cross reference frames resulting in the overall Double Cross Calculus reference frame.

Figure 2.8: The Single and Double Cross reference systems.

prepositions. The original linguistic terms are: straight-front (**0**), left-front (**1**), left-neutral (**2**), left-back (**3**), straight-back (**4**), right-back (**5**), right-neutral (**6**), and right-front (**7**) (cf. Freksa, 1992b). Relations **0**, **2**, **4**, **6** are linear ones, while relations **1**, **3**, **5**, **7** are planar. In addition, three special relations exist for the cases $A \neq B - C$ (**bc**), $A = B \neq C$ (**dou**), and $A = B = C$ (**tri**). A Single Cross relation rel_{SCC} is written as $A, B\ rel_{SCC}\ C$, e.g. $A, B\ \mathbf{4}\ C$ or $A, B\ \mathbf{dou}\ C$. The relation depicted in Fig. 2.8(a) is the relation $A, B\ \mathbf{5}\ C$.

2.4.3   Double Cross Calculus (DCC)

The Double Cross Calculus (Freksa, 1992b) can be seen as an extension of the Single Cross calculus adding another perpendicular, this time at A (see Fig. 2.8(b) (right)). It can also be interpreted as the combination of two Single Cross relations, the first describing the position of C wrt. B as seen from A and the second wrt. A as seen from B (cf. Fig. 2.8(b) (left)). The resulting partition distinguishes 13 relations (7 linear and 6 planar) derived from the two underlying SCC reference frames[12] and four special cases, $A = C \neq B$ (relax(a)), $A \neq B = C$ (**b**), $A = B \neq C$ (**dou**), and $A = B = C$ (**tri**), resulting in 17 base relations overall. Fig. 2.8(b) depicts the relation A, B **9** C.

2.4.4 The Dipole Calculus and Dipole Relation Algebras ($\mathcal{DRA}$)

Schlieder (1995) proposes a two-dimensional generalization of Allen's interval relations. The 2D generalization permits representation of the relative position of two line segments. Schlieder then exploits that linear ordering is the one-dimensional specialization of generalized n-dimensional point ordering. The two-dimensional case, like the one-dimensional case, also induces a set of interval relations to represent the relative position of two line segments in the plane. These directed line segments, in the following also called *dipoles*, are used for representing spatial objects with intrinsic orientation. A dipole A is defined by two points, the start point s_A and the end point e_A. Schlieder assumes four pairwise different points in general position. General position is defined such that no three points are on one line. Thereby a left/right dichotomy is specified for each point regarding the dipole the point is not contained in. This approach, in the following also called Dipole Calculus (DC), leads to 14 base relations[13].

Each base relation is a quaternary tuple (r_1, r_2, r_3, r_4) of, so to speak, restricted FlipFlop relations relating a point from one of the dipoles with the other dipole. r_1 describes the relation of s_B with respect to the dipole A, r_2 of e_B with respect to A, r_3 of s_A with respect to B, and r_4 of e_A with respect to B. Due to the restrictions of the point positions only **l**eft and **r**ight are possible for each r_i with $i \in \{1, ..., 4\}$. Dipole relations are usually written without commas and parentheses, e.g. **rrll**. The example in Fig. 2.9 shows the relation A **rlll** B.

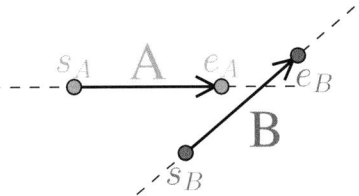

Figure 2.9: A dipole configuration: A **rlll** B in the Dipole Calculus (DC).

Moratz et al. (2000) relax the restriction of unique points, so that only the start

---

[12]Originally the relation names were derived from the relation tuples defined by the two individual reference frames, e.g. **5_3** corresponds to **9** or **4_a** corresponds to **a**.

[13]Out of the $4^2 = 16$ configurations only 14 are geometrically realizable.

point and end point of one dipole have to be unique. In their representation two dipoles may have the same start point or end point, but no three disjoint points are collinear. This leads to ten additional base relations resulting in 24 JEPD base relations overall (cf. Fig. 2.10). We call this framework the coarse Dipole Relation Algebra ($\mathcal{DRA}_c$).

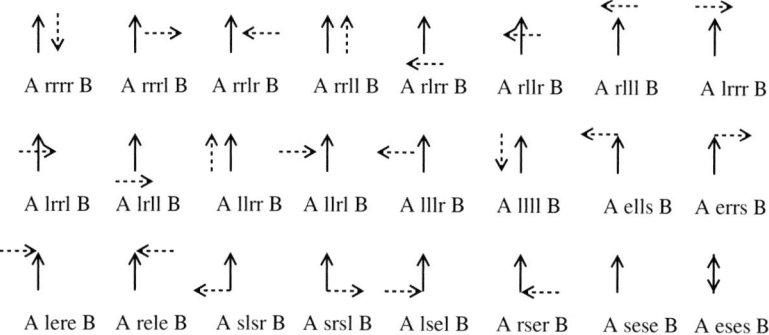

Figure 2.10:   The 24 atomic relations of the coarse dipole calculus. In the dipole calculus orthogonality is not defined, although the graphic presentation might suggest this.

In (Moratz et al., 2000) a fine-grained variant of the Dipole Relation Algebra ($\mathcal{DRA}_f$) was sketched, and further elaborated in (Dylla & Moratz, 2005). Without restrictions on the point positions, except that start and end point of a dipole must be disjoint, each r_i with $i \in \{1, ..., 4\}$ can carry any of the FlipFlop relations *front*, *end*, *inside*, *start*, *back*, *left*, or *right*. The number of base relations is 72 for $\mathcal{DRA}_f$ as not all combinations are physically possible.

2.4.5   The Qualitative Trajectory Calculus (QTC)

The Qualitative Trajectory Calculus (van de Weghe, 2004; van de Weghe et al., 2005)[14] was recently developed. QTC takes into account changes between two moving objects on a plane. For the relations a 'double cross' reference system is built up by the observation of two objects' positions A and B at a certain time point t_i, denoted by A_{t_i} and B_{t_i} in the following. The relative position changes between t_i and t_j (with $j > i$) are expressed within this reference system. The relations are denoted by four letters each taking the values $+$, $-$, or 0. The first letter describes the change in distance of A with respect to the perpendicular to the line $A_{t_i}B_{t_i}$ at point B_{t_i} that occurred during t_i and t_j. In Fig. 2.11, A_{t_j} is on the same side of the perpendicular at A_{t_i} as B_{t_i}, and

---

[14]Although van de Weghe (2004) defines different variants of the calculus, we present only the most complex variant which deals with orientation QTC_{C21}. We do not regard simpler variants or variants extended with information on qualitative speed.

thus it is closer and the letter takes the value $-$. The second letter expresses the change in distance of B_{t_j} compared to the perpendicular at A_{t_i}. B_{t_j} is further away from it, therefore the value is $+$. The third and fourth letter abstract the relative motion to the side regarding the directed line from A_{t_i} to B_{t_i}, respectively from B_{t_i} to A_{t_i}. In our example A moves to the left $(-)$ of $A_{t_i}B_{t_i}$ and B to the left $(-)$ of $B_{t_i}A_{t_i}$. This results in the relation $A\,(-+--)\,B$.

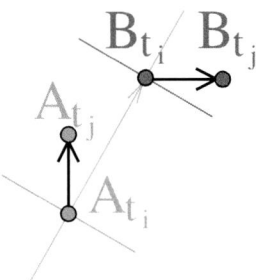

Figure 2.11: An example of the Qualitative Trajectory Calculus relation $A\,(-+\allowbreak--)\,B$.

2.4.6   The Oriented Point Relation Algebra with Adjustable Granularity ($\mathcal{OPRA}_m$)

The domain of the Oriented Point Relation Algebra ($\mathcal{OPRA}_m$) (Moratz, 2006; Moratz et al., 2005) is the set of oriented points (points in the plane with an additional direction parameter). The calculus relates two oriented points with respect to their relative orientation towards each other. An oriented point $\vec{O}$ can be described by its Cartesian coordinates $x_O, y_O \in \mathbb{R}$ and a direction $\phi_{\vec{O}} \in [0, 2\pi]$ with respect to a reference direction and thus $D = \mathbb{R}^2 \times [0, 2\pi]$.

The $\mathcal{OPRA}_m$ calculus is suited for dealing with objects that have an intrinsic front or move in a particular direction and can be abstracted as points. The exact set of base relations distinguished in $\mathcal{OPRA}_m$ depends on the granularity parameter $m \in \mathbb{N}$. For each of the two related oriented points, m lines are used to partition the plane into $2m$ planar and $2m$ linear regions. Fig. 2.12 shows the partitions for the cases $m = 2$ (a) and $m = 4$ (b). The orientation of the two points is depicted by the arrows starting at $\vec{A}$ and $\vec{B}$, respectively. The regions are numbered from 0 to $4m - 1$, region 0 always coincides with the orientation of the point. An $\mathcal{OPRA}_m$ base relation consists of a pair (i, j) where i is the number of the region of $\vec{A}$ which contains $\vec{B}$, while j is the number

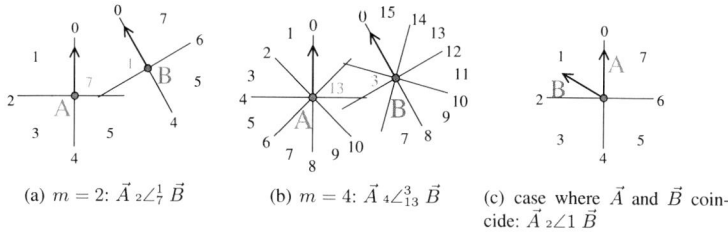

(a) $m = 2$: $\vec{A}\ _2\angle_7^1\ \vec{B}$ (b) $m = 4$: $\vec{A}\ _4\angle_{13}^3\ \vec{B}$ (c) case where $\vec{A}$ and $\vec{B}$ coincide: $\vec{A}\ _2\angle1\ \vec{B}$

Figure 2.12: Two oriented points related at different granularities.

of the region of $\vec{B}$ that contains $\vec{A}$. These relations are usually written as $\vec{A}\ _m\angle_i^j\ \vec{B}$ with $i, j \in \mathcal{Z}_{4m}$[15]. Thus, the examples in Fig. 2.12 depict the relations $\vec{A}\ _2\angle_7^1\ \vec{B}$ and $\vec{A}\ _4\angle_{13}^3\ \vec{B}$. Additional base relations called *'same' relations* describe situations in which both oriented points coincide. In these cases, the relation is determined by the number s of the region of $\vec{A}$ in which the orientation arrow of $\vec{B}$ is positioned (as illustrated in Figure 2.12(c)). These relations are written as $\vec{A}\ _2\angle s\ \vec{B}$ ($\vec{A}\ _2\angle1\ \vec{B}$ in the example). The total number of base relations with respect to granularity m is $(4m)^2 + 4m$.

2.4.7 Dependencies Between Relative Orientation Calculi

In the following we summarize the dependencies of the point-based calculi dealing with relative orientation in a plane.

The first orientation calculi dealing with points in a two-dimensional plane were the Single Cross Calculus and the Double Cross Calculus (Freksa, 1992b). The Qualitative Trajectory Calculus (van de Weghe, 2004) is based directly on the idea of the Double Cross Calculus, namely conjoining two Single Cross reference frames. Instead of only relating a single point to both reference frames, two different points – the perceptions of A and B at a successive times – are related to the reversed reference frame. The FlipFlop Calculus is based on qualitative trigonometry (Ligozat, 1993). Ligozat discovers that the idea of reasoning about partially known angular values gives rise to a whole family of spatial calculi. This family also contains the Double Cross Calculus as a special member. Although the Dipole Calculus (Schlieder, 1995) was derived on a two-dimensional generalization of Allen's interval relations, i.e. a two-dimensional linear ordering, it turns out that it is a logical conjunction of four FlipFlop relations with certain restrictions to the point positions. These restrictions were relaxed at different levels regarding other variants of the Dipole Relation Algebras. The Oriented Point Relation Algebra is derived from the Dipole Relation Algebras by assuming an infinitesimal distance between start point and end point of a dipole. So, the reference

---

[15] $\mathcal{Z}_{4m}$ defines a cyclic group with $4m$ elements ($\{0, ..., (4m - 1)\}$).

frame is reduced to a single point with an intrinsic reference direction. In addition, granularity is grounded in the algebraic relation specifications.

Chapter 3

A General Approach to Representing Relative Orientation Information

In this chapter we give an algorithm for composing relations of the Oriented Point Relation Algebra ($\mathcal{OPRA}_m$). In addition, we consider reasoning properties of $\mathcal{OPRA}_m$ relations. $\mathcal{OPRA}_m$ is the most general qualitative calculus representing relative orientation information currently defined. We show this by representing other orientation calculi in terms of $\mathcal{OPRA}_m$ relations and sketch how composition tables and neighborhood graphs of the mapped calculi can be derived by means of the mappings to $\mathcal{OPRA}_m$.

3.1 Introduction

A considerable part of everyday human activities is guided by regulations or recommendations. These rules are usually formulated in natural language and so in many cases *qualitative terms* are used to describe the situations that are governed by the rules. For example, in traffic laws qualitative spatial concepts like "from the right" are used to describe situations governed as well as "correct" behavior of agents.

For example, the set of Collision Regulations in Sea Navigation (ColRegs) as presented by the International Maritime Organization (IMO, 1972) contains rules like:

- When two power-driven vessels are meeting on reciprocal or nearly reciprocal courses so as to involve risk of collision each shall alter her course to starboard[1] so that each shall pass on the port side of the other. (Rule 14(a))

---

[1] *Starboard* is the nautical term that refers to the right side of a vessel with respect to its *bow* (front); *port* refers to the left hand side, *stern* to the back.

- When two power-driven vessels are crossing so as to involve risk of collision, the vessel which has the other on her own starboard side shall keep out of the way and shall, if the circumstances of the case admit, avoid crossing ahead of the other vessel. (Rule 15(a))

Relevant aspects for this kind of rules dealing with dynamic scenarios are orientation, distance, and speed of the objects involved. To make such rules processable by artificial agents, they need to be formalized. The formalizations should be easy and intuitive for developers of the agents. To make a start we will concentrate on relative 2D orientation information. From our point of view, orientation is the most important aspect, out of the list of relevant aspects, if we assume a "sufficient" distance between the vessels, such that "enough reaction time" is given to execute actions like turning or stopping successfully.

In recent years many different calculi dealing with relative orientation have been presented. Among them we find the FlipFlop Calculus (FFC), the Single Cross Calculus (SCC), the Double Cross Calculus (DCC), the coarse Dipole Relation Algebra ($\mathcal{DRA}_c$), and the Qualitative Trajectory Calculus (QTC). For details on these calculi we refer to Section 2.4. For developers it is a hard task to find out which of these calculi is sufficient to represent the rule set at hand, e.g. to represent collision regulations as mentioned in the beginning of this chapter. Additionally, it is not reasonable – and not to be expected at all – that developers of cognitive agents are familiar with all of these calculi. Furthermore, in some context it might be reasonable to switch between two calculi to solve a task, e.g. the Double Cross Calculus and the Dipole Relation Algebra. In general, defining a mapping between the relations of two calculi is not a trivial task. Therefore, it is reasonable to develop a representation for orientation that is able to subsume the expressiveness of other relative orientation calculi. We call a calculus that may serve as a general representation for orientation *umbrella calculus*.

All the calculi mentioned above have in common that they represent relative orientation at a fixed level of granularity, either a left/right dichotomy defined by two of the points (origin and relatum)[2], or with additional perpendiculars at one or both of the points spanning the reference line. As it turned out in our investigations on representing collision regulations in sea navigation, these levels of granularity are not sufficient. Although more fine-grained variants could be derived for these calculi, the only one capable of dealing with different levels of granularity within the original definition of base relations and its operations is the Oriented Point Relation Algebra ($\mathcal{OPRA}_m$). Refining the other calculi would be possible, but this entails that compositions and neighborhood structures must be derived from scratch. These two tasks are very time consuming and error prone. Therefore, we favor the Oriented Point Relation Algebra as an umbrella calculus for relative orientation calculi. Given the composition for $\mathcal{OPRA}_m$ relations we are then able to generate composition tables for the calculus represented by means of the transformation to $\mathcal{OPRA}_m$ relations. Additionally,

---

[2]We disregard here that the Dipole Relation Algebra contains two different frames of reference (cf. Sec. 2.4.4)

neighborhood graphs can be derived based on the $\mathcal{OPRA}_m$ neighborhood structure as well.

To reach our goal of developing a unifying and superior representation of relative orientation, we first discuss composition issues of $\mathcal{OPRA}_m$ relations. Furthermore, we derive the neighborhood structure for relations with arbitrary granularity m afterwards. In addition, we take a closer look on properties of reasoning with $\mathcal{OPRA}_m$ relations. Afterwards, we represent other relative orientation calculi in terms of $\mathcal{OPRA}_m$ relations. In the end, we apply these mappings for deriving composition tables and neighborhood structures for the formalized calculi. Before, we introduce several abbreviations, e.g. for disjunctions of $\mathcal{OPRA}_m$ relations, for better readability.

3.2 Notation

In the following we deal extensively with $\mathcal{OPRA}_m$ relations (cf. Sec. 2.4.6). On the one hand we are concerned with *normal* or *regular points*, e.g. P being defined by their position in the plane ($P = (x_P, y_P) \in \mathbb{R}^2$). On the other hand, we will talk about *oriented points* (o-points) as required for the $\mathcal{OPRA}_m$ calculus, written as $\vec{O}$. The following notations will be used assuming A, B, and C are normal points: the direction ϕ^{BC} is defined as the direction from B towards C. We write $\vec{A}^{BC}$ for the oriented point $((x_A, y_A), \phi^{BC})$; it has the same position as the normal point A and the direction ϕ^{BC}. We write $\vec{A}$ if the direction is unknown or unspecified, e.g. if we want to define an oriented point that coincides with A that can have an arbitrary fixed direction. Note that $\vec{A}^{AB}$, $\vec{A}^{AC}$, and $\vec{A}$ are three different oriented points coinciding in position but possibly differing in orientation. Additionally, we want to emphasize that oriented point names like $\vec{A}^{AC}$ are only identifiers we use for making their role intuitively comprehensible. The semantics is completely given by the $\mathcal{OPRA}_m$ relations between the identifiers. The knowledge that one oriented point either coincides with or is oriented towards another has to be explicitly represented by respective relations.

We will speak of *'same' relations* if point positions coincide ($m\angle s$) and *non-'same' relations* otherwise ($m\angle_i^j$). For reasons of simplicity we refer to i, j, and s as regions or sectors, although they denote lines if $i \mod 2 = 0$, j and s respectively.

In the following, we will speak about disjunctions of base relations instead of unions of base relations (cf. Sec. 2.3), because they are better to handle for the following considerations. We will use the abbreviation $\vec{A} \ m\angle_{i..j}^{k..l} \ \vec{B}$ with $i, j, k, l \in \mathcal{Z}_{4m}{}^3$ for the disjunction

$$\vec{A} \ m\angle_{i..j}^{k..l} \ \vec{B} = \bigvee_{a=i}^{j} \bigvee_{b=k}^{l} \vec{A} \ m\angle_a^b \ \vec{B} \ .$$

As the values are elements of the cyclic group $\mathcal{Z}_{4m}$, we point out that $m\angle_{i..j}^x$ denotes different relations than $m\angle_{j..i}^x$. For example, $m\angle_{3..5}^x$ denotes a disjunction

---

[3] $\mathcal{Z}_{4m}$ defines a cyclic group with $4m$ elements ($\{0, ..., (4m - 1)\}$).

of three relations $m\angle_3^x \lor m\angle_4^x \lor m\angle_5^x$, whereas $m\angle_{5..3}^x$ denotes the disjunction $m\angle_{5..(4m-1)}^x \lor m\angle_{0..3}^x$.

A star $(*)$ abbreviates all members 0 to $(4m - 1)$ of $\mathcal{Z}_{4m}$ and (i, j) a disjunction of i and j such that for example $\vec{A}\; m\angle_{(i,j)}^*\; \vec{B}$ denotes:

$$\vec{A}\; m\angle_{(i,j)}^*\; \vec{B} = \vec{A}\; m\angle_{i,j}^*\; \vec{B} = \left(\bigvee_{b=0}^{4m-1} \vec{A}\; m\angle_i^b\; \vec{B} \right) \lor \left(\bigvee_{b=0}^{4m-1} \vec{A}\; m\angle_j^b\; \vec{B} \right).$$

3.3 Reasoning With $\mathcal{OPRA}_m$ Relations

In Qualitative Spatial Reasoning (QSR) two variants of reasoning are predominant: on the one hand constraint-based reasoning and on the other hand neighborhood-based reasoning. Roughly, in constraint-based reasoning additional knowledge about objects can be derived by combining and manipulating the existing relations. The most important operation is composition where two relations are combined. Neighborhood-based reasoning assumes continuous transformation of the objects involved and reflects the direct reachability of relations, i.e. without traversing other relations in between, in a conceptual neighborhood graph (cf. Sec. 2.3.3 for details).

We first define an algorithm for composing $\mathcal{OPRA}_m$ relations and derive the conceptual neighborhood structure afterwards.

3.3.1 Composition

Relations of $\mathcal{OPRA}_m$ represent relative orientation information at a certain granularity with respect to the granularity parameter m. The parameter m divides the angular range in $2m$ equidistant angular planar sectors and additional $2m$ linear sectors in between. Because of the well-defined algebraic semantics of $\mathcal{OPRA}_m$ base relations, we are able to define composition algorithmically. Moreover, due to the variable granularity of the calculus, a tabular representation of the composition operation for arbitrary m is infeasible. The algorithm can be applied easily for deriving the composition table for specific m.

Algorithms for composing $\mathcal{OPRA}_m$ relations were already presented in Moratz et al. (2005) and Moratz (2006), but these algorithms need further consideration. Moratz presents a weak composition which narrows down the solution space significantly. However, in some cases the solution space can be reduced even further. The algorithm sketched here, is in principle based on the same idea presented by Moratz (2006). Both algorithms rely on the determination of valid triangle configurations described by the two relations to compose. Some of the configurations derived by Moratz do not necessarily constitute valid triangles. Our algorithm differs in the way the triangle configurations are derived and evaluated. In addition, we consider composition including 'same' relations. Both algorithms have a complexity of

$O(m^2)$. The complete algorithm and further details on the derivation are presented in (Frommberger et al., 2007).

Given the three o-points $\vec{A}$, $\vec{B}$, and $\vec{C}$ and their relative orientation represented by $\mathcal{OPRA}_m$ relations r_{AB}, r_{BC}, and r_{CA} ($\vec{A}\, r_{AB}\, \vec{B}$, $\vec{B}\, r_{BC}\, \vec{C}$, and $\vec{C}\, r_{CA}\, \vec{A}$) three classes can be differentiated:

1. configurations without 'same' relations, i.e. $\vec{A}$, $\vec{B}$, and $\vec{C}$ do not pairwise coincide in point position,

2. configurations with one 'same' relation regarding $\vec{A}$ and $\vec{B}$, $\vec{B}$ and $\vec{C}$, or $\vec{A}$ and $\vec{C}$, and

3. configurations with only 'same' relations, i.e. $\vec{A}$, $\vec{B}$, and $\vec{C}$ all coincide in point position.

Within these categorizations further subclasses with specific properties can be identified which we present below. Based on these categories the composition algorithm is defined.

Without 'Same' Relations

In this case, the three o-point positions are different and a triangle is defined by them. It follows that the inner angles sum up to π, although the triangle might be degenerate. We assume w.l.o.g. that the three o-points defining the triangle to be positively oriented. Assuming all three relations r_{AB}, r_{BC}, and r_{AC} are given the triangle is defined completely, e.g. a triangle as in Fig. 3.1. We define the relations by $r_{AB} = {}_m\angle_i^j$, $r_{BC} = {}_m\angle_k^l$, and $r_{CA} = {}_m\angle_s^t$ with $i, j, k, l, s, t \in \mathcal{Z}_{4m}$. Three vectors $v_{\vec{A}} = \binom{j}{i}$, $v_{\vec{B}} = \binom{l}{k}$, and $v_{\vec{C}} = \binom{t}{s}$ can be defined giving the relative position of two points regarding the reference frame of a specific o-point, e.g. $v_{\vec{A}}$ regarding the reference frame defined by $\vec{A}$. The properties of a triangle defined by three o-points depend on whether the angular orientations are precisely given (linear sector) or not (planar sector). Based on the vectors v_x with $x \in \{\vec{A}, \vec{B}, \vec{C}\}$ we can define vectors v'_x giving this information by calculating the individual components modulo 2. This yields three different kinds of vectors: both parameters define linear sectors ($\binom{0}{0}$), one parameter defines a linear sector and the other a planar sector ($\binom{1}{0}$, $\binom{0}{1}$), and both parameters define planar sectors ($\binom{1}{1}$). Based on the 3-tuples of $(v'_{\vec{A}}, v'_{\vec{B}}, v'_{\vec{C}})$ 10 different categories can be defined. From the category $\mathcal{K}_1$ where all $v'_x = \binom{0}{0}$ over the category $\mathcal{K}_4$ where all $v'_x \in \{\binom{0}{1}, \binom{1}{0}\}$ to the category $\mathcal{K}_{10}$ where all $v'_x = \binom{1}{1}$. For further details we refer to Frommberger et al. (2007).

Now, by using the fact that the inner angles of a triangle sum up to π the sets K_n with $n \in \{1, .., 10\}$ of valid triangle configurations can be determined for each class $\mathcal{K}_n$. For example, the triangle depicted in Fig. 3.1 with $r_{AB} = {}_4\angle_{12}^1$, $r_{BC} = {}_4\angle_{14}^{11}$, and $r_{CA} = {}_4\angle_{13}^8$ belongs to K_4, because the three o-points define a triangle and $(v'_{\vec{A}}, v'_{\vec{B}}, v'_{\vec{C}}) = (\binom{1}{0}, \binom{1}{0}, \binom{1}{0}) \in \mathcal{K}_4$. The proofs for each class can be found in Frommberger et al. (2007).

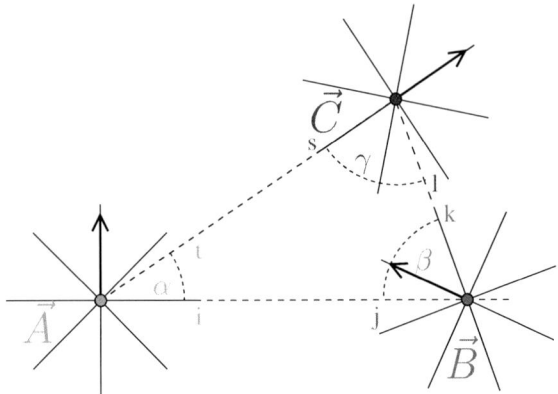

Figure 3.1: A completely specified triangle: $r_{AB} = 4\angle_{12}^1$, $r_{BC} = 4\angle_{14}^{11}$, and $r_{CA} = 4\angle_{13}^8$. The corresponding vectors are given by $v_{\vec{A}} = \binom{13}{12}$, $v_{\vec{B}} = \binom{1}{14}$, $v_{\vec{C}} = \binom{11}{8}$, and $v'_{\vec{A}} = \binom{1}{0}$, $v'_{\vec{B}} = \binom{1}{0}$, $v'_{\vec{C}} = \binom{1}{0}$.

Only 'Same' Relations

In this case we assume the configuration is specified by $r_{AB} = m\angle i$, $r_{BC} = m\angle k$, $r_{CA} = m\angle s$. Applying the same idea on linear and planar specification of the angles as above, we can define $w_{\vec{A}} = i$, $w_{\vec{B}} = k$, $w_{\vec{C}} = s$, and w'_x accordingly, only this time on single values instead of vectors, i.e. instead of four different vectors we only have values 0 or 1. This yields four different categories ($\mathcal{S}_1$ to $\mathcal{S}_4$) of three tuples: all values are 0, two values are 0, only one value is 0, and finally, all values are 1.

One 'Same' Relation

In this case two o-points coincide in position, i.e. we have one 'same' relation and two non-'same' relations. W.l.o.g. we assume that the configuration is given by $r_{AB} = m\angle i$, $r_{BC} = m\angle_k^l$, $r_{CA} = m\angle_s^t$. The categorization is similar to the case with only 'same' relations. Here t is the relevant value for the categorization into the four classes $\mathcal{T}_1$ to $\mathcal{T}_4$. Instead of s being relevant for the categories $\mathcal{S}_n$ with $n \in \{1, .., 4\}$, here, t is relevant for the categories $\mathcal{T}_n$. So, we define $y_{\vec{A}} = i$, $y_{\vec{B}} = k$, $y_{\vec{C}} = t$, and y'_x accordingly.

The Composition Algorithm

Based on the categorizations above the composition algorithm can be defined. If relations r_{AB} and r_{BC} for three disjoint points are given, r_{CA} is part of the solution, if the according three tuple $(v_{\vec{A}}, v_{\vec{B}}, v_{\vec{C}})$ is a member of one of the sets K_1 to K_{10}. Instead of referring to the classes S_n or T_n for cases with one 'same' relation or only 'same' relations we give the composition for configurations belonging to one of them directly:

- $r_{AB} = m\angle i \wedge r_{BC} = m\angle k :$

$$m\angle i \circ m\angle k = \begin{cases} m\angle(i+k) & i \mod 2 = 0 \vee k \mod 2 = 0 \\ \bigcup_{a=i+k-1}^{i+k+1} m\angle a & \text{else} \end{cases}$$

- $r_{AB} = m\angle i \wedge r_{BC} = m\angle_k^l$ or $r_{AB} = m\angle_i^j \wedge r_{BC} = m\angle k :$

  - $m\angle i \circ m\angle_k^l \begin{cases} m\angle_{i+k}^t & i \mod 2 = 0 \vee k \mod 2 = 0 \\ \bigcup_{a=i+k-1}^{i+k+1} m\angle_a^l & \text{else} \end{cases}$

  - $m\angle_i^j \circ m\angle k \begin{cases} m\angle_i^{j-k} & j \mod 2 = 0 \vee k \mod 2 = 0 \\ \bigcup_{a=j-k-1}^{j-k+1} m\angle_i^a & \text{else} \end{cases}$

- $r_{AB} = m\angle_i^j \wedge r_{BC} = m\angle_k^l :$
  check for all $s, t \in \mathcal{Z}_{4m}$ whether $(v_{\vec{A}}, v_{\vec{B}}, v_{\vec{C}}) \in \mathcal{K}_{n_K}$ with $(v'_{\vec{A}}, v'_{\vec{B}}, v'_{\vec{C}}) \in \mathcal{K}_{n_K}$ and additionally, whether $(i, k, t) \in \mathcal{T}_{n_T}$ with $(y'_{\vec{A}}, y'_{\vec{B}}, y'_{\vec{C}}) \in \mathcal{T}_{n_T}$ ('same' relations as result).

In the worst case of r_{AB} and r_{BC} being non-'same' relations, the algorithm loops $4m \cdot (4m + 1)$ times. Calculation of K_n, S_n, and T_n is done in constant time for each configuration, so the overall complexity of the algorithm is $O(m^2)$. Because m is a constant granularity, the algorithm computes composition for every instance of $\mathcal{OPRA}_m$ in constant time.

3.3.2 Reasoning Properties of $\mathcal{OPRA}_m$

Renz & Ligozat (2005) show that algebraic closure decides consistency for CSPs over a set of atomic relations if and only if this set is closed under constraints (cf. Sec. 2.3.1). Unfortunately, $\mathcal{OPRA}_m$ is not closed under constraints.

Consequently, standard constraint reasoning techniques can only be applied for $\mathcal{OPRA}_m$ as approximations of consistency. Even in the case of atomic networks inconsistencies might not be detected by algebraic-closure. Thus, algebraic-closure is not sufficient to decide consistency even for atomic networks. For finding these inconsistencies we need to extend the syntactic method of algebraic-closure with semantic post processing.

In Fig. 3.2 we depict a configuration with four disjoint o-points $\vec{A}, \vec{B}, \vec{C}$, and $\vec{D}$ to illustrate that $\mathcal{OPRA}_m$ is not closed under constraints. $\vec{D}$ is supposed to be on the line

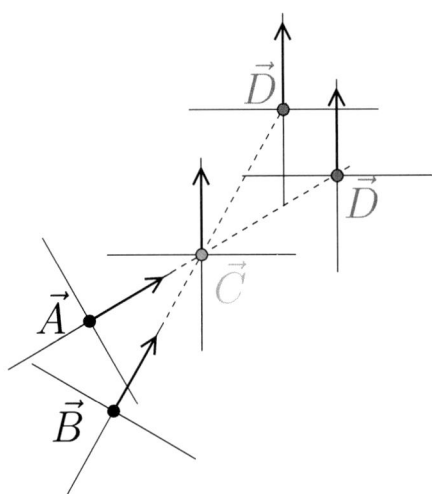

Figure 3.2: In this example two different lines are defined by the tuples $(\vec{A}, \vec{C})$ and $(\vec{B}, \vec{C})$. $\vec{D}$ is supposed to lie on both lines: $\vec{A} \, _2\angle_5^1 \, \vec{B}$, $\vec{A} \, _2\angle_0^3 \, \vec{C}$, $\vec{A} \, _2\angle_0^3 \, \vec{D}$, $\vec{B} \, _2\angle_0^3 \, \vec{C}$, $\vec{B} \, _2\angle_0^3 \, \vec{D}$, and $\vec{C} \, _2\angle_7^3 \, \vec{D}$.

defined by $\vec{A}$ and $\vec{C}$ as well as on the line defined by $\vec{B}$ and $\vec{C}$. But because $\vec{B}$ is not on the line defined by $\vec{A}$ and $\vec{C}$, $\vec{D}$ is supposed to be on two different lines at the same time, which is inconsistent. In terms of Renz & Ligozat (2005) the relation between $\vec{C}$ and $\vec{D}$ is refined by stating that $\vec{A}$ and $\vec{B}$ also point at $\vec{D}$ ($\vec{A} \, _2\angle_0^3 \, \vec{D}$ and $\vec{B} \, _2\angle_0^3 \, \vec{D}$). As indicated by the dashed lines, this refines the relation $\vec{C} \, _2\angle_7^3 \, \vec{D}$ into two different linear subatomic relations which have an empty intersection. This configuration is evaluated as consistent with respect to the algebraic-closure algorithm[4]. The complete atomic constraint network is given by:

$$\vec{A} \, _2\angle_5^1 \, \vec{B}, \; \vec{A} \, _2\angle_0^3 \, \vec{C}, \; \vec{A} \, _2\angle_0^3 \, \vec{D}, \; \vec{B} \, _2\angle_0^3 \, \vec{C}, \; \vec{B} \, _2\angle_0^3 \, \vec{D}, \text{ and } \vec{C} \, _2\angle_7^3 \, \vec{D}.$$

In the following we present a method for detecting inconsistent atomic constraint networks by making the refinement explicit, i.e. by adding further o-points with specific orientations to the original configuration. Although we cannot prove in general that all inconsistent atomic networks can be found, at least some inconsistencies can

---

[4]The computations were performed with SparQ (Wallgrün et al., 2006), a generic toolbox for reasoning with qualitative calculi (http://www.sfbtr8.uni-bremen.de/project/r3/sparq/). We introduce SparQ in Sec. 6.2.1.

be detected. To construct the necessary points, we need two additional operations on the relations:

- *orientation rotation* and
- *o-point projection.*

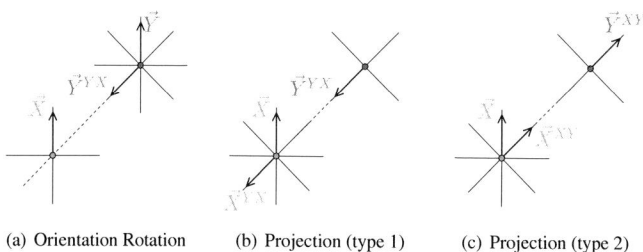

(a) Orientation Rotation   (b) Projection (type 1)   (c) Projection (type 2)

Figure 3.3: Diagrammatic sketch showing how new o-points can be constructed by orientation rotation and projection.

Assume $\vec{X} \ _m\angle_i^j \ \vec{Y}$ as given. With orientation rotation we rotate the orientation of $\vec{Y}$ such that it is oriented towards $\vec{X}$. This results in a new o-point $\vec{Y}^{YX}$ with $\vec{X} \ _m\angle_i^0 \ \vec{Y}^{YX}$ (cf. Fig. 3.3(a)) Now that we have an o-point that directly points to $\vec{X}$, we can move $\vec{Y}^{YX}$ straight forward until it coincides with $\vec{X}$. This yields the new point $\vec{X}^{YX}$ with $\vec{X} \ _m\angle(2m+i) \ \vec{X}^{YX}$ (projection type 1). Accordingly, we can derive 'same' relations for o-points pointing away from $\vec{X}$ by straight backward motion (projection type 2). For example, given relation $\vec{X} \ _m\angle_i^{2m} \ \vec{Y}^{XY}$ we can construct a new o-point $\vec{X}^{XY}$ so that $\vec{X} \ _m\angle i \ \vec{X}^{XY}$. We depict these two cases in Fig. 3.3(b) and Fig. 3.3(c). We summarize the propositions below:

$$\vec{X} \ _m\angle_i^j \ \vec{Y} : \quad \vec{X} \ _m\angle_i^0 \ \vec{Y}^{YX} \qquad \text{(orientation rotation)} \qquad (3.1)$$

$$\vec{X} \ _m\angle_i^0 \ \vec{Y}^{YX} : \quad \vec{X} \ _m\angle(2m+i) \ \vec{X}^{YX} \qquad \text{(projection type 1)} \qquad (3.2)$$

$$\vec{X} \ _m\angle_i^{2m} \ \vec{Y}^{XY} : \quad \vec{X} \ _m\angle i \ \vec{X}^{XY} \qquad \text{(projection type 2)} \qquad (3.3)$$

Referring to the example in Fig. 3.2 we can derive relations like:

$$\vec{C}^{CB} \ _2\angle_0^0 \ \vec{B}, \ \vec{C}^{BC} \ _2\angle_4^0 \ \vec{B}, \text{ and } \vec{D}^{DC} \ _2\angle_0^7 \ \vec{C} \ .$$

In the example these relations are sufficient to detect the inconsistency. We depict the extended configuration in Fig. 3.4. We will show another example where the operations are applied in Section 3.5.2.

By applying the constructive operations orientation rotation and projection the contradiction is detected and the constraint network is evaluated as inconsistent. With this

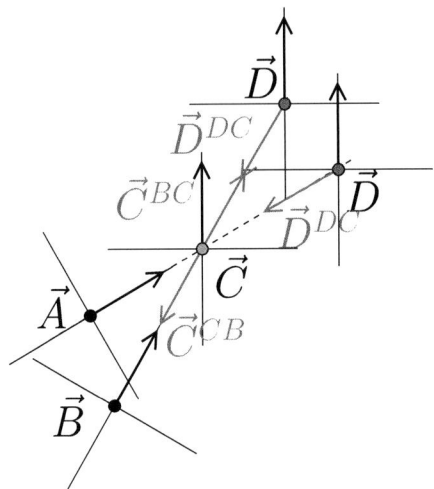

Figure 3.4: The o-point configuration from Fig. 3.2 extended by three o-points with the relations $\vec{C}^{CB}\ _2\angle_0^0\ \vec{B}$, $\vec{C}^{BC}\ _2\angle_4^0\ \vec{B}$, and $\vec{D}^{DC}\ _2\angle_4^0\ \vec{C}$.

constructive method we are able to detect inconsistencies of several atomic constraint networks with four o-points. In addition, we detected inconsistencies in configurations containing more than four o-points. Wether all inconsistencies for arbitrary point configurations represented in $\mathcal{OPRA}_m$ can be found with this method remains an open question.

3.3.3 Conceptual Neighborhood of $\mathcal{OPRA}_m$ relations

We now derive the neighborhood structure of $\mathcal{OPRA}_m$ relations ($\mathcal{CNG} =< \mathcal{BR}, \sim>$). This means that we specify the function $\mathrm{cn}(b) = \{b'|(b,b') \in \sim\}$ for each $b \in \mathcal{BR}$ (cf. Sec. 2.3.3). The construction of the conceptual neighborhood for $\mathcal{OPRA}_m$ relations is straightforward. Neighboring relations can be identified by moving around the o-points arbitrarily, i.e. shifting and twisting. As yet no method is known for deriving the neighborhood structure automatically, we must do this by hand. First, we consider non-'same' relations as start configurations and afterwards, 'same' relations as start configurations.

Start Configuration is of kind $m\angle_i^j$

Given a non-'same' relation $m\angle_i^j$ as start configuration we need to consider two different cases. On the one hand cases where both objects do not move onto the same position and afterwards if they do so.

First, if motion does not end up with both points in the same position, $\vec{B}$ can reach all regions next to i with respect to the reference frame of $\vec{A}$, i.e. $(i-1)$ and $(i+1)$, and $\vec{A}$ can reach all sectors next to j with respect to the reference frame of $\vec{B}$, i.e. $(j-1)$ and $(j+1)$. Additionally, one of the o-points $\vec{A}$ or $\vec{B}$ may stay in the sector it is currently in. If both o-points stay in their original regions, no relational change occurred at all. Subtracting the relation where no change occurred, we gain eight neighboring relations, if point positions of the o-points do not coincide after motion. We depict some examples of conceptual neighbors for $2\angle_1^1$ in Fig. 3.5 and for $2\angle_1^2$ in Fig. 3.6. We denote the eight neighboring relations of a relation $m\angle_i^j$ by cn_1:

$$\mathrm{cn}_1\left(m\angle_i^j \right) = \{ \quad m\angle_{i-1}^{j-1} \,,\; m\angle_{i-1}^{j} \,,\; m\angle_{i-1}^{j+1} \,,\; m\angle_{i}^{j-1} \,,$$
$$m\angle_{i}^{j+1} \,,\; m\angle_{i+1}^{j-1} \,,\; m\angle_{i+1}^{j} \,,\; m\angle_{i+1}^{j+1} \}\,.$$

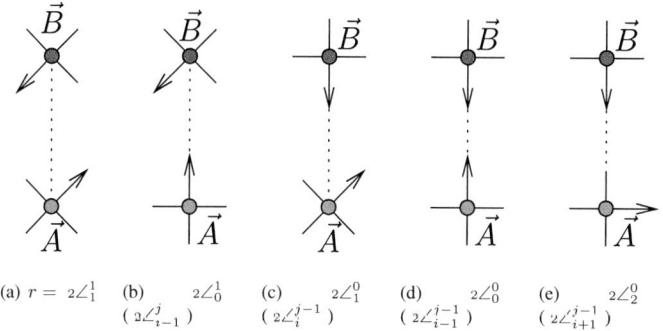

(a) $r = 2\angle_1^1$ (b) $2\angle_0^1$ (c) $2\angle_1^0$ (d) $2\angle_0^0$ (e) $2\angle_2^0$

                ($2\angle_{i-1}^j$)   ($2\angle_i^{j-1}$)   ($2\angle_{i-1}^{j-1}$)   ($2\angle_{i+1}^{j-1}$)

Figure 3.5: Examples of conceptual neighbors regarding $\mathrm{cn}_1(r)$ with $r = 2\angle_1^1$.

The second category we have to concider is, if the objects' point positions coincide after moving. We have to regard two different cases. First, the case where both orientations i and j describe planar sectors, and second, if at least one orientation is a linear sector.

If we for example take relation $\vec{A}$ $2\angle_1^1$ $\vec{B}$ as start configuration and move the o-points straight towards each other the result is one of three relations: $2\angle(3..5)$. If the orientations of $\vec{A}$ and $\vec{B}$ are parallel (which is not identifyable for all $\mathcal{OPRA}_m$ relations unambiguously) we result in $2\angle4$ (cf. Fig. 3.7(c)). But if the orientations

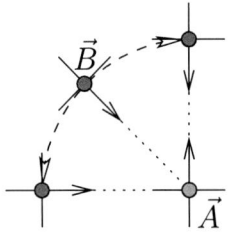

Figure 3.6: Two conceptual neighbors of $r = {}_2\angle_1^0$ regarding $\text{cn}_1(r)$: ${}_2\angle_0^0$ (${}_2\angle_{i-1}^j$) and ${}_2\angle_2^0$ (${}_2\angle_{i+1}^j$).

are turned towards each other, i.e. the reference lines intersect in front of $\vec{B}$ the result is ${}_2\angle 5$ (cf. Fig. 3.7(d)). If turned away from each other, i.e. the reference lines intersect behind $\vec{B}$ the result is ${}_2\angle 3$ (cf. Fig. 3.7(b)). In addition, we need to consider the extreme cases being "close to" $\vec{A}$ ${}_2\angle_2^0$ $\vec{B}$ or $\vec{A}$ ${}_2\angle_0^2$ $\vec{B}$. Roughly, with twisting the o-points "the last moment before" the positions coincide, relations ${}_2\angle 2$ and ${}_2\angle 6$ are reachable as well (cf. Fig. 3.7(a) and Fig. 3.7(e)).

In contrast, if we take relation ${}_2\angle_1^2$ as start configuration, for example, and move the o-points straight towards each other the result is relation ${}_2\angle 3$ (cf. Fig. 3.8(b)). If we do not move the points straight towards each other we result in another non-'same' relation in between. This case was already considered before. According to the extreme case above if we are "close to" ${}_2\angle_0^2$, or ${}_2\angle_2^2$ respectively, relations ${}_2\angle 2$ and ${}_2\angle 4$ are reachable as well (cf. Fig. 3.8(a) and Fig. 3.8(c)). Generalizing these findings the conceptual neighbors of $m\angle_i^j$ in this category are $m\angle(2m + i - j - 1)$, $m\angle(2m + i - j)$, and $m\angle(2m + i - j + 1)$ if one of the orientations i or j is linear, and $m\angle(2m + i - j - 2)$, $m\angle(2m + i - j - 1)$, $m\angle(2m + i - j)$, $m\angle(2m + i - j - 1)$, and $m\angle(2m + i - j + 2)$ if both orientations are planar.

$$
\begin{aligned}
\text{cn}_2(\, m\angle_i^j \,) &= \{ \, m\angle(2m + i - j - 2) \,,\; m\angle(2m + i - j - 1) \,, \\
&\quad m\angle(2m + i - j) \,,\; m\angle(2m + i - j - 1) \,, \\
&\quad m\angle(2m + i - j + 2) \, | i \mod 2 = 1 \wedge j \mod 2 = 1 \} \\
\text{cn}_3(\, m\angle_i^j \,) &= \{ \, m\angle(2m + i - j - 1) \,,\; m\angle(2m + i - j) \,,\; m\angle(2m + i - j + 1) \, | \\
&\quad i \mod 2 = 0 \vee j \mod 2 = 0 \}
\end{aligned}
$$

Start Configuration is of kind $m\angle s$

If the starting relation is a 'same' relation, we first consider cases where the result is also a 'same' relation and afterwards cases where the result is a non-'same' relation.

It is the simplest case to derive neighboring relations of a 'same' relation, if the

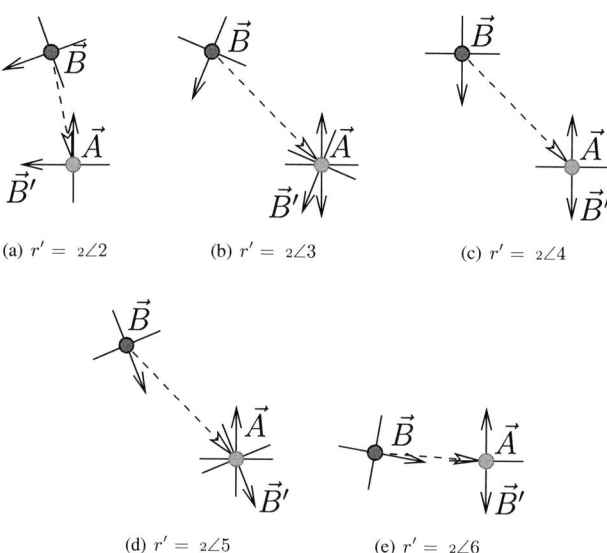

(a) $r' = {}_2\angle 2$ (b) $r' = {}_2\angle 3$ (c) $r' = {}_2\angle 4$

(d) $r' = {}_2\angle 5$ (e) $r' = {}_2\angle 6$

Figure 3.7: Examples of conceptual neighbors r' regarding $\text{cn}_2(r)$ with $r = {}_2\angle_1^1$.

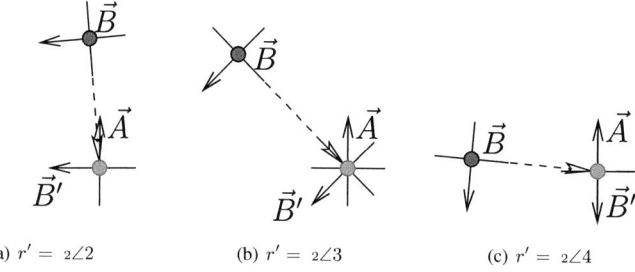

(a) $r' = {}_2\angle 2$ (b) $r' = {}_2\angle 3$ (c) $r' = {}_2\angle 4$

Figure 3.8: Examples of conceptual neighbors r' regarding $\text{cn}_3(r)$ with $r = {}_2\angle_1^2$.

result is again a 'same' relation. Here, only the orientation of $\vec{A}$ or $\vec{B}$ may change, but not the position of the o-points itself. Therefore, only the relations which are directly located next to the starting relation, regarding rotation of the orientation, are reachable, i.e. $(s - 1)$ and $(s + 1)$ (cf. Fig. 3.9).

$$\text{cn}_4(\ m\angle s\ ) \;=\; \{\ m\angle(s+1)\ ,\ m\angle(s-1)\ \}$$

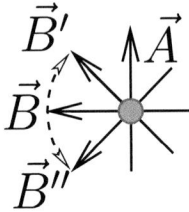

Figure 3.9: Two conceptual neighbors of $r = {}_2\angle 2$ regarding $\text{cn}_4(r)$: ${}_2\angle 1$ (${}_2\angle s - 1$) and ${}_2\angle 3$ (${}_2\angle s + 1$).

If one of the points moves away from the original position we gain a non-'same' relation $m\angle_i^j$ as result. We assume that o-point $\vec{B}$ moves in arbitrary direction. Thus, $\vec{B}$ can be positioned in any region with respect to $\vec{A}$. If $\vec{B}$ moves in region i regarding $\vec{A}$ j cannot take arbitrary values, instead j depends on s and i. For example, assume ${}_2\angle 1$ as given. Moving straight forward in the reference direction $\vec{B}$ ends in ${}_2\angle_1^4$ (cf. Fig. 3.10(b)). Moving forward, but a little to the left of the reference direction ends in ${}_2\angle_1^5$ (cf. Fig. 3.10(c)), and a little to the right in ${}_2\angle_1^3$ (cf. Fig. 3.10(a)). Now we assume that $\vec{B}$ moves so that $i = 2$, then we end in ${}_2\angle_2^5$ (cf. Fig. 3.11(b)). Again, if we are "close to" ${}_2\angle 0$ or ${}_2\angle 2$ with a little turn it is also possible to end in ${}_2\angle_2^4$ or ${}_2\angle_2^6$ (cf. Fig. 3.11(a) and (cf. Fig. 3.11(c))). In Fig. 3.12 we additionally depict the neighbors regarding a transition in region 3 regarding $\vec{A}$ to point out the systematics of the neighborhood structure.

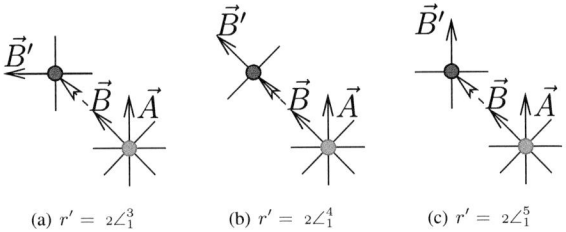

(a) $r' = {}_2\angle_1^3$ (b) $r' = {}_2\angle_1^4$ (c) $r' = {}_2\angle_1^5$

Figure 3.10: Examples of conceptual neighbors: ${}_2\angle_1^j \in \text{cn}_5({}_2\angle 1)$.

Generalizing these results for $\vec{B}$ moving in arbitrary direction results in $m\angle_i^{2m+i-s-1}$, $m\angle_i^{2m+i-s}$, and $m\angle_i^{2m+i-s+1}$. Finally, we need to consider that $\vec{A}$ moves instead of $\vec{B}$ and so, the cases with i and j interchanged are also neighbors of $m\angle s$ ($m\angle_{2m+j-s-1}^j$, $m\angle_{2m+j-s}^j$, $m\angle_{2m+j-s+1}^j$). We denote these cases with cn_5.

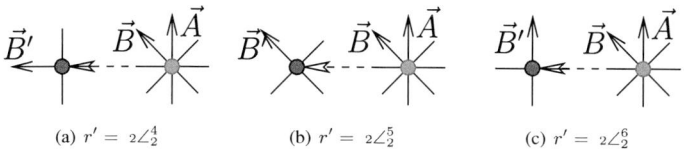

(a) $r' = {}_2\angle_2^4$ (b) $r' = {}_2\angle_2^5$ (c) $r' = {}_2\angle_2^6$

Figure 3.11: Examples of conceptual neighbors: ${}_2\angle_2^j \in cn_5({}_2\angle 1)$.

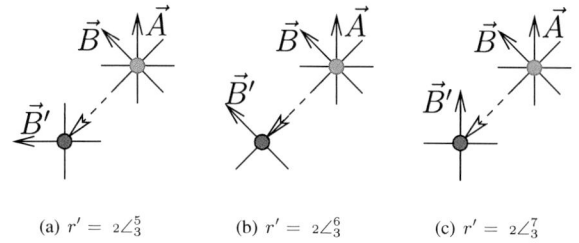

(a) $r' = {}_2\angle_3^5$ (b) $r' = {}_2\angle_3^6$ (c) $r' = {}_2\angle_3^7$

Figure 3.12: Examples of conceptual neighbors: ${}_2\angle_3^j \in cn_5({}_2\angle 1)$.

$$cn_5({}_m\angle s) = \{ {}_m\angle_i^{2m+i-s-1} , {}_m\angle_i^{2m+i-s} , {}_m\angle_i^{2m+i-s+1} ,$$
$$ {}_m\angle_{2m+j-s-1}^{j} , {}_m\angle_{2m+j-s}^{j} , {}_m\angle_{2m+j-s+1}^{j} \}$$

Overall, the neighboring function $cn(r)$ for an $\mathcal{OPRA}_m$ relation r is given by the union of all the results above[5]:

$$cn(r) = cn_1(r) \cup cn_2(r) \cup cn_3(r) \cup cn_4(r) \cup cn_5(r)$$

3.4 Representing Orientation Calculi in $\mathcal{OPRA}_m$

We now show how relations from different orientation calculi can be encoded within a single framework such that they can be combined in a single reasoning system and information can be translated from one calculus to another. As we will see, the $\mathcal{OPRA}_m$ calculus is a suitable candidate for this framework, as it is expressive enough to encode the relations from other calculi considered. In the following, we will give transformations for representing the base relations of other calculi with a set of $\mathcal{OPRA}_m$ relations.

---

[5]If r is a 'same' relation in case of cn_1, cn_2, and cn_3 or a non-'same' relation in case of cn_4, and cn_5, the return value is the empty set, e.g. $cn_1({}_m\angle s) = \{\}$.

In Sec. 2.4 we presented a variety of calculi dealing with relative orientation, among them the FlipFlop Calculus and the Double Cross Calculus. While some relationships between these calculi are rather obvious, e.g. the Double Cross Calculus is a logical conjunction of two Single Cross reference frames with origin and relatum interchanged and can be seen as a refinement of the Single Cross Calculus, other connections are less obvious.

The relationships between orientation calculi have not been investigated exhaustively. We argue that knowing the relationships of several calculi to another calculus can be exploited to build tools that reduce the typically complex tasks involved in designing and implementing a spatial calculus. For instance, for every calculus the composition operation has to be specified, which usually has to be done by hand, and thus is a difficult, time-consuming, and error-prone process. If the calculus can be expressed in another already completely specified calculus this can facilitate the automatic generation or verification of the composition table. We take a step towards understanding the relationships between the calculi listed in Sec. 2.4 by showing that and how they all can be mapped to the $\mathcal{OPRA}_m$ calculus. Mapping other calculi into the algebraically well-defined framework of $\mathcal{OPRA}_m$ facilitates reasoning over relations from different calculi. Furthermore, these mappings can support the derivation of the neighborhood structure of a spatial calculus.

We give the mappings of the FlipFlop Calculus, the Double Cross Calculus, the $\mathcal{DRA}_f$, and QTC to sets of $\mathcal{OPRA}_m$ relations in the remainder of this section. We give examples how these assignments can be applied in Section 3.5.

3.4.1 Encoding FlipFlop Calculus and $\mathcal{LR}$ in $\mathcal{OPRA}_m$

To encode the nine ternary FlipFlop relations $A, B \; rel_{FFC} \; C$ within $\mathcal{OPRA}_1$, we utilize three oriented points: $\vec{A}^{AB}$, $\vec{B}^{AB}$, and $\vec{C}^{BC}$. For cases with $A \neq B$, the FlipFlop relations right, left, front, inside, back, start and end are distinguished.

To formulate the condition $A \neq B$ in $\mathcal{OPRA}_m$ and to define the reference frame, we introduce the following *reference frame constraint 1* (rfc_1^{FFC}), that has to hold for all these relations:

$$ rfc_1^{FFC} = \vec{A}^{AB} \; {}_1\angle_0^2 \; \vec{B}^{AB} \; . $$

This describes first, that $\vec{A}^{AB}$ and $\vec{B}^{AB}$ have different positions but the same orientation, and second, that $\vec{B}^{AB}$ is in front of $\vec{A}^{AB}$.

We can now describe the individual FlipFlop relations as configurations of the three oriented points $\vec{A}^{AB}$, $\vec{B}^{AB}$ and $\vec{C}^{BC}$. We always provide a complete description of the configuration, though it is often sufficient to relate the referent to only one point of the reference frame. For instance, for the front case the following $\mathcal{OPRA}_1$ relations hold in addition to rfc_1^{FFC}: $\vec{A}^{AB} \; {}_1\angle_0^2 \; \vec{C}^{BC}$ and $\vec{B}^{AB} \; {}_1\angle_0^2 \; \vec{C}^{BC}$ (cf. Fig. 3.13(a)). It would be sufficient to give only rfc_1^{FFC} and $\vec{B}^{AB} \; {}_1\angle_0^2 \; \vec{C}^{BC}$ as $\vec{A}^{AB} \; {}_1\angle_0^2 \; \vec{C}^{BC}$ would result by determining the algebraic closure of the previous relations. Neverthe-

less, we will always give the complete description although some information represented in the relations might be redundant. For **inside**, we get the following relations:
$\vec{A}^{AB}\ _1\angle_0^0\ \vec{C}^{BC}$ and $\vec{B}^{AB}\ _1\angle_2^2\ \vec{C}$ (cf. Fig. 3.13(c)). And for **left** the resulting relations
are $\vec{A}^{AB}\ _1\angle_1^1\ \vec{C}^{BC}$ and $\vec{B}^{AB}\ _1\angle_1^2\ \vec{C}^{BC}$ (cf. Fig. 3.13(f)).

We now turn to the special cases **dou** and **tri**. We need to formalize that $\vec{A}$ and $\vec{B}$
have the same position in our second reference frame constraint that has to hold only
for **dou** and **tri**:

$$rfc_2^{FFC} = \vec{A}\ _1\angle*\ \vec{B}\ .$$

The orientation of the o-points for $\vec{A}$ and $\vec{B}$ is unimportant in this case and thus,
we leave it unspecified. In the **dou** case, we have to make sure that C is different from
A and B. We achieve this by the following relations: $\vec{A}\ _1\angle_*^2\ \vec{C}^{BC}$ and $\vec{B}\ _1\angle_*^2\ \vec{C}^{BC}$.
For **tri**, C has to be the same as A and B: $\vec{A}\ _1\angle*\ \vec{C}$ and $\vec{B}\ _1\angle*\ \vec{C}$.

A pictorial representation of all relations but **dou** and **tri** is given in Fig. 3.13.
The complete listing of formalizations for all FlipFlop relations is given in Table 3.1.
The set of $\mathcal{OPRA}_1$ relations describes a jointly exhaustive and pairwise disjoint set of
configurations of three oriented points that can be used to translate between FlipFlop
and $\mathcal{OPRA}_m$.

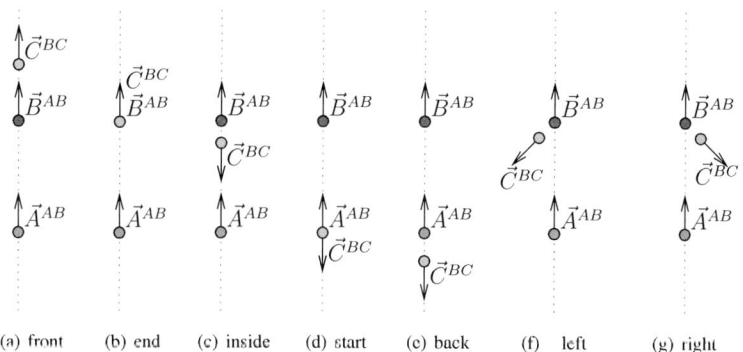

Figure 3.13: Pictorial representations of FlipFlop relations in $\mathcal{OPRA}_1$.

3.4.2 Encoding DCC in $\mathcal{OPRA}_m$

As stated above, the Double Cross Calculus is a combination of two Single Cross
reference frames[6] with not all combinations possible. We adopt the original idea to
conjoin the two reference frames used in Freksa (1991). Nevertheless, we are not

---

[6]We omit an $\mathcal{OPRA}_m$ specification for the Single Cross Calculus here, as it can be derived easily
from the DCC representation.

$A, B \; rel_{FFC} \; C$	$\mathcal{OPRA}_1$ representation		
front	rfc_1^{FFC}	$\wedge \quad \vec{A}^{AB} \; {}_1\angle_0^2 \; \vec{C}^{BC}$	$\wedge \quad \vec{B}^{AB} \; {}_1\angle_0^2 \; \vec{C}^{BC}$
end	rfc_1^{FFC}	$\wedge \quad \vec{A}^{AB} \; {}_1\angle_0^* \; \vec{C}$	$\wedge \quad \vec{B}^{AB} \; {}_1\angle* \; \vec{C}$
inside	rfc_1^{FFC}	$\wedge \quad \vec{A}^{AB} \; {}_1\angle_0^0 \; \vec{C}^{BC}$	$\wedge \quad \vec{B}^{AB} \; {}_1\angle_2^2 \; \vec{C}^{BC}$
start	rfc_1^{FFC}	$\wedge \quad \vec{A}^{AB} \; {}_1\angle 2 \; \vec{C}^{BC}$	$\wedge \quad \vec{B}^{AB} \; {}_1\angle_2^2 \; \vec{C}^{BC}$
back	rfc_1^{FFC}	$\wedge \quad \vec{A}^{AB} \; {}_1\angle_2^2 \; \vec{C}^{BC}$	$\wedge \quad \vec{B}^{AB} \; {}_1\angle_2^2 \; \vec{C}^{BC}$
left	rfc_1^{FFC}	$\wedge \quad \vec{A}^{AB} \; {}_1\angle_1^1 \; \vec{C}^{BC}$	$\wedge \quad \vec{B}^{AB} \; {}_1\angle_1^2 \; \vec{C}^{BC}$
right	rfc_1^{FFC}	$\wedge \quad \vec{A}^{AB} \; {}_1\angle_3^3 \; \vec{C}^{BC}$	$\wedge \quad \vec{B}^{AB} \; {}_1\angle_3^2 \; \vec{C}^{BC}$
dou	rfc_2^{FFC}	$\wedge \quad \vec{A} \quad {}_1\angle_*^2 \; \vec{C}^{BC}$	$\wedge \quad \vec{B} \quad {}_1\angle_*^2 \; \vec{C}^{BC}$
tri	rfc_2^{FFC}	$\wedge \quad \vec{A} \quad {}_1\angle* \; \vec{C}$	$\wedge \quad \vec{B} \quad {}_1\angle* \; \vec{C}$

Table 3.1: A mapping of FlipFlop relations to $\mathcal{OPRA}_1$ relations.

using the inverse orientation for the second reference frame for reasons of simplicity, i.e. we also use orientation AB for the second reference frame instead of orientation BA (compare Fig. 2.8(b)). We will now give the mapping of the 17 base relations based on the three oriented points $\vec{C}^{BC}$, $\vec{A}^{AB}$, and $\vec{B}^{AB}$ and summarize it in Table 3.2.

For building the reference frame for the cases with $A \neq B$ we need to define the *reference frame constraint 1* as for the FlipFlop calculus, but this time on the basis of granularity $m = 2$, because the perpendiculars to $\vec{A}^{AB}$ and $\vec{B}^{AB}$ are needed for classification:

$$rfc_1^{DCC} = \vec{A}^{AB} \; {}_2\angle_0^4 \; \vec{B}^{AB}.$$

The second reference frame constraint required for **dou** and **tri** is:

$$rfc_2^{DCC} = \vec{A} \; {}_2\angle* \; \vec{B} \;.$$

We need to relate referent $\vec{C}^{BC}$ to $\vec{A}^{AB}$ and $\vec{B}^{AB}$ for representing DCC relations. Given $A, B \; \mathbf{1} \; C$ in DCC C is left-front of $\vec{A}^{AB}$ ($\mathcal{OPRA}_2$ region 1) as well as left-front of $\vec{B}^{AB}$. $\vec{B}^{AB}$ is straight-back of $\vec{C}^{BC}$ (region 4) and $\vec{A}^{AB}$ can only be positioned in region 3 of $\vec{C}^{BC}$ (cf. Fig. 3.14(a)). Therefore, it follows that $A, B \; \mathbf{1} \; C$ has to be encoded as $rfc_1^{DCC} \wedge \vec{A}^{AB} \; {}_2\angle_1^3 \; \vec{C}^{BC} \wedge \vec{B}^{AB} \; {}_2\angle_1^4 \; \vec{C}^{BC}$.

Cases with C being positioned between $\vec{A}^{AB}$ and $\vec{B}^{AB}$ ($rel_{DCC} \in \{3, 9, 12\}$) are a little more complex. For instance, assume $A, B \; \mathbf{3} \; C$ is given. We depict this case in Fig. 3.14(b). Then, $\vec{C}^{BC}$ is left front of $\vec{A}^{AB}$ (region 1) and left back of $\vec{B}^{AB}$ (region 3) and $\vec{B}^{AB}$ is straight back of $\vec{C}^{BC}$ (region 4). Now imagine $\vec{C}^{BC}$ being positioned quite close to the line segment AB. Then $\vec{A}^{AB}$ is positioned in region 1 of $\vec{C}^{BC}$ (cf. $\vec{C}_1^{BC}$). But $\vec{C}^{BC}$ could be also positioned very far away from this line, then $\vec{A}^{AB}$ is positioned in region 3 of $\vec{C}^{BC}$ (cf. $\vec{C}_3^{BC}$). The case with $\vec{A}^{AB}$ being straight left is also valid (cf. $\vec{C}_2^{BC}$). Therefore $rfc_1^{DCC} \wedge \vec{A}^{AB} \; {}_2\angle_1^{1..3} \; \vec{C}^{BC} \wedge \vec{B}^{AB} \; {}_2\angle_3^4 \; \vec{C}^{BC}$ follows as the correct encoding.

The special cases with $A \neq B = C$ **(b)** $A = C \neq B$ **(a)** as well as **dou** and **tri** can be handled just like the according cases in FFC. **Dou** results in $rfc_2^{DCC} \wedge$

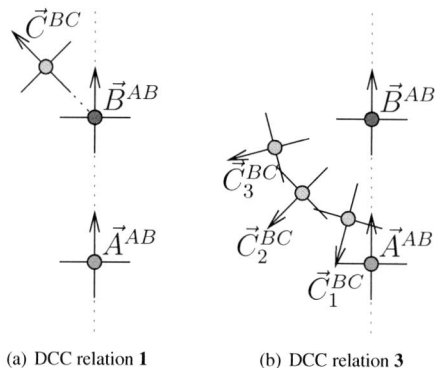

(a) DCC relation **1**   (b) DCC relation **3**

Figure 3.14: A mapping of Double Cross relations to $\mathcal{OPRA}_2$ relations.

$\vec{A} \; _2\angle_*^4 \; \vec{C}^{BC} \wedge \vec{B} \; _2\angle_*^4 \; \vec{C}^{BC}$ and **tri** in $rfc_2^{DCC} \wedge \vec{A} \; _2\angle_* \; \vec{C} \wedge \vec{B} \; _2\angle_* \; \vec{C}$. A complete list is given in Table 3.2.

3.4.3 Encoding $\mathcal{DRA}_f$ in $\mathcal{OPRA}_m$

We now give a mapping of the 72 base relations of the fine-grained Dipole Relation Algebra ($\mathcal{DRA}_f$). We do not give the mapping of the 24 base relations of $\mathcal{DRA}_c$, because they can be derived from the $\mathcal{DRA}_f$ mapping. The first dipole is given by start point A and end point B, and the second dipole by start point C and end point D. In contrast to FFC and DCC we have two different reference frames. We have to define the reference frame constraint such that $A \neq B \wedge C \neq D$ and line AB as well as CD form a reference line:

$$rfc_1^{\mathcal{DRA}_f} - \vec{A}^{AB} \; _1\angle_0^2 \; \vec{B}^{AB} \wedge \vec{C}^{CD} \; _1\angle_0^2 \; \vec{D}^{CD}.$$

A $\mathcal{DRA}_f$ relation consists of four relations each of the case left, right, front, back, inside, start, or end (cf. Sec. 2.4.4). Since each letter is derived in the same way, just for different triples of points, and each describes a FlipFlop relation, we begin by providing the FlipFlop encodings from Table 3.1, but with the concrete oriented points replaced by variables X, Y, and Z in Table 3.3. **dou** and **tri** are not listed because of the preliminaries $A \neq B$ and $C \neq B$. Table 3.4 lists the instantiations that have to be chosen for X, Y, and Z for each of the four letters. The first letter describes the FlipFlop relation between A, B and C, the second for A, B and D, the third for C, D and A, and the fourth C, D and B. We give two examples on how complete $\mathcal{DRA}_f$ relations are mapped:

$A, B\ rel_{DCC}\ C$	$\mathcal{OPRA}_m$ representation		
0	rfc_1^{DCC}	$\wedge\quad \vec{A}^{AB}\ _2\angle_0^4\ \vec{C}^{BC}$	$\wedge\quad \vec{B}^{AB}\ _2\angle_0^4\ \vec{C}^{BC}$
1	rfc_1^{DCC}	$\wedge\quad \vec{A}^{AB}\ _2\angle_1^4\ \vec{C}^{BC}$	$\wedge\quad \vec{B}^{AB}\ _2\angle_1^4\ \vec{C}^{BC}$
2	rfc_1^{DCC}	$\wedge\quad \vec{A}^{AB}\ _2\angle_1^4\ \vec{C}^{BC}$	$\wedge\quad \vec{B}^{AB}\ _2\angle_2^4\ \vec{C}^{BC}$
3	rfc_1^{DCC}	$\wedge\quad \vec{A}^{AB}\ _2\angle_1^{1..3}\ \vec{C}^{BC}$	$\wedge\quad \vec{B}^{AB}\ _2\angle_3^4\ \vec{C}^{BC}$
4	rfc_1^{DCC}	$\wedge\quad \vec{A}^{AB}\ _2\angle_2^3\ \vec{C}^{BC}$	$\wedge\quad \vec{B}^{AB}\ _2\angle_3^4\ \vec{C}^{BC}$
5	rfc_1^{DCC}	$\wedge\quad \vec{A}^{AB}\ _2\angle_2^3\ \vec{C}^{BC}$	$\wedge\quad \vec{B}^{AB}\ _2\angle_3^4\ \vec{C}^{BC}$
6	rfc_1^{DCC}	$\wedge\quad \vec{A}^{AB}\ _2\angle_4^4\ \vec{C}^{BC}$	$\wedge\quad \vec{B}^{AB}\ _2\angle_4^4\ \vec{C}^{BC}$
7	rfc_1^{DCC}	$\wedge\quad \vec{A}^{AB}\ _2\angle_5^5\ \vec{C}^{BC}$	$\wedge\quad \vec{B}^{AB}\ _2\angle_5^4\ \vec{C}^{BC}$
8	rfc_1^{DCC}	$\wedge\quad \vec{A}^{AB}\ _2\angle_6^5\ \vec{C}^{BC}$	$\wedge\quad \vec{B}^{AB}\ _2\angle_5^4\ \vec{C}^{BC}$
9	rfc_1^{DCC}	$\wedge\quad \vec{A}^{AB}\ _2\angle_7^{5..7}\ \vec{C}^{BC}$	$\wedge\quad \vec{B}^{AB}\ _2\angle_5^4\ \vec{C}^{BC}$
10	rfc_1^{DCC}	$\wedge\quad \vec{A}^{AB}\ _2\angle_7^5\ \vec{C}^{BC}$	$\wedge\quad \vec{B}^{AB}\ _2\angle_6^4\ \vec{C}^{BC}$
11	rfc_1^{DCC}	$\wedge\quad \vec{A}^{AB}\ _2\angle_7^5\ \vec{C}^{BC}$	$\wedge\quad \vec{B}^{AB}\ _2\angle_7^4\ \vec{C}^{BC}$
12	rfc_1^{DCC}	$\wedge\quad \vec{A}^{AB}\ _2\angle_0^0\ \vec{C}^{BC}$	$\wedge\quad \vec{B}^{AB}\ _2\angle_4^4\ \vec{C}^{BC}$
a	rfc_1^{DCC}	$\wedge\quad \vec{A}^{AB}\ _2\angle_0 4\ \vec{C}^{BC}$	$\wedge\quad \vec{B}^{AB}\ _2\angle_4^4\ \vec{C}^{BC}$
b	rfc_1^{DCC}	$\wedge\quad \vec{A}^{AB}\ _2\angle_\angle^*\ \vec{C}$	$\wedge\quad \vec{B}^{AB}\ _2\angle_\angle^*\ \vec{C}$
dou	rfc_2^{DCC}	$\wedge\quad \vec{A}\ _2\angle_*^4\ \vec{C}^{BC}$	$\wedge\quad \vec{B}\ _2\angle_*^4\ \vec{C}^{BC}$
tri	rfc_2^{DCC}	$\wedge\quad \vec{A}\ _2\angle_*\ \vec{C}$	$\wedge\quad \vec{B}\ _2\angle_*\ \vec{C}$

Table 3.2: A mapping of DCC relations to $\mathcal{OPRA}_m$ relations.

Example 1: $\vec{d}_{AB}\,(rfll)\,\vec{d}_{CD}\ \equiv\ rfc_1^{\mathcal{DRA}_f}$
$\wedge\quad \vec{A}^{AB}\ _1\angle_3^3\ \vec{C}^{BC}\qquad \wedge\quad \vec{B}^{AB}\ _1\angle_3^2\ \vec{C}^{BC}$
$\wedge\quad \vec{A}^{AB}\ _1\angle_0^2\ \vec{D}^{BD}\qquad \wedge\quad \vec{B}^{AB}\ _1\angle_0^2\ \vec{D}^{BD}$
$\wedge\quad \vec{C}^{CD}\ _1\angle_1^1\ \vec{A}^{DA}\qquad \wedge\quad \vec{D}^{CD}\ _1\angle_1^2\ \vec{A}^{DA}$
$\wedge\quad \vec{C}^{CD}\ _1\angle_1^1\ \vec{B}^{DB}\qquad \wedge\quad \vec{D}^{CD}\ _1\angle_1^2\ \vec{B}^{DB}$

Example 2: $\vec{d}_{AB}\,(ebis)\,\vec{d}_{CD}\ \equiv\ rfc_1^{\mathcal{DRA}_f}$
$\wedge\quad \vec{A}^{AB}\ _1\angle_0^2\ \vec{C}^{AB}\qquad \wedge\quad \vec{B}^{AB}\ _1\angle 0\ \vec{C}^{AB}$
$\wedge\quad \vec{A}^{AB}\ _1\angle_2^2\ \vec{D}^{BD}\qquad \wedge\quad \vec{B}^{AB}\ _1\angle_2^2\ \vec{D}^{BD}$
$\wedge\quad \vec{C}^{CD}\ _1\angle_0^0\ \vec{A}^{DA}\qquad \wedge\quad \vec{D}^{CD}\ _1\angle_2^2\ \vec{A}^{DA}$
$\wedge\quad \vec{C}^{CD}\ _1\angle 2\ \vec{B}^{DB}\qquad \wedge\quad \vec{D}^{CD}\ _1\angle_2^2\ \vec{B}^{DB}$

3.4.4 Encoding QTC in $\mathcal{OPRA}_m$

QTC relations are based on a double cross reference frame spanned by the objects' original positions A_{t_i} and B_{t_i} at time point t_i. The relations are defined on the differentiated motion direction given by the positions of A and B at t_j with $i < j$. We

	$\vec{X}^{XY}\ _1\angle_i^j\ \vec{Z}$ $\wedge$ $\vec{Y}^{XY}\ _1\angle_k^l\ \vec{Z}$
front	$\vec{X}^{XY}\ _1\angle_0^2\ \vec{Z}^{YZ}$ $\wedge$ $\vec{Y}^{XY}\ _1\angle_0^2\ \vec{Z}^{YZ}$
end	$\vec{X}^{XY}\ _1\angle_0^*\ \vec{Z}$ $\wedge$ $\vec{Y}^{XY}\ _1\angle*\ \vec{Z}$
inside	$\vec{X}^{XY}\ _1\angle_0^0\ \vec{Z}^{YZ}$ $\wedge$ $\vec{Y}^{XY}\ _1\angle_2^2\ \vec{Z}^{YZ}$
start	$\vec{X}^{XY}\ _1\angle2\ \vec{Z}^{YZ}$ $\wedge$ $\vec{Y}^{XY}\ _1\angle_2^2\ \vec{Z}^{YZ}$
back	$\vec{X}^{XY}\ _1\angle_2^2\ \vec{Z}^{YZ}$ $\wedge$ $\vec{Y}^{XY}\ _1\angle_2^2\ \vec{Z}^{YZ}$
left	$\vec{X}^{XY}\ _1\angle_1^1\ \vec{Z}^{YZ}$ $\wedge$ $\vec{Y}^{XY}\ _1\angle_1^2\ \vec{Z}^{YZ}$
right	$\vec{X}^{XY}\ _1\angle_3^3\ \vec{Z}^{YZ}$ $\wedge$ $\vec{Y}^{XY}\ _1\angle_3^2\ \vec{Z}^{YZ}$

Table 3.3: Describing the local $\mathcal{DRA}_f$ point configurations (cf. Table 3.1).

position		X	Y	Z
1st position	(r_1)	A	B	C
2nd position	(r_2)	A	B	D
3rd position	(r_3)	C	D	A
4th position	(r_4)	C	D	B

Table 3.4: Instantiation mapping of X, Y, Z in Table 3.3 according to the position in the $\mathcal{DRA}_f$ relation tuple.

abbreviate A_{t_i} with A_i and A_{t_j} with A_j. We define the reference frame in DCC manner based on A_i and B_i.

$$rfc^{QTC} = \vec{A_i}^{A_iB_i}\ _2\angle_0^4\ \vec{B_i}^{A_iB_i}.$$

Table 3.5 shows the corresponding mapping of the four single $-, 0, +$ literals of the QTC relation string. The first two literals are defined by the front/back dichotomy regarding the perpendiculars relative to the reference orientation from A_i to B_i, the last two by left/right regarding the reference orientation. For the example in Figure 2.11 ($A\ (\ \ |\ \ )\ B$) it follows $\vec{A_i}^{A_iB_i}\ _2\angle_{7..1}^4\ \vec{A_j}^{A_iA_j} \wedge \vec{B_i}^{A_iB_i}\ _2\angle_{7..1}^4\ \vec{B_j}^{B_iB_j}$ for the front/back part and $\vec{A_i}^{A_iB_i}\ _1\angle_1^2\ \vec{A_j}^{A_iA_j} \wedge \vec{B_i}^{A_iB_i}\ _1\angle_3^2\ \vec{B_j}^{B_iB_j}$ for the left/right part.

	$-$	0	$+$
1st literal	$\vec{A_i}^{A_iB_i}\ _2\angle_{7..1}^4\ \vec{A_j}^{A_iA_j}$	$\vec{A_i}^{A_iB_i}\ _2\angle_{2,6}^4\ \vec{A_j}^{A_iA_j}$	$\vec{A_i}^{A_iB_i}\ _2\angle_{3..5}^4\ \vec{A_j}^{A_iA_j}$
2nd literal	$\vec{B_i}^{A_iB_i}\ _2\angle_{3..5}^4\ \vec{B_j}^{B_iB_j}$	$\vec{B_i}^{A_iB_i}\ _2\angle_{2,6}^4\ \vec{B_j}^{B_iB_j}$	$\vec{B_i}^{A_iB_i}\ _2\angle_{7..1}^4\ \vec{B_j}^{B_iB_j}$
3rd literal	$\vec{A_i}^{A_iB_i}\ _1\angle_1^2\ \vec{A_j}^{A_iA_j}$	$\vec{A_i}^{A_iB_i}\ _1\angle_{0,2}^2\ \vec{A_j}^{A_iA_j}$	$\vec{A_i}^{A_iB_i}\ _1\angle_3^2\ \vec{A_j}^{A_iA_j}$
4th literal	$\vec{B_i}^{A_iB_i}\ _1\angle_3^2\ \vec{B_j}^{B_iB_j}$	$\vec{B_i}^{A_iB_i}\ _1\angle_{0,2}^2\ \vec{B_j}^{B_iB_j}$	$\vec{B_i}^{A_iB_i}\ _1\angle_1^2\ \vec{B_j}^{B_iB_j}$

Table 3.5: An $\mathcal{OPRA}_m$ representation schema for each literal of a QTC relation.

3.5   Applications of $\mathcal{OPRA}_m$ Mappings

In this section we demonstrate how the mappings in the previous section can be applied to mediate between different calculi. First, we show how FlipFlop relations are derived from Double Cross relations. Second, we derive the composition of Double Cross relations by the mapping, and finally, we derive the conceptual neighborhood structure of the FlipFlop Calculus and the $\mathcal{DRA}_f$.

3.5.1   From DCC relations to FlipFlop relations

So far, it was not possible to translate relations between different calculi without an explicit description of such a mapping, or to reason with relations represented in different calculi. By expressing arbitrary orientation calculi in $\mathcal{OPRA}_m$ we provide the facilities to do so. We give a simple example how an FFC relation can be derived from a DCC relation on the basis of the $\mathcal{OPRA}_m$ representation. The idea can be generalized for more complex transformations as well.

For example, given the DCC relation $r = A, B\ \mathbf{3}\ C$ we get

$$r f c_1^{DCC} \wedge \vec{A}^{AB}\ {}_2\angle_1^{1..3}\ \vec{C}^{BC} \wedge \vec{B}^{AB}\ {}_2\angle_3^4\ \vec{C}^{BC}$$

as $\mathcal{OPRA}_m$ representation from Table 3.2. By changing the granularity from $m = 2$ to $m = 1$ we get the FFC relation between A, B, and C. How to map relations between different granularities that are a multiple of each other is explained in Moratz et al. (2005).

From $r f c_1^{DCC} = \vec{A}^{AB}\ {}_2\angle_0^4\ \vec{B}^{AB}$ follows $\vec{A}^{AB}\ {}_1\angle_0^2\ \vec{B}^{AB} = r f c_1^{FFC}$. From $\vec{A}^{AB}\ {}_2\angle_1^{1..3}\ \vec{C}^{BC}$ follows $\vec{A}^{AB}\ {}_1\angle_1^1\ \vec{C}^{BC}$ and from $\vec{B}^{AB}\ {}_2\angle_3^4\ \vec{C}^{BC}$ follows $\vec{B}^{AB}\ {}_1\angle_1^2\ \vec{C}^{BC}$. The combined result

$$r f c_1^{FFC} \wedge \vec{A}^{AB}\ {}_1\angle_1^1\ \vec{C}^{BC} \wedge \vec{B}^{AB}\ {}_1\angle_1^2\ \vec{C}^{BC}$$

is the $\mathcal{OPRA}_m$ formalization for the FlipFlop relation $A, B\ \mathbf{l}\ C$ (cf. Table 3.1).

Transformations of base relations do not necessarily yield a base relation. Taking the example above translating the FlipFlop relation $A, B\ \mathbf{l}\ C$ back into DCC results in a complex Double Cross relation: $A, B\ (\mathbf{1..5})\ C$.

3.5.2   Deriving Composition Tables From $\mathcal{OPRA}_m$ Representations (Example DCC)

We want to derive the composition table for DCC based on the completely specified composition of $\mathcal{OPRA}_m$. Thus, we have four points A, B, C, and D and want to infer the relation $A, B\ rel_{DCC}\ D$ from the given relations $A, B\ rel_{DCC}\ C$ and $B, C\ rel_{DCC}\ D$ (cf. Fig. 3.15(a)). The according configuration modeled in $\mathcal{OPRA}_m$ is shown in Fig. 3.15(b).

To demonstrate the process of deriving the composition, we consider the composition example depicted in Fig. 3.16. We compose the DCC relations $\mathbf{12}$ and $\mathbf{9}$

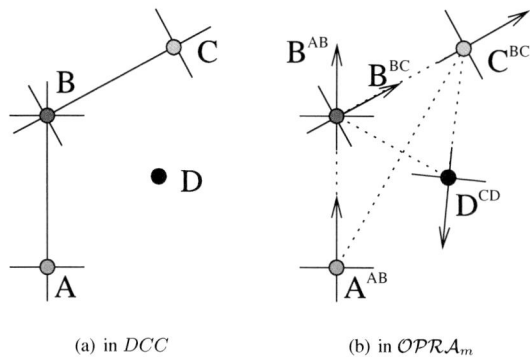

(a) in DCC (b) in $\mathcal{OPRA}_m$

Figure 3.15: A general spatial configuration for composition.

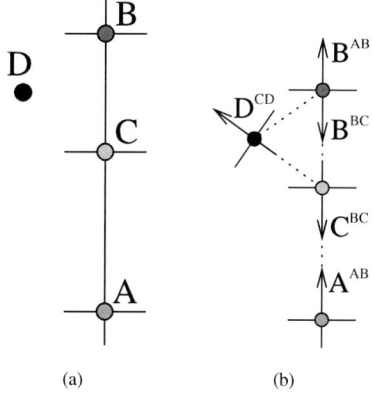

(a)   (b)

Figure 3.16: A, B **12** C and B, C **9** D for composition in DCC and $\mathcal{OPRA}_m$.

(cf. Fig. 3.16(a)). We employ the standard operations composition, converse, and intersection, but also the additional operations orientation rotation and projection which were introduced in Sec. 3.3.2. In the example we only utilize o-points and operations necessary for deriving the result for this specific case. Other operations or o-points do not further constrain the composition result. For deriving the composition result in general, all potential o-points and operations must be applied to the $\mathcal{OPRA}_m$ representation.

We start by turning the given DCC relations into $\mathcal{OPRA}_m$ relations as described in Sec. 3.4.2 (cf. Table 3.2). To do this, five oriented points have to be introduced (see Fig. 3.16(b)). A, B **12** C and B, C **9** D yield the following relations:

$$\vec{A}^{AB} \ _2\angle_0^0 \ \vec{C}^{BC} \tag{3.4}$$

$$\vec{B}^{AB} \ _2\angle_4^4 \ \vec{C}^{BC} \tag{3.5}$$

$$\vec{A}^{AB} \ _2\angle_0^4 \ \vec{B}^{AB} \quad (rfc_1^{DCC}) \tag{3.6}$$

$$\vec{B}^{BC} \ _2\angle_7^{5..7} \ \vec{D}^{CD} \tag{3.7}$$

$$\vec{C}^{BC} \ _2\angle_5^4 \ \vec{D}^{CD} \tag{3.8}$$

$$\vec{B}^{BC} \ _2\angle_0^4 \ \vec{C}^{BC} \quad (rfc_1^{DCC}) \tag{3.9}$$

We will later need the relation between $\vec{D}^{CD}$ and $\vec{D}^{BD}$. This can be derived from (3.7) by first applying converse operation, then the orientation rotation operation (3.1), and finally projection type 1 (3.2):

$$\vec{B}^{BC} \ _2\angle_7^{5..7} \ \vec{D}^{CD} \ \xrightarrow{(converse)} \ \vec{D}^{CD} \ _2\angle_{5..7}^7 \ \vec{B}^{BC} \ \xrightarrow{(3.1)}$$

$$\vec{D}^{CD} \ _2\angle_{5..7}^0 \ \vec{B}^{BD} \ \xrightarrow{(3.2)} \ \vec{D}^{CD} \ _2\angle 1..3 \ \vec{D}^{BD} \tag{3.10}$$

From applying projection type 2 to (3.5) follows:

$$\vec{B}^{AB} \ _2\angle_4^4 \ \vec{C}^{BC} \ \xrightarrow{(3.3)} \ \vec{B}^{AB} \ _2\angle 4 \ \vec{B}^{BC} \tag{3.11}$$

There are two paths that allow to derive information about the position of $\vec{B}^{AB}$ and $\vec{D}^{CD}$. First, by composing (3.11) with (3.9) and then with (3.8). And second, by composing (3.11) with (3.7). Since both can constrain the possible position, we need to compute both and take the intersection of the resulting disjunctions of base relations. Overall, we thus compute (3.11) ∘ (((3.9) ∘ (3.8)) ∩ (3.7)). Composing (3.9) and (3.8) yields:

$$\vec{B}^{BC} \ _2\angle_0^4 \ \vec{C}^{BC} \circ \vec{C}^{BC} \ _2\angle_5^4 \ \vec{D}^{CD} = \vec{B}^{BC} \ \left(_2\angle_{5..7}^5 \vee {}_2\angle_7^{6..7} \right) \ \vec{D}^{CD} \tag{3.12}$$

Taking the intersection with (3.7) we get:

$$\vec{B}^{BC} \ _2\angle_7^{5..7} \ \vec{D}^{CD} \tag{3.13}$$

And composing this with (3.11) results in the following disjunction for the relation between $\vec{B}^{AB}$ and $\vec{D}^{CD}$:

$$\vec{B}^{AB} \ _2\angle 4 \ \vec{B}^{BC} \circ \vec{B}^{BC} \ _2\angle_7^{5..7} \ \vec{D}^{CD} = \vec{B}^{AB} \ _2\angle_3^{5..7} \ \vec{D}^{CD} \tag{3.14}$$

We can now apply orientation rotation to (3.14) to derive the following relation between $\vec{B}^{AB}$ and $\vec{D}^{BD}$:

$$\vec{B}^{AB} \; _2\angle_3^{5..7} \; \vec{D}^{CD} \overset{(3.1)}{\Longrightarrow} \vec{B}^{AB} \; _2\angle_3^4 \; \vec{D}^{BD} \qquad (3.15)$$

To compute the relation between $\vec{A}^{AB}$ and $\vec{D}^{BD}$ there are again two paths to consider. First, composing (3.6) with (3.15) and second, composing (3.4) and (3.8) and (3.10). This results in the overall computation of $((3.6) \circ (3.15)) \cap ((3.4) \circ (3.8) \circ (3.10))$. Composing (3.6) and (3.15) yields:

$$\vec{A}^{AB} \; _2\angle_0^4 \; \vec{B}^{AB} \circ \vec{B}^{AB} \; _2\angle_3^4 \; \vec{D}^{BD} = \vec{A}^{AB} \left(_2\angle_1^{1..3} \vee \; _2\angle_2^3 \vee \; _2\angle_3^3 \right) \vec{D}^{BD} \qquad (3.16)$$

Composing (3.4) and (3.8) and (3.10) yields:

$$\vec{A}^{AB} \; _2\angle_0^0 \; \vec{C}^{BC} \circ \vec{C}^{BC} \; _2\angle_5^4 \; \vec{D}^{CD} \circ \vec{D}^{CD} \; _2\angle 1..3 \; \vec{D}^{BD} = \vec{A}^{AB} \; _2\angle_1^{7..3} \; \vec{D}^{BD} \qquad (3.17)$$

Taking the intersection of (3.16) and (3.17) we get:

$$\vec{A}^{AB} \; _2\angle_1^{1..3} \; \vec{D}^{BD} \qquad (3.18)$$

The resulting $\mathcal{OPRA}_m$ relations (3.15) and (3.18) together with rfc_1^{DCC} can be looked up in Table 3.2. Inspection reveals that they describe the DCC relation **3**. Thus we have correctly derived that **3** is the composition of **12** and **9**.

We applied the generalized process for deriving composition tables to the calculi presented in Sec. 3.4. We compared the results to the composition tables available in the literature or, if not available, to composition results derived by hand. We found no mistakes in the composition results derived by the method based on the $\mathcal{OPRA}_m$ mappings.

3.5.3 Deriving the $\mathcal{CNG}$ for FFC

Now we derive the neighborhood structure of FFC from the $\mathcal{OPRA}_1$ neighborhood structure. Since A and B are not allowed to coincide in the FFC definition, we can restrict ourselves to consider cases in which only C is allowed to move. The corresponding oriented point $\vec{C}^{BC}$ is part of two relations in the $\mathcal{OPRA}_1$ formalization and thus, these two relations can change simultaneously.

The general idea of the algorithm for deriving the $\mathcal{CNG}$ is to combine the individual conceptual neighbors of the $\mathcal{OPRA}_1$ relations and check the resulting constraint networks for consistency to find out whether the generated formalizations describe valid FFC relations. We abbreviate the $\mathcal{OPRA}_1$ model $\vec{A}^{AB} \; S_1 \; \vec{B}^{AB} \wedge \vec{A}^{AB} \; S_2 \; \vec{C}^{BC} \wedge \vec{B}^{AB} \; S_3 \; \vec{C}^{BC}$ of an FFC relation (as provided by Table 3.1) as a

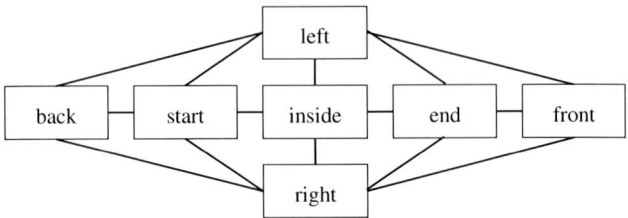

Figure 3.17: The conceptual neighborhood structure of the FlipFlop Calculus.

triple (S_1, S_2, S_3) where the S_i again are sets of base relations. The set of combinations that need to be checked for a given triple (S_1, S_2, S_3) can then be specified with the help of the relax function[7] as $(S_1 \times \text{relax}(S_2) \times \text{relax}(S_3)) \setminus (S_1 \times S_2 \times S_3)$.
For the FFC relation front $(\vec{A}^{AB} {}_1\angle_0^2 \vec{B}^{AB} \wedge \vec{A}^{AB} {}_1\angle_0^2 \vec{C}^{BC} \wedge \vec{B}^{AB} {}_1\angle_0^2 \vec{C}^{BC})$, we check all combinations from the following sets except those which are combinations of base relations already contained in S_1, S_2, and S_3:

$$\text{relax}(S_2) \; = $$
$$\text{relax}(S_3) \; = \; \{ {}_1\angle_0^2 \, , {}_1\angle_3^1 \, , {}_1\angle_3^2 \, , {}_1\angle_3^3 \, , {}_1\angle_0^1 \, , {}_1\angle_0^3 \, , {}_1\angle_1^1 \, , {}_1\angle_1^2 \, , {}_1\angle_1^3 \, ,$$
$${}_1\angle 3 \, , {}_1\angle 0 \, , {}_1\angle 1 \}$$

From all these combinations that were checked for consistency[8], all consistent networks fall into one of three classes from Table 3.1. These are $({}_1\angle_0^2, {}_1\angle_1^1, {}_1\angle_1^2)$ for left, $({}_1\angle_0^2, {}_1\angle_3^3, {}_1\angle_3^2)$ for right, and $({}_1\angle_0^2, {}_1\angle_*^2, {}_1\angle*)$ for end. These three FFC relations are indeed the correct conceptual neighbors of the front relation. Applying this method to the other base relations yields the $\mathcal{CNG}$ shown in Figure 3.17, which is the same structure as presented by Ligozat (1993). Regarding the $\mathcal{LR}$ refinement, S_1 may also be relaxed, but only to same relations. Otherwise we would violate the reference frame constraints. In this case, **dou** and **tri** are also neighbors of front.
Other neighborhood structures, e.g. of the Double Cross Calculus can be derived in the same manner based on the mapping to $\mathcal{OPRA}_2$ relations.

3.5.4   Deriving the $\mathcal{CNG}$ for $\mathcal{DRA}_f$

For deriving the $\mathcal{CNG}$ for $\mathcal{DRA}_f$ we use the same algorithmic scheme as for FFC: composing the individual neighbors of the relations occurring in the $\mathcal{OPRA}_1$ translation, checking the results for consistency, and retranslating the consistent ones.

---

[7]$\text{relax}(S) = \left(\bigcup_{b \in S} \text{cn}(b) \right) \cup S$ (cf. Sec. 2.3.3).

[8]The computations were performed with SparQ (Wallgrün et al., 2006), a generic toolbox for reasoning with qualitative calculi (http://www.sfbtr8.uni-bremen.de/project/r3/sparq/). We introduce SparQ in Sec. 6.2.1.

For a single FFC relation about 140 potential neighboring relations exist. Applying this scheme naively to $\mathcal{DRA}_f$ relations, we get about 140^4 potential neighbors for each relation. However, after eliminating the inconsistent ones for FFC, we ended up with an average of four consistent networks per FFC relation. We therefore chose to employ these results to reduce the number of networks that need to be checked for consistency for $\mathcal{DRA}_f$. The constraints responsible for the inconsistencies in the FFC networks will also be contained in the potential neighbors for $\mathcal{DRA}_f$ relations and thus the overall constraint network would be classified as inconsistent as well. After that, only an average of $5^4 - 1 = 624$ potential neighboring configurations needed to be checked per $\mathcal{DRA}_f$ relation.

For example, out of the approximately 850 potential neighbors of *rfll* only 14 are consistent. The neighboring relations derived are: *rrll, rlll, rele, rlli, rrlf, flll, brll, rrbl, ffbb, efbs, ifbi, bfii, sfsi,* and *ffff*. To give another example, for relation *ebis* 30 neighbors were derived: *fbii, ibib, ells, errs, eses, lbll, rbrr, rlir, lril, llll, lllb, lllr, llrl, llrr, lril, lrll, lrlr, lrrl, lrri, lrrr, flll, frrr, illr, rlll, rlli, rllr, rlrl, rlrr, rrll,* and *rlrl*. The neighborhood structure derived is consistent with the neighborhood structure we derived in the context of Dylla & Moratz (2005).

3.6 Summary

In this chapter we derived an algorithm for composing $\mathcal{OPRA}_m$ relations. We described an example showing that the composition is not closed under constraints. Due to this, standard constraint-based reasoning methods can only be applied as approximations to consistency of constraint networks. By introducing the constructive operations orientation rotation and projection, we are able to determine inconsistencies for configurations with four o-points. Whether all inconsistencies for arbitrary o-point configurations can be found by constructing additional o-points and adding them to the constraint network remains an open question. In addition, we derived the neighborhood structure for $\mathcal{OPRA}_m$ relations.

Based on $\mathcal{OPRA}_m$ we presented mappings of several point-based orientation calculi to sets of $\mathcal{OPRA}_m$ relations, among them the FlipFlop Calculus, the Double Cross Calculus, the $\mathcal{DRA}_f$, and the QTC. Finally, we applied these mappings to mediate between calculi other than $\mathcal{OPRA}_m$, to derive their composition tables, and to determine their neighborhood structures.

The method for deriving the composition tables and neighborhood structures described in this section yields the correct results for the calculi considered. However, whether the method is applicable for qualitative orientation calculi in general is still an open question. So far, manual verification of the composition tables and neighborhood graphs computed for different orientation calculi indicates that this might be the case, but further research is needed on this issue.

Chapter 4

$\mathcal{OPRA}_m^\star$: Combining $\mathcal{OPRA}_m$ and Alignment Knowledge

$\mathcal{OPRA}_m$ is a very expressive calculus dealing with relative orientation information. However, $\mathcal{OPRA}_m$ is not sufficient for controlling agents in an adequate manner. Considering a subpart of $\mathcal{OPRA}_m$ relations we cannot distinguish whether two moving objects approach each other, depart from each other, or are moving on parallel paths. To overcome this shortcoming, we define the Alignment Calculus ($\mathcal{AC}$) and combine it with $\mathcal{OPRA}_m$ resulting in the new calculus $\mathcal{OPRA}_m^\star$ which is more adequate for agent control.

4.1 Introduction

Relative orientation information is fundamental for controlling agents, e.g. in the context of right-of-way regulations or collision detection in traffic scenarios. In traffic situations it is necessary to know whether an object moves towards another object, moves away, moves in parallel in the same direction, or moves in parallel in the opposite direction. We subsume these four cases under the term *alignment knowledge*. Current relative orientation calculi are not capable of representing alignment in an adequate manner.

We have shown in Section 3 that $\mathcal{OPRA}_m$ is a good candidate for an umbrella calculus for orientation knowledge. Many other orientation calculi can be represented in terms of $\mathcal{OPRA}_m$. Additionally, $\mathcal{OPRA}_m$ has the advantage that the angular resolution can be changed due to the granularity parameter m. $\mathcal{OPRA}_m$ cannot represent alignment properly, an thus, it is necessary to extend $\mathcal{OPRA}_m$ to also representing alignment regarding o-points so that $\mathcal{OPRA}_m$ is better suited for agent control purposes.

For some $\mathcal{OPRA}_m$ relations alignment is given by the algebraic definition of the relations, but for others alignment is ambiguous. For example, for linear relations ($i \mod 2 = 0$) with $m\angle_i^i$ or $m\angle_i^{i+2m}$, the lines induced by the reference directions of the o-points are parallel. e.g. $_2\angle_2^2$ or $_2\angle_2^6$. In contrast, planar relations (i mod $2 = 1$) with $m\angle_i^i$ or $m\angle_i^{i+2m}$, are ambiguous as they may be aligned arbitrarily. Assuming $m \to \infty$ it would be possible to represent alignment with an accuracy of $\frac{2\pi}{m}$ for ambiguous relations, but this would result in great computational effort for composition, because the complexity of the composition algorithm presented in the previous chapter is dependent on m (cf. Sec. 3.3.1).

In the following we first investigate alignment separately by defining the Alignment Calculus ($\mathcal{AC}$). We give the neighboring structure and the composition table. Afterwards, we integrate $\mathcal{OPRA}_m$ and $\mathcal{AC}$ into the compound calculus $\mathcal{OPRA}_m^\star$. We clarify the dependencies between both calculi and give a composition algorithm based on the original $\mathcal{OPRA}_m$ composition and an additional set of inequalities representing the dependencies. Finally, we determine the neighboring structure of $\mathcal{OPRA}_m^\star$ relations.

4.2   The Alignment Calculus ($\mathcal{AC}$)

In this section we give the Alignment Calculus ($\mathcal{AC}$) representing alignment of two directed lines. Given two o-points $\vec{A}$ and $\vec{B}$, dipoles respectively, two oriented lines are induced by their reference direction, which we call *o-lines*. We denote these o-lines by $\vec{A}_l$ and $\vec{B}_l$. We can distinguish four different alignment relations regarding two o-lines $\vec{A}_l$ and $\vec{B}_l$:

- the o-lines are parallel and point in the same direction,

- the o-lines are parallel and point in the opposite direction,

- $\vec{B}_l$ is rotated mathematically positive by $0 < \alpha < \pi$ with respect to $\vec{A}_l$ (positive alignment), and

- $\vec{B}_l$ is rotated mathematically negative by $0 < \alpha < \pi$ with respect to $\vec{A}_l$ (negative alignment).

Thus, we define the four base relations *parallel* (P), *opposite-parallel* (O), *positive* ($+$), and *negative* ($-$). We depict these four cases in Fig. 4.1. For intersecting o-lines the enclosed angle between $\vec{A}_l$ and B_l is denoted by α. If o-lines are parallel, angles α and β are the enclosed angles with respect to a third line intersecting $\vec{A}_l$ and B_l. The set of $\mathcal{AC}$ base relations is denoted by $\mathcal{BR}_{\mathcal{AC}}$.

Isli & Cohn (1998, 2000) present a calculus with the same base relations as the $\mathcal{AC}$. The calculus is called an algebra of binary relations. They derive the four basic relations *equal*, *left*, *opposite*, and *right* on the basis of a 2D generalization of Allen's Temporal Interval Algebra (Allen, 1983). In addition, they derive a ternary variant of this calculus with 24 base relations. They give converse and composition for both variants. The two algebras are applied to refine the *CYCORD* theory (Röhrig, 1994) and to investigate the reasoning properties of the *CYCORD* refinements.

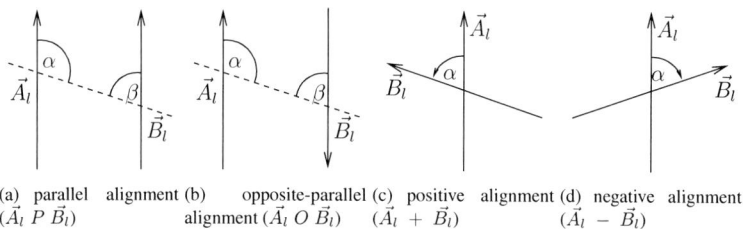

(a) parallel alignment ($\vec{A}_l$ P $\vec{B}_l$)   (b) opposite-parallel alignment ($\vec{A}_l$ O $\vec{B}_l$)   (c) positive alignment ($\vec{A}_l$ $+$ $\vec{B}_l$)   (d) negative alignment ($\vec{A}_l$ $-$ $\vec{B}_l$)

Figure 4.1: Different alignments between oriented line segments $\vec{A}$ and $\vec{B}$.

We now derive the neighborhood structure of $\mathcal{AC}$. The alignment of two lines can only be changed by rotating the orientation of at least one line. Assuming that two lines are parallel ($\vec{A}_l$ P $\vec{B}_l$) and $\vec{B}_l$ rotates to the left the alignment changes consecutively to *positive*, to *opposite-parallel*, to *negative*, and finally, back to *parallel*. If $\vec{B}_l$ rotates to the right, alignment changes from *negative* to *opposite-parallel*, to *positive*, and back to *parallel*. $\vec{A}_l$ rotating left (right), results in the same changes as if $\vec{B}_l$ rotates right (left). Assuming both objects are rotating at the same time does not results in additional neighborhood relations. A direct transition from P to O and from $+$ to $-$ and vice versa is not possible. The neighborhood structure for $\mathcal{AC}$ relations is depicted in Fig. 4.2.

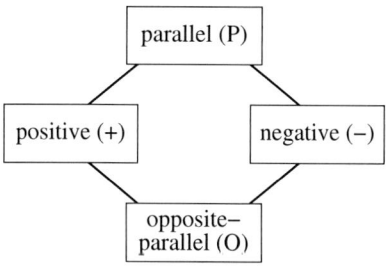

Figure 4.2: The conceptual neighborhood graph for $\mathcal{AC}$.

For making expressions simpler in the remainder of this thesis, we define the labels $P, +, O$, and $-$ as a cyclic group. Thereupon, we define the operators $\oplus$ and $\ominus$ based on the order of the symbols as given above. Thus, it follows:

$$
\begin{aligned}
P \oplus 1 &= + \\
+ \oplus 1 &= O \\
O \oplus 1 &= - \\
- \oplus 1 &= P
\end{aligned}
\qquad \text{and} \qquad
\begin{aligned}
P \ominus 1 &= - \\
+ \ominus 1 &= P \\
O \ominus 1 &= + \\
- \ominus 1 &= O\,.
\end{aligned}
$$

The converse of $\mathcal{AC}$ relations is easy to derive. If $\vec{A}_l$ is parallel to $\vec{B}_l$ than $\vec{B}_l$ is also parallel to $\vec{A}_l$. If $\vec{A}_l$ is opposite-parallel to $\vec{B}_l$ than $\vec{B}_l$ is also opposite-parallel to $\vec{A}_l$. If $\vec{A}_l$ is aligned positively to $\vec{B}_l$ than $\vec{B}_l$ is aligned negatively to $\vec{A}_l$ and vice versa. The converse operation is summarized in Table 4.1.

Now we derive the composition table for $\mathcal{AC}$ informally. Assume the orientation relations x and $y \in \mathcal{BR}_{\mathcal{AC}}$ are given. If both orientations are aligned in *parallel* the resulting relation will also be *parallel*. The same holds, if both relations are *opposite-parallel*. If one relation is *parallel* and the other is *positive* (*negative*), the result is *positive* (*negative*). In the case of one relation is *opposite-parallel* and the other positive (*negative*) the composition result is *negative* (*positive*). Therefore P can be interpreted as the identity relation, whereas O can be interpreted as the inverse relation. Only in the case of both relations being *positive* or *negative* the composition result is more uncertain. If both relations are *positive* or *negative* the result can never be *parallel*, but the other three alternatives are possible ($\{-, O, +\}$). If one relation is *positive* and the other *negative* the result can never be *opposite-parallel*. Again, the other three alternatives are possible ($\{+, P, -\}$). We give the complete $\mathcal{AC}$ composition table in Table 4.2.

x	$x^{\smile}$
P	P
$+$	$-$
O	O
$-$	$+$

$x \circ y$	P	$+$	O	$-$
P	P	$+$	O	$-$
$+$	$+$	$-, O, +$	$-$	$+, P, -$
O	O	$-$	P	$+$
$-$	$-$	$+, P, -$	$+$	$-, O, +$

Table 4.1: The converse of $\mathcal{AC}$ relations.

Table 4.2: The $\mathcal{AC}$ composition table.

4.3 Integrating $\mathcal{OPRA}_m$ and $\mathcal{AC}$

We now demonstrate how $\mathcal{OPRA}_m$ and $\mathcal{AC}$ can be combined resulting in $\mathcal{OPRA}_m^{\star}$. First, we define $\mathcal{OPRA}_m^{\star}$ relations as tuples of $\mathcal{OPRA}_m$ relations and $\mathcal{AC}$ relations. We will start our investigations with the lowest granularity for $\mathcal{OPRA}_m$, i.e. $m = 1$, and transfer the result to finer granularities, i.e. $m > 1$.

First, we define a compound $\mathcal{OPRA}_m^{\star}$ relation as tuple of the original $\mathcal{OPRA}_m$ relation $r_{\mathcal{OPRA}_m}$ and an $\mathcal{AC}$ relation $r_{\mathcal{AC}}$: $(r_{\mathcal{OPRA}_m}, r_{\mathcal{AC}})$. In the following we will not distinguish between the o-points regarding the $\mathcal{OPRA}_m$ relation and the o-lines induced by the o-points which are the basic entities regarding the $\mathcal{AC}$ relation. We denote a compound $\mathcal{OPRA}_m^{\star}$ relation by $\,_m^{r_{\mathcal{AC}}}\angle_i^j$, if $r_{\mathcal{OPRA}_m} = m\angle_i^j$, or $\,_m^{r_{\mathcal{AC}}}\angle i$, if $r_{\mathcal{OPRA}_m} = m\angle i$.

The question for each $\mathcal{OPRA}_m^{\star}$ relation is, which potential alignment relations $r_{\mathcal{AC}}$ are valid. First, we consider $\mathcal{OPRA}_1$ relations and generalize afterwards.

i/j	0	1	2	3	$same$
0	O	$+$	P	$-$	P
1	$-$	$-,O,+$	$+$	$+,P,-$	$+$
2	P	$-$	O	$+$	O
3	$+$	$+,P,-$	$-$	$-,O,+$	$-$

Table 4.3: The possible $\mathcal{AC}$ orientations for $\mathcal{OPRA}_1$ relations ($1\angle_i^j$ and $1\angle i$).

For each 'same' relation only a single base relation is valid. The alignment of relation $1\angle 0$ is always *parallel* as the o-lines are identical. In case of $1\angle 2$ the o-lines are parallel, but they have opposite orientation, therefore alignment is *opposite-parallel*. Relation $1\angle 1$ is aligned *positively* and $1\angle 3$ is aligned *negatively*. Henceforth, we consider non-'same' $\mathcal{OPRA}_1$ relations. For twelve relations of the remaining sixteen relations the alignment is given by the definition of the $\mathcal{OPRA}_1$ relations. The alignment regarding $1\angle_0^0$ and $1\angle_2^2$ is *parallel* and the alignment regarding $1\angle_0^2$ and $1\angle_2^0$ is *opposite-parallel*. Relations $1\angle_1^0$, $1\angle_2^1$, $1\angle_3^2$, and $1\angle_0^3$ are aligned *positively*, whereas $1\angle_0^1$, $1\angle_1^2$, $1\angle_2^3$, and $1\angle_3^0$ are aligned *negatively*. Now, the four relations $1\angle_1^1$, $1\angle_3^1$, $1\angle_1^3$, and $1\angle_3^3$ remain.

Regarding $1\angle_1^1$ three different alignments are possible: *positive, opposite-parallel*, and *negative*. So $1\angle_1^1$ refines to $1^+\angle_1^1$, $1^O\angle_1^1$, and $1^-\angle_1^1$. Similarly, $1\angle_3^3$ refines to $1^+\angle_3^3$, $1^O\angle_3^3$, and $1^-\angle_3^3$. Regarding $1\angle_1^3$ the alignments *positive, parallel*, and *negative* are possible. So $1\angle_1^3$ is refined to $1^+\angle_1^3$, $1^P\angle_1^3$, and $1^-\angle_1^3$. In the same manner $1\angle_3^1$ refines to $1^+\angle_3^1$, $1^P\angle_3^1$, and $1^-\angle_3^1$. We summarize the potential alignments of $\mathcal{OPRA}_1^*$ base relations with respect to $\mathcal{OPRA}_1$ relations in Table 4.3. The extension for $m = 1$ results in $20 - 4 + (3 * 4) = 28$ base relations.

We now generalize our considerations for arbitrary m. Assume relation $\vec{A}\ m\angle_i^j\ \vec{B}$ is given. For the following argumentation it is important that the region denoted by i, j respectively, correspond to a precise angle if it is an even number and to an interval of angles if it is an odd number.

We first regard relations where $i - j$ holds. If i and j are even numbers then two linear regions are given. These two linear regions define a distinct line between the o-points. The induced o-lines do not intersect. The angle α is determined by i and angle β by $2m-j$ (cf. Fig. 4.1). With $i = j$ we can follow that $i+(2m-j) = 2m$. Regarding the algebraic specification of $\mathcal{OPRA}_m$ relations we can infer that $2m$ corresponds to the angle π. So, the orientations of the o-points are opposite to each other. Therefore, we can conclude from the definition of $\mathcal{OPRA}_m$ relations that all relations with $i = j$ and i is even are *opposite-parallel*. If i and j are odd two planar regions are given. The o-points may still be opposite-parallel, but there are also instantiations regarding the intervall of angles where one of the o-points is 'rotated to the right or left', and thus α and β may not sum up to π. Therefore, it follows that all relations with $i = j$ and i is odd may have an *opposite-parallel, positive*, or *negative* alignment.

We now regard relations with $i = 2m + j^1$. In this case α is determined by i and β by j. Again, if i and $j + 2m$ are even the sum up to $2m$ which corresponds to the angle π. Contrary to the first case the o-points are aligned in the same direction and thus, can only be *parallel*. If i is odd the case is similar to the case above. $\vec{A}$ and $\vec{B}$ can be rotated so that the inferred angles α and β do not exactly sum up to π, and thus, the alignment may be *parallel*, *positive*, or *negative*.

Now all relations we have not categorized so far have to be considered. These are all relations where the induced lines are not parallel and thus, will have a definite intersection point. We need to determine the angle α (cf. Fig. 4.1) from i and j. We will consider 'same' relations further below because α is determined by i directly. We can distinguish three different cases for the remaining relations. First, i and j are linear and thus α is precisely determined. Second, either i or j is linear and the other planar, then α is in an angular interval of size $\frac{\pi}{m}$. And finally, i and j are planar then α is in an interval of size $\frac{2\pi}{m}$.

From the algebraic specification of $\mathcal{OPRA}_m$ relations it can be derived that, if one of the remaining relations either fulfills the conditions $i > j$ and $i < (j+2m)$ or $i < j$ and $j > (i + 2m)$ the exact value or the interval α is completely in the range between zero and $-\pi$, i.e. the o-points are aligned *negatively*. For all remaining relations the alignment is *positive*.

The 'same' relations can be derived uniquely as in the case of $\mathcal{OPRA}_1$. For $m\angle 0$ the alignment is *parallel*. In the case of $m\angle 2m$ the o-points point in opposite directions and therefore, are aligned *opposite-parallel*. For all relations $m\angle i$ with $0 < i < 2m$ the alignment is *positive* and for all relations $m\angle i$ with $2m < i < 4m$ the alignment is *negative*.

We summarize the results in Table 4.4 for non-'same' relations and in Table 4.5 for 'same' relations. We define the function

$$\texttt{align}(r) = \mathcal{O}_r$$

where $r \in \mathcal{BR}_{\mathcal{OPRA}_m}$ and $\mathcal{O}_r$ is the set of potential alignments of the underlying $\mathcal{OPRA}_m$ relation. An overview of the results of this algorithm for arbitrary m is depicted in Table 4.6. The number of base relations $\mathcal{BR}$ for $\mathcal{OPRA}_m^\star$ can be determined by $|\mathcal{BR}_{\mathcal{OPRA}_m^\star}| = 4m(4m + 1) - 4m + (3 * 4m) = 4m(4m + 3)$. Hence, there are $8m$ more base relations in $\mathcal{OPRA}_m^\star$ compared to $\mathcal{OPRA}_m$ for a given granularity m.

The $\mathcal{OPRA}_m^\star$ refinement of an $\mathcal{OPRA}_m$ relation ($r = m\angle_i^j$) can now be defined as the set

$$\mathcal{R}_r = \{ {}_m^o\angle_i^j \, | o \in \mathcal{O}_r = \texttt{align}(\, m\angle_i^j \,)\}.$$

We will denote this refinement function by $\texttt{refine}(r)$. The $\mathcal{OPRA}_m^\star$ refinement of a set of $\mathcal{OPRA}_m$ relations $\mathcal{S}$ is then given by the union of all $\mathcal{R}_s$ with $s \in \mathcal{S}$:

$$\texttt{refine}(\mathcal{S}) = \bigcup_{s \in \mathcal{S}} \texttt{refine}(s).$$

---

[1] We do not need to distinguish the case where $j = 2m + i$ here as i and j are members of the cyclic group $\mathcal{Z}_{4m}$, and thus, these cases are symmetric to relations with $i = 2m + j$

$$\text{align}(\,{}_m\angle_i^j\,) \;=\; \begin{cases} \{O\} & \text{, if } i = j \wedge i \mod 2 = 0\,, \\ \{-,O,+\} & \text{, if } i = j \wedge i \mod 2 = 1\,, \\ \{P\} & \text{, if } i = j + 2m \wedge i \mod 2 = 0\,, \\ \{+,P,-\} & \text{, if } i = j + 2m \wedge i \mod 2 = 1\,, \\ \{-\} & \text{, if } (i > j \wedge i < j + 2m) \vee (i < j \wedge j > i + 2m) \\ \{+\} & \text{, else.} \end{cases}$$

Table 4.4: Alignment of a non-'same' relation ${}_m\angle_i^j$.

$$\text{align}(\,{}_m\angle s\,) \;=\; \begin{cases} \{P\} & \text{, if } s = 0, \\ \{+\} & \text{, if } 0 < s < 2m, \\ \{O\} & \text{, if } s = 2m, \\ \{-\} & \text{, if } 2m < s < 4m. \end{cases}$$

Table 4.5: Alignment of a 'same' relation ${}_m\angle s$.

We define an $\mathcal{OPRA}_m^{\star}$ relation $r^{\star} = \{\,{}_m^o\angle_i^j\,\}$ to be *valid* if $o \in \text{align}(\,{}_m\angle_i^j\,)$, $r^{\star} = \{\,{}_m^o\angle i\,\}$ and $o \in \text{align}(\,{}_m\angle i\,)$ respectively.

It is easy to see that the converse of $\mathcal{OPRA}_m^{\star}$ relations can be defined by the individual components. The converse of $\mathcal{OPRA}_m$ relations is $(\,{}_m\angle_i^j\,)^{\smile} = {}_m\angle_j^i$ and $(\,{}_m\angle s\,)^{\smile} = {}_m\angle(4m - s)$. The converse of $\mathcal{AC}$ relations is the exchange of $+$ and $-$, and for P and O the identity. We give the converse of $\mathcal{OPRA}_m^{\star}$ relations by

$$\begin{aligned} (\,{}_m^x\angle_i^j\,)^{\smile} &= {}_m^{x^{\smile}}\angle_j^i \\ (\,{}_m^x\angle s\,)^{\smile} &= {}_m^{x^{\smile}}\angle(4m - s)\,. \end{aligned}$$

i/j	0	1	2	...	2m-2	2m-1	2m	2m+1	2m+2	...	4m-3	4m-2	4m-1	same
0	O	+	+	:	+	+	P	-	-	:	-	-	-	P
1	-	-,O,+	+	:	+	+	+	+,P,-	P	:	-	-	-	+
2	-	-	O	:	+	+	+	+	+	:	-	-	-	+
...	:	:	:	:	:	:	:	:	:	:	:	:	:	:
2m-2	-	-	-	:	O	+	+	+	+	:	+	P	+,P,-	+
2m-1	-	-	-	:	-	-,O,+	+	+	+	:	+	+	+	+
2m	P	-	-	:	-	-	O	+	+	:	+	+	+	O
2m+1	+	+,P,-	-	:	-	-	-	-,O,+	+	:	+	+	+	-
2m+2	+	+	-	:	-	-	-	-	O	:	+	+	+	-
...	:	:	:	:	:	:	:	:	:	:	:	:	:	:
4m-3	+	+	+	:	-	-	-	-	-	:	-,O,+	+	+	-
4m-2	+	+	+	:	P	-	-	-	-	:	-	O	+	-
4m-1	+	+	+	:	+	+,P,-	-	-	-	:	-	-	-,O,+	-

Table 4.6: The possible $\mathcal{AC}$ orientations for $\mathcal{OPRA}_m$ relations.

4.4 Composition of $\mathcal{OPRA}_m^\star$ relations

We now consider the composition operation for $\mathcal{OPRA}_m^\star$ relations. Given two $\mathcal{OPRA}_m^\star$ relations $r_1 = {}_m^x\angle_i^j$ and $r_2 = {}_m^y\angle_k^l$ a composition result can be derived on the basis of the separate composition tables of $\mathcal{OPRA}_m$ and $\mathcal{AC}$. This means that all relations $r = {}_m^a\angle_s^t \in ({}_m^x\angle_i^j \circ {}_m^y\angle_k^l)$ with $a \in (x \circ y)$ are considered as correct result. It is known from results on other combined calculi, e.g. the INDU Calculus (Pujari & Sattar, 1999), that this kind of composition does not necessarily give the correct result, i.e. not the minimal set of base relations possible. We call this process *naive composition*. We depict an example in Fig. 4.3. Given the base configuration $\vec{A}\;{}_1^-\angle_0^3\;\vec{B}$ and $\vec{B}\;{}_1^+\angle_0^1\;\vec{C}$ (cf. Fig. 4.3(a)) one of the resulting relations is $\vec{A}\;{}_1^+\angle_3^3\;\vec{C}$ (cf. Fig. 4.3(c)) which is an invalid configuration considering the base configuration.

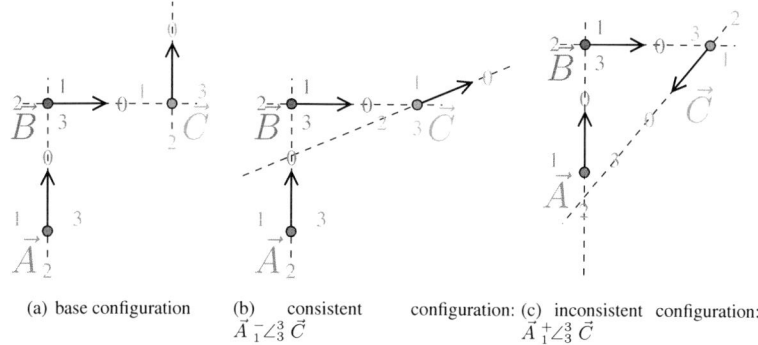

(a) base configuration   (b) consistent   configuration: (c) inconsistent configuration:
$\vec{A}\;{}_1^-\angle_3^3\;\vec{C}$ $\vec{A}\;{}_1^+\angle_3^3\;\vec{C}$

Figure 4.3: Examples of naive composition results for $\mathcal{OPRA}_m^\star$ relations $\vec{A}\;{}_1^-\angle_0^3\;\vec{B}$ and $\vec{B}\;{}_1^+\angle_0^1\;\vec{C}$.

Now we take a closer look at the geometric properties of $\mathcal{OPRA}_m^\star$ relations and exploit them to create an algorithm for deriving the composition table. Given three $\mathcal{OPRA}_m^\star$ objects $\vec{A}, \vec{B}$, and $\vec{C}$ with two $\mathcal{OPRA}_m^\star$ relations for the pair $(\vec{A}, \vec{B})$ and $(\vec{B}, \vec{C})$ we already have the composition table to get the plain $\mathcal{OPRA}_m$ relation between $\vec{A}$ and $\vec{C}$ (cf. Sec. 3.3.1). Using this information and geometric constraints that arise in the triangle configuration of three o-points we realize that resulting $\mathcal{OPRA}_m^\star$ relations should fulfill certain requirements that will be stated in the following.

4.4.1 A Composition Algorithm Based on Geometric Properties

We assume that we have three o-points $\vec{A}, \vec{B}$, and $\vec{C}$ that constitute a positively oriented triangle, i.e. the vertices are positioned in anticlockwise order. We denote the three corresponding $\mathcal{OPRA}_m^\star$ relations with $\vec{A}\;{}_m^x\angle_i^j\;\vec{B}$, $\vec{B}\;{}_m^y\angle_k^l\;\vec{C}$, and $\vec{A}\;{}_m^z\angle_t^s\;\vec{C}$. Let the line that connects the points A and C be denoted l_{AC}. Then we call the angle between

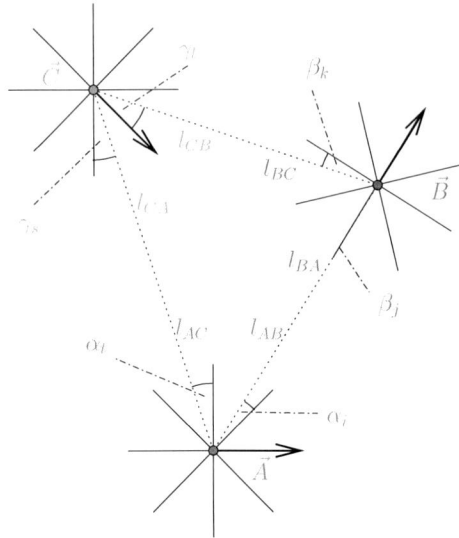

Figure 4.4: An exemplary triangle configuration for $\vec{A} \, {}^x_m\angle^j_i \, \vec{B}$, $\vec{B} \, {}^y_m\angle^l_k \, \vec{C}$, and $\vec{A} \, {}^z_m\angle^s_t \, \vec{C}$.

l_{AC} and the linear region positioned clockwise next to it α_t. In the same way we define the angles α_i, β_j, β_k, γ_l, and γ_s (cf. Fig. 4.4). Using these notations we are able to find equivalent expressions for the relations $+$, $-$, P, and O added in $\mathcal{OPRA}_m^\star$, e.g.

$$\vec{A} \, {}^O_m\angle^s_t \, \vec{C} \iff \vec{A} \, {}_m\angle^s_t \, \vec{C} \text{ and} \tag{4.1}$$

$$\left(\alpha_t + \frac{\tilde{t}}{2} \cdot \frac{\pi}{m} - \left(\gamma_S + \frac{\tilde{s}}{2} \cdot \frac{\pi}{m} \right) \right) \bmod 2\pi = 0$$

where the operator $\tilde{\ }$ is defined as

$$\tilde{t} := \begin{cases} t & \text{if } t \text{ is even, i.e. the } t\text{-th sector of } \vec{A} \text{ is linear} \\ t - 1 & \text{if } t \text{ is odd, i.e. the } t\text{-th sector of } \vec{A} \text{ is planar} \end{cases}$$

The interpretation of this formula is simple: the term $\alpha_t + \frac{\tilde{t}}{2} \cdot \frac{\pi}{m}$ stands for the angle between the o-point's reference direction (0-th linear sector) of $\vec{A}$ and the line l_{AC}. If this is equal to $\gamma_s + \frac{\tilde{s}}{2} \cdot \frac{\pi}{m}$ which stands for the angle between the reference direction of $\vec{C}$ and l_{AC}, than they make up alternate interior angles arisen from the line l_{AC} and the two reference directions. Thus, the oriented points $\vec{A}$ and $\vec{C}$ are opposite-parallel to each other. In the same manner, we restate the remaining potential alignments as follows:

$$\vec{A} \, {}_m^{-}\angle_t^s \, \vec{C} \iff \vec{A} \, {}_m\angle_t^s \, \vec{C} \text{ and} \tag{4.2}$$

$$0 < \left(\left(\alpha_t + \frac{\tilde{t}}{2} \cdot \frac{\pi}{m} - \left(\gamma_s + \frac{\tilde{s}}{2} \cdot \frac{\pi}{m} \right) \right) \right) \bmod 2\pi < \pi,$$

$$\vec{A} \, {}_m^{P}\angle_t^s \, \vec{C} \iff \vec{A} \, {}_m\angle_t^s \, \vec{C} \text{ and} \tag{4.3}$$

$$\left(\left(\alpha_t + \frac{\tilde{t}}{2} \cdot \frac{\pi}{m} - \left(\gamma_s + \frac{\tilde{s}}{2} \cdot \frac{\pi}{m} \right) \right) \right) \bmod 2\pi = \pi, \text{ and}$$

$$\vec{A} \, {}_m^{+}\angle_t^s \, \vec{C} \iff \vec{A} \, {}_m\angle_t^s \, \vec{C} \text{ and} \tag{4.4}$$

$$\pi < \left(\left(\alpha_t + \frac{\tilde{t}}{2} \cdot \frac{\pi}{m} - \left(\gamma_s + \frac{\tilde{s}}{2} \cdot \frac{\pi}{m} \right) \right) \right) \bmod 2\pi < 2\pi.$$

The other relations can be constructed in the same way. We will now make use of the results above and calculate the composition

$$\vec{A} \, {}_m^{x}\angle_i^j \, \vec{B} \circ \vec{B} \, {}_m^{y}\angle_k^l \, \vec{C}.$$

Assume that

$$\vec{A} \, {}_m^{z}\angle_t^s \, \vec{C} \in \vec{A} \, {}_m^{x}\angle_i^j \, \vec{B} \circ \vec{B} \, {}_m^{y}\angle_k^l \, \vec{C}.$$

Then

$$\vec{A} \, {}_m\angle_t^s \, \vec{C} \in \vec{A} \, {}_m\angle_i^j \, \vec{B} \circ \vec{B} \, {}_m\angle_k^l \, \vec{C}$$

should be satisfied beforehand, i.e. the pair s, t is in the result of the corresponding composition under plain $\mathcal{OPRA}_m$.

We now set up sufficient and necessary constraints for the geometrical feasibility of the given triangle construction. The variables in these constraints are α_t, α_i, β_j, β_k, γ_l, and γ_s, having real numbers as values. First of all, restating the three given relations $_m\angle_t^s$, $_m\angle_i^j$, and $_m\angle_k^l$ according to (4.1) - (4.4) yields three constraints. Let α, β, and γ be the internal angles of the triangle corresponding to the points A, B, and C, respectively. Then

$$\alpha = \left(\left(\alpha_t + \frac{\tilde{t}}{2} \cdot \frac{\pi}{m} - \left(\alpha_i + \frac{\tilde{i}}{2} \cdot \frac{\pi}{m} \right) \right) \right) \bmod 2\pi \tag{4.5}$$

$$\beta = \left(\left(\beta_j + \frac{\tilde{j}}{2} \cdot \frac{\pi}{m} - \left(\beta_k + \frac{\tilde{k}}{2} \cdot \frac{\pi}{m} \right) \right) \right) \bmod 2\pi \tag{4.6}$$

$$\gamma = \left(\left(\gamma_l + \frac{\tilde{l}}{2} \cdot \frac{\pi}{m} - \left(\gamma_s + \frac{\tilde{s}}{2} \cdot \frac{\pi}{m} \right) \right) \right) \bmod 2\pi \tag{4.7}$$

and since each of α, β, and γ should be in $[0; \pi]$ we get three additional constraints. The construction of α_t, α_i, β_j, β_k, γ_l, and γ_s, gives again six new constraints, e.g.

$$\alpha_t \in \begin{cases} \{0\} & \text{if } t \text{ is even} \\ ]0; \frac{\pi}{m}[& \text{if } t \text{ is odd} \end{cases} \tag{4.8}$$

The very last constraint arises from the fact that the sum of the internal angles of a triangle is π. Altogether there are 13 constraints which can be written as a system of linear inequalities with the variables α_t, α_i, β_j, β_k, γ_l, and γ_s. With Fourier-Motzkin elimination (e.g. cf. Bik & Wijshoff, 1995) for solving a system of linear inequalities[2] we are able to decide solvability of the 13 constraints. We give an example how this algorithm works in Section 4.4.2. Although, the worst case complexity of the algorithm is $O(n^{2^k})$, where n is the number of constraints and k the number of variables to eliminate, the algorithm is applicable in our case, because (a) the average case behavior is considered much better and (b) we only deal with a comparatively small set of constraints and variables. For our computations we applied the ECLiPSe Constraint Logic Programming Library[3].

In the beginning of this section we assumed a positively oriented triangle as the underlying construction. In the case of a negatively orientated triangle, we only have to switch the order of the letters in each of the formulas from (4.5) - (4.7). So, we can derive the according formulas for α, β, and γ for negatively orientated triangles:

$$\alpha = \left(\left(\alpha_i + \frac{\tilde{i}}{2} \cdot \frac{\pi}{m} - \left(\alpha_t + \frac{\tilde{t}}{2} \cdot \frac{\pi}{m} \right) \right) \right) \mod 2\pi \tag{4.9}$$

$$\beta = \left(\left(\beta_k + \frac{\tilde{k}}{2} \cdot \frac{\pi}{m} - \left(\beta_j + \frac{\tilde{j}}{2} \cdot \frac{\pi}{m} \right) \right) \right) \mod 2\pi \tag{4.10}$$

$$\gamma = \left(\left(\gamma_s + \frac{\tilde{s}}{2} \cdot \frac{\pi}{m} - \left(\gamma_l + \frac{\tilde{l}}{2} \cdot \frac{\pi}{m} \right) \right) \right) \mod 2\pi \tag{4.11}$$

We now further investigate cases containing modulo operations. In our case the general form of the terms involving modulo operations looks as follows

$$\left(\alpha_t + \frac{\tilde{t}}{2} \cdot \frac{\pi}{m} - \left(\alpha_i + \frac{\tilde{i}}{2} \cdot \frac{\pi}{m} \right) \right) \mod 2\pi = \left(\alpha_t - \alpha_i + (\tilde{t} - \tilde{i})\frac{\pi}{2m} \right) \mod 2\pi .$$

From $\alpha_t, \alpha_i \in [0; \frac{\pi}{m}[$ and $\tilde{t}, \tilde{i} \in \{0, \dots 2m - 2\}$ it follows that

$$-\pi < \alpha_t - \alpha_i + (\tilde{t} - \tilde{i})\frac{\pi}{2m} < \pi. \tag{4.12}$$

---

[2]A great variety of algorithms for solving linear inequalities exits. For further details we refer to Schrijver (1989), Kessler (1996), and Bik & Wijshoff (1995).
[3]http://eclipse.crosscoreop.com/

Thus $\left(\alpha_t - \alpha_i + (\tilde{t} - \tilde{i})\frac{\pi}{2m}\right)$ mod 2π is

$$\alpha_t - \alpha_i + (\tilde{t} - \tilde{i})\frac{\pi}{2m} \qquad \text{or}$$

$$\alpha_t - \alpha_i + (\tilde{t} - \tilde{i})\frac{\pi}{2m} + 2\pi \quad .$$

In other words, from one constraint we get two constraints combined with disjunction. As a system of inequalities is nothing but a set of inequalities combined via conjunctions, a modulo operation in a system of inequalities induces two systems of inequalities by distributive law (e.g. $X_1 \wedge (X_2 \vee X_2') \wedge X_3 \wedge X_4 = (X_1 \wedge X_2 \wedge X_3 \wedge X_4) \vee (X_1 \wedge X_2' \wedge X_3 \wedge X_4)$). Altogether we have 6 constraints including one modulo operation and the constraint $\pi = \alpha + \beta + \gamma$ which includes 3 modulo operations. From a constraint with 3 modulo operations we can derive 4 different constraints without modulo operation. So the resulting number of systems of inequalities is $2^6 \cdot 4 = 256$. However, several approaches reducing the branching factor exist (cf. Sec. 4.4.3).

4.4.2 Examples

Example 1 Here we consider the example from Fig. 4.3:

$$_1^+\angle_3^3 \notin {}_1^-\angle_0^3 \circ {}_1^+\angle_0^1 \,,$$

i.e. $i = 0$, $j = 3$, $k = 0$, $l = 1$, $s = 3$ and $t = 3$. In this case, a contradiction can be easily inferred. According to (4.9) - (4.11) we obtain from $0 \leq \alpha, \beta, \gamma \leq \pi$ and $\pi = \alpha + \beta + \gamma$

$$
\begin{aligned}
0 &\leq & \alpha_t & \leq \pi \,, \\
0 &\leq & \beta_j & \leq \pi \,, \\
0 &\leq & \gamma_l - \gamma_s & \leq \pi \,, \text{ and} \\
& & -\alpha_t - \beta_j + \gamma_s - \gamma_l & = 2\pi \,.
\end{aligned}
\tag{4.13}
$$

Note that the underlying triangle here is negatively oriented. Besides, as the reader can check easily, each inequality above is the only true one from the two that arise from disintegrating the modulo operation. So, the systems of inequalities, which possess no solution because they contain the false one, are not considered here.

Substituting β_j in (4.13) with the last equation yields

$$2\pi + \gamma_l + \alpha_t \leq \gamma_s \leq 3\pi + \gamma_l + \alpha_t \tag{4.14}$$

Since γ_l and α_t are positive numbers and $\gamma_s \in \,]0; \pi[$ due to (4.8), this gives a contradiction.

Example 2 (with Fourier-Motzkin elimination) Take the example above. Since the critical inequalities for creating a contradiction are the one from (4.14) with $\gamma_l, \alpha_t \geq 0$ and $0 < \gamma_S < \pi$, we consider only these. At first we transform the inequalities so, that the one variable we want to eliminate, say γ_s, stands on the left-hand side and the remaining terms on the right-hand side. Thus we have

$$
\begin{aligned}
\gamma_s &\leq 3\pi + \gamma_l + \alpha_t \\
\gamma_s &< \pi \\
-\gamma_s &\leq -2\pi - \gamma_l - \alpha_t \\
-\gamma_s &< 0 \\
-\gamma_l &\leq 0 \\
-\alpha_t &\leq 0 .
\end{aligned}
$$

Then we eliminate γ_s by combining the first two lines with the third and fourth lines

$$
\begin{aligned}
2\pi + \gamma_l + \alpha_t &\leq \gamma_s \leq 3\pi + \gamma_l + \alpha_t \\
2\pi + \gamma_l + \alpha_t &\leq \gamma_s < \pi \\
0 &\leq \gamma_s \leq 3\pi + \gamma_l + \alpha_t \\
0 &\leq \gamma_s < \pi
\end{aligned}
$$

and removing γ_s from each line

$$
\begin{aligned}
2\pi + \gamma_l + \alpha_t &\leq 3\pi + \gamma_l + \alpha_t \\
2\pi + \gamma_l + \alpha_t &< \pi \\
0 &\leq 3\pi + \gamma_l + \alpha_t \\
0 &< \pi .
\end{aligned}
$$

In the end the remaining inequalities are altogether

$$
\begin{aligned}
\gamma_l &< -\pi - \alpha_t \\
-\gamma_l &\leq 3\pi + \alpha_t \\
-\gamma_l &\leq 0 \\
-\alpha_t &\leq 0 .
\end{aligned}
$$

Again we choose a variable, say γ_l, and eliminate it with the same method. We then have

$$
\begin{aligned}
\alpha_t &< -\pi \\
-\alpha_t &\leq 0 ,
\end{aligned}
$$

which is a contradiction.

4.4.3   The Algorithm for Composing Two $\mathcal{OPRA}_m^*$ Relations

The preceding section dealt with a specific combination of the values for t,s, and z with given values for i, j, x, k, l, and y. Then we set up a system of linear inequalities and it followed that their solvability determine whether the underlying geometric configuration is feasible or not. To get the complete composition, this procedure is then to be extended to all combinations of the values for t, s, and z. Fortunately, we do not need to iterate this procedure for all values for t, s, and z, because we only have to consider those values for t and s that come from the plain $\mathcal{OPRA}_m$ composition. The complete algorithm is presented in Alg. 1. In addition, there are further possibilities for optimization:

1. As we discussed in the Sec. 4.3, z takes multiple values if and only if s and t are both odd, where $s = t$ or $s = (m + t) \bmod 4m$. Otherwise we are able to derive a unique $\mathcal{OPRA}_m^*$ relation from the given $\mathcal{OPRA}_m$ relation. In the latter case we can spare the step for solving a system of inequalities.

2. There are cases where we can transform a constraint with modulo operation into just one constraint instead of two constraints combined with disjunction. Let us consider the middle term in (4.12). If we can foresee that the term may take on either positive or negative values, e.g. if i is an even number and $\tilde{t} - \tilde{i} \geq 0$, or t is an even number and $\tilde{t} - \tilde{i} \leq 0$, then we obtain from a constraint involving a modulo operation only one constraint instead of two.

4.5   Conceptual Neighborhood

We now convey the neighborhood structure of $\mathcal{OPRA}_m$ and $\mathcal{AC}$ relations to a neighborhood structure for $\mathcal{OPRA}_m^*$ relations. In comparison to the neighborhood structure for $\mathcal{OPRA}_m$ relations we need to adapt the neighborhood relations for those relations which have been refined into several $\mathcal{OPRA}_m^*$ relations based on $\mathcal{AC}$ relations and those which are directly neighbored to these relations. Therefore, we integrate the neighborhood graphs of $\mathcal{OPRA}_m^*$ (cn_1 - cn_5) and $\mathcal{AC}$. Although, some of the neighborhood transitions are rather unlikely to occur, e.g. because of complex motion patterns the objects would have to perform, they are theoretically possible. Nevertheless, at this point we give a complete definition of potential neighborhood relations. In Chapter 5 we take a closer look which of these transitions are more or less likely under different conditions.

For keeping the structure well arranged we assume that any relation ${}_m^x\angle_i^j$ with $x \in \{P, +, O, -\}$ and $i, j \in \mathcal{Z}_{4m}$ occurring in the definitions below has to be a valid relation in terms of the definition of $\mathcal{OPRA}_m^*$ relations, i.e. $x \in \mathtt{align}(\ {}_m\angle_i^j\ )$. As the original relation must not be a neighbor of itself at least one neighborhood transition in $\mathcal{OPRA}_m$ or $\mathcal{AC}$ must occur, i.e. ${}_m^x\angle_i^j \neq {}_m^y\angle_{i'}^{j'}$ and ${}_m^x\angle i \neq {}_m^y\angle i'$ respectively

---

Algorithm 1: A algorithm for deriving $\mathcal{OPRA}_m^*$ composition

function: $\mathrm{comp}(r_1, r_2)$ with $r_1 = {}_{m}^{x}\angle_i^j$ and $r_2 = {}_{m}^{y}\angle_k^l$

1:   $\mathcal{C} = \emptyset$
2:   $S = {}_{m}\angle_i^j \circ {}_{m}\angle_k^l$ /* the 'pure' $\mathcal{OPRA}_m$ composition */
3:   **while** $S \neq \phi$ **do**
4:     Choose ${}_{m}\angle_t^s \in S$
5:     $S = S \backslash \{ {}_{m}\angle_t^s \}$
6:     $M = \mathtt{align}({}_{m}\angle_t^s)$
7:     **if** $|M| = 1$ **then**
8:       $\mathcal{C} = \mathcal{C} \cup \{ {}_{m}^{z}\angle_t^s \}$ with $z \in M$
9:     **else**
10:      **while** $M \neq \phi$ **do**
11:        Choose $z \in M$
12:        $M = M \backslash \{z\}$
13:        Generate systems of inequalities according to 4.4.1
14:        Apply Fourier-Motzkin elimination on the systems of inequalities
15:        /* cf. Schrijver (1989), Kessler (1996), Bik & Wijshoff (1995) */
16:        **if** One of the systems has a solution **then**
17:          $\mathcal{C} = \mathcal{C} \cup \{ {}_{m}^{z}\angle_t^s \}$
18:        **end if**
19:      **end while**
20:     **end if**
21: **end while**
22: **return** $\mathcal{C}$ /* the composition result of r_1 and r_2 */

with i' and j' are values determined regarding cn_1 to cn_5 and $y \in cn(x)$. For the systematic construction of the neighborhood structure we take each of the sets derived by cn_1 to cn_5 and derive three refined functions. First we only consider changes in the $\mathcal{OPRA}_m$-part of the relation (cn'), second only changes in the $\mathcal{AC}$-part of the relation (cn''), and finally, changes in both parts of the compound relation (cn'''). cn_5'', i.e. only the $\mathcal{AC}$-part of the relation changes, does not exist as all orientations are fixed for 'same' relations and therefore, no changes are possible without changing the $\mathcal{OPRA}_m$-part of the relation as well. The compound neighborhood structure is then given as:

$$
\begin{aligned}
cn_1'({}_{m}^{x}\angle_{i}^{j}) &= \{ \; {}_{m}^{x}\angle_{i-1}^{j-1} \, , \; {}_{m}^{x}\angle_{i-1}^{j} \, , \; {}_{m}^{x}\angle_{i-1}^{j+1} \, , \; {}_{m}^{x}\angle_{i}^{j-1} \, , \\
&\qquad {}_{m}^{x}\angle_{i}^{j+1} \, , \; {}_{m}^{x}\angle_{i+1}^{j-1} \, , \; {}_{m}^{x}\angle_{i+1}^{j} \, , \; {}_{m}^{x}\angle_{i+1}^{j+1} \; \} \\
cn_1''({}_{m}^{x}\angle_{i}^{j}) &= \{ \; {}_{m}^{x\oplus 1}\angle_{i}^{j} \, , \; {}_{m}^{x\ominus 1}\angle_{i}^{j} \; \} \\
cn_1'''({}_{m}^{x}\angle_{i}^{j}) &= \{ \; {}_{m}^{x\oplus 1}\angle_{i-1}^{j-1} \, , \; {}_{m}^{x\oplus 1}\angle_{i-1}^{j} \, , \; {}_{m}^{x\oplus 1}\angle_{i-1}^{j+1} \, , \; {}_{m}^{x\oplus 1}\angle_{i}^{j-1} \, , \; {}_{m}^{x\oplus 1}\angle_{i}^{j+1} \, , \; {}_{m}^{x\oplus 1}\angle_{i+1}^{j-1} \, , \\
&\qquad {}_{m}^{x\oplus 1}\angle_{i+1}^{j} \, , \; {}_{m}^{x\oplus 1}\angle_{i+1}^{j+1} \, , \; {}_{m}^{x\ominus 1}\angle_{i-1}^{j-1} \, , \; {}_{m}^{x\ominus 1}\angle_{i-1}^{j} \, , \; {}_{m}^{x\ominus 1}\angle_{i-1}^{j+1} \, , \; {}_{m}^{x\ominus 1}\angle_{i}^{j-1} \, , \\
&\qquad {}_{m}^{x\ominus 1}\angle_{i}^{j+1} \, , \; {}_{m}^{x\ominus 1}\angle_{i+1}^{j-1} \, , \; {}_{m}^{x\ominus 1}\angle_{i+1}^{j} \, , \; {}_{m}^{x\ominus 1}\angle_{i+1}^{j+1} \; \}
\end{aligned}
$$

$$
\begin{aligned}
cn_2'({}_{m}^{x}\angle_{i}^{j}) &= \{ \; {}_{m}^{x}\angle(2m+i-j-2) \, , \; {}_{m}^{x}\angle(2m+i-j-1) \, , \\
&\qquad {}_{m}^{x}\angle(2m+i-j) \, , \; {}_{m}^{x}\angle(2m+i-j-1) \, , \\
&\qquad {}_{m}^{x}\angle(2m+i-j+2) \, | \, i \mod 2 = 1 \wedge j \mod 2 = 1 \} \\
cn_2''({}_{m}^{x}\angle_{i}^{j}) &= \{ \; {}_{m}^{x\oplus 1}\angle i \, , \; {}_{m}^{x\ominus 1}\angle i \, | \, i \mod 2 = 1 \wedge j \mod 2 = 1 \} \\
cn_2'''({}_{m}^{x}\angle_{i}^{j}) &= \{ \; {}_{m}^{x\oplus 1}\angle(2m+i-j-2) \, , \; {}_{m}^{x\oplus 1}\angle(2m+i-j-1) \, , \\
&\qquad {}_{m}^{x\oplus 1}\angle(2m+i-j) \, , \; {}_{m}^{x\oplus 1}\angle(2m+i-j-1) \, , \\
&\qquad {}_{m}^{x\oplus 1}\angle(2m+i-j+2) \, , \; {}_{m}^{x\oplus 1}\angle(2m+i-j-2) \, , \\
&\qquad {}_{m}^{x\ominus 1}\angle(2m+i-j-1) \, , \; {}_{m}^{x\ominus 1}\angle(2m+i-j) \, , \\
&\qquad {}_{m}^{x\ominus 1}\angle(2m+i-j-1) \, , \; {}_{m}^{x\ominus 1}\angle(2m+i-j+2) \, | \\
&\qquad i \mod 2 = 1 \wedge j \mod 2 = 1 \}
\end{aligned}
$$

$$
\begin{aligned}
cn_3'({}_{m}^{x}\angle_{i}^{j}) &= \{ \; {}_{m}^{x}\angle(2m+i-j-1) \, , \; {}_{m}^{x}\angle(2m+i-j) \, , \; {}_{m}^{x}\angle(2m+i-j+1) \, | \\
&\qquad i \mod 2 = 0 \vee j \mod 2 = 0 \} \\
cn_3''({}_{m}^{x}\angle_{i}^{j}) &= \{ \; {}_{m}^{x\oplus 1}\angle i \, , \; {}_{m}^{x\ominus 1}\angle i \, | \, i \mod 2 = 0 \vee j \mod 2 = 0 \} \\
cn_3'''({}_{m}^{x}\angle_{i}^{j}) &= \{ \; {}_{m}^{x\oplus 1}\angle(2m+i-j-1) \, , \; {}_{m}^{x\oplus 1}\angle(2m+i-j) \, , \; {}_{m}^{x\oplus 1}\angle(2m+i-j+1) \, , \\
&\qquad {}_{m}^{x\ominus 1}\angle(2m+i-j-1) \, , \; {}_{m}^{x\ominus 1}\angle(2m+i-j) \, , \; {}_{m}^{x\ominus 1}\angle(2m+i-j+1) \, | \\
&\qquad i \mod 2 = 0 \vee j \mod 2 = 0 \}
\end{aligned}
$$

$$\mathrm{cn}'_4(\,{}^x_m\!\angle s\,) \;=\; \{\; {}^x_m\!\angle(s+1)\,,\, {}^x_m\!\angle(s-1)\,\}$$
$$\mathrm{cn}''_4(\,{}^x_m\!\angle s\,) \;=\; \{\; {}^{x\oplus1}_m\!\angle s\,,\, {}^{x\ominus1}_m\!\angle s\,\}$$
$$\mathrm{cn}'''_4(\,{}^x_m\!\angle s\,) \;=\; \{\; {}^{x\oplus1}_m\!\angle(s+1)\,,\, {}^{x\oplus1}_m\!\angle(s-1)\,,\, {}^{x\ominus1}_m\!\angle(s+1)\,,\, {}^{x\ominus1}_m\!\angle(s-1)\,\}$$

$$\mathrm{cn}'_5(\,{}^x_m\!\angle s\,) \;=\; \{\; {}^x_m\!\angle^{2m+i-s-1}_i\,,\, {}^x_m\!\angle^{2m+i-s}_i\,,\, {}^x_m\!\angle^{2m+i-s+1}_i\,,$$
$$\qquad\qquad\qquad {}^x_m\!\angle^{j}_{2m+j-s-1}\,,\, {}^x_m\!\angle^{j}_{2m+j-s}\,,\, {}^x_m\!\angle^{j}_{2m+j-s+1}\,\}$$
$$\mathrm{cn}'''_5(\,{}^x_m\!\angle s\,) \;=\; \{\; {}^{x\oplus1}_m\!\angle^{2m+i-s-1}_i\,,\, {}^{x\oplus1}_m\!\angle^{2m+i-s}_i\,,\, {}^{x\oplus1}_m\!\angle^{2m+i-s+1}_i\,,$$
$$\qquad\qquad\qquad {}^{x\oplus1}_m\!\angle^{j}_{2m+j-s-1}\,,\, {}^{x\oplus1}_m\!\angle^{j}_{2m+j-s}\,,\, {}^{x\oplus1}_m\!\angle^{j}_{2m+j-s+1}$$
$$\qquad\qquad\qquad {}^{x\ominus1}_m\!\angle^{2m+i-s-1}_i\,,\, {}^{x\ominus1}_m\!\angle^{2m+i-s}_i\,,\, {}^{x\ominus1}_m\!\angle^{2m+i-s+1}_i\,,$$
$$\qquad\qquad\qquad {}^{x\ominus1}_m\!\angle^{j}_{2m+j-s-1}\,,\, {}^{x\ominus1}_m\!\angle^{j}_{2m+j-s}\,,\, {}^{x\ominus1}_m\!\angle^{j}_{2m+j-s+1}\,\}$$

Following this definition we gain a maximum number of twelve conceptual neighbors for non-'same' $\mathcal{OPRA}_m$ relations, i.e. ${}^x_m\!\angle^j_i$, if 'same' relations are not considered as neighbors. The minimum number results in six. The average number of conceptually neighboring relations is just about eight. If 'same' relations are allowed for each non-'same' relation three additional neighbors are possible. Each 'same' relation ${}^x_m\!\angle s$ has two neighboring 'same' relations (${}^x_m\!\angle s - 1$ and ${}^x_m\!\angle s + 1$) where orientation x is fixed for 'same' relations (cf. cn'_4 to cn'''_4). Additionally, each 'same' relation has at least $4m$ conceptually neighboring non-'same' relations (cf. cn'_5). For this case we have not further investigated how the number of neighborhood relations behaves with respect to a growing granularity m. This remains an interesting question for future investigations.

4.6   Iconic Representation of $\mathcal{OPRA}^*_m$ Relations

In this section we give an iconic representation of $\mathcal{OPRA}^*_m$ relations to give a better impression of $\mathcal{OPRA}^*_m$ relations and making the examples in the following chapters more vivid.

As a basis we take relation $\vec{X}\,{}^x_m\!\angle^j_i\,\vec{Y}$ with the two o-points $\vec{X}$ and $\vec{Y}$. Both o-points define a reference direction to relate the other o-point, but $\vec{X}$ defines the reference direction for the alignment additionally. So, $\vec{X}$ is always positioned in the center of the icon with its orientation facing upwards, depicted by a large circle, and will not change position. Object $\vec{Y}$ is depicted by a small circle and is positioned around the center according to the current relation (cf. Fig. 4.5(a)). For better discrimination which relation is illustrated we connect $\vec{X}$ and $\vec{Y}$ by a line.

In cases where the alignments of the relations may have multiple values with respect to the depicted $\mathcal{OPRA}_m$ relation, e.g. ${}_2\!\angle^3_3$ and ${}^{\{+,O,-\}}_2\!\angle^3_3$, we additionally introduce dashed lines to point out the alignment of $\vec{Y}$ regarding $\vec{X}$ (cf. Fig. 4.5(b) to Fig. 4.5(d)).

Illustrating 'same' relations results in superpositioning the small circle for $\vec{Y}$ and the large circle for $\vec{X}$ in the center of the representation. According to non-'same' relations the orientation of $\vec{X}$ is always facing upwards and the orientation of $\vec{Y}$ is drawn relative to this direction (cf. Fig. 4.5(e)).

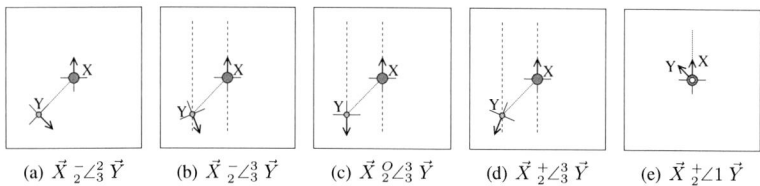

(a) $\vec{X}\,{}^{-}_{2}\angle{}^{2}_{3}\,\vec{Y}$ (b) $\vec{X}\,{}^{-}_{2}\angle{}^{3}_{3}\,\vec{Y}$ (c) $\vec{X}\,{}^{O}_{2}\angle{}^{3}_{3}\,\vec{Y}$ (d) $\vec{X}\,{}^{+}_{2}\angle{}^{3}_{3}\,\vec{Y}$ (e) $\vec{X}\,{}^{+}_{2}\angle 1\,\vec{Y}$

Figure 4.5: Exemplary icons for $\mathcal{OPRA}_2^\star$ relations.

The complete set of icons for $\mathcal{OPRA}_1^\star$ is given in Table 4.7 ('same' relations) and Table 4.9 (non-'same' relations), and for $\mathcal{OPRA}_2^\star$ relations in Table 4.8 ('same' relations), Table 4.10, and Table 4.11 (non-'same' relations).

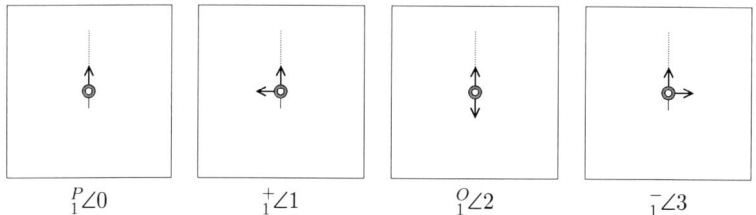

$${}^{P}_{1}\angle 0 \qquad {}^{+}_{1}\angle 1 \qquad {}^{O}_{1}\angle 2 \qquad {}^{-}_{1}\angle 3$$

Table 4.7: An iconic representation of $\mathcal{OPRA}_1^\star$ 'same' relations $\vec{X}\,{}^{x}_{1}\angle s\,\vec{Y}$. Both objects $\vec{X}$ and $\vec{Y}$ are in the same position. The reference direction given by $\vec{X}$ always points to the top.

4.7 Summary

In this section we demonstrated how two different calculi dealing with relative orientation, the Oriented Point Relation Algebra ($\mathcal{OPRA}_m$) and the Alignment Calculus ($\mathcal{AC}$), can be combined to a compound calculus ($\mathcal{OPRA}_m^\star$).

We presented the Alignment Calculus ($\mathcal{AC}$) to represent geometric alignment. We gave composition and converse of $\mathcal{AC}$. Based on the individual calculi we refined

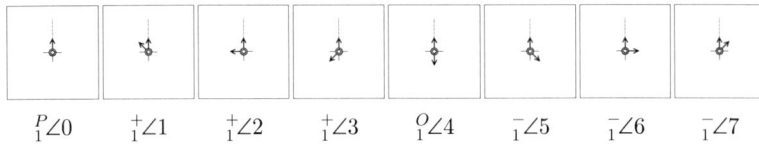

$$\begin{array}{cccccccc}
{}^P_1\angle 0 & {}^+_1\angle 1 & {}^+_1\angle 2 & {}^+_1\angle 3 & {}^O_1\angle 4 & {}^-_1\angle 5 & {}^-_1\angle 6 & {}^-_1\angle 7
\end{array}$$

Table 4.8: An iconic representation of $\mathcal{OPRA}_2^\star$ 'same' relations $\vec{X} \, {}^x_2\angle s \, \vec{Y}$. Both objects $\vec{X}$ and $\vec{Y}$ are in the same position. The reference direction given by $\vec{X}$ always points to the top.

the representation of $\mathcal{OPRA}$ by $\mathcal{AC}$ to $\mathcal{OPRA}_m^\star$. We illustrated that only $4m$ relations out of $(4m)^2 + 4m$ base relations of $\mathcal{OPRA}_m$ were affected by this refinement. With $\text{align}(r) = \mathcal{O}_r$ we presented an algorithm for deriving the set of potential alignments of the underlying $\mathcal{OPRA}_m$ relation r. Because naive composition (based on the two separate composition tables) is not optimal, we further investigated the geometric properties of $\mathcal{OPRA}_m^\star$ relations. We extracted geometric constraints that arise in the triangle configuration of the three o-points involved. We encoded these constraints in systems of linear inequalities. By solving these systems of inequalities with a standard method, e.g. the Fourier-Motzkin elimination, we were able to eliminate infeasible or inconsistent solutions for the composition of two $\mathcal{OPRA}_m^\star$ relations.

Furthermore, we derived the refined conceptual neighborhood structure for $\mathcal{OPRA}_m^\star$ and presented an iconic representation for $\mathcal{OPRA}_1^\star$ and $\mathcal{OPRA}_2^\star$.

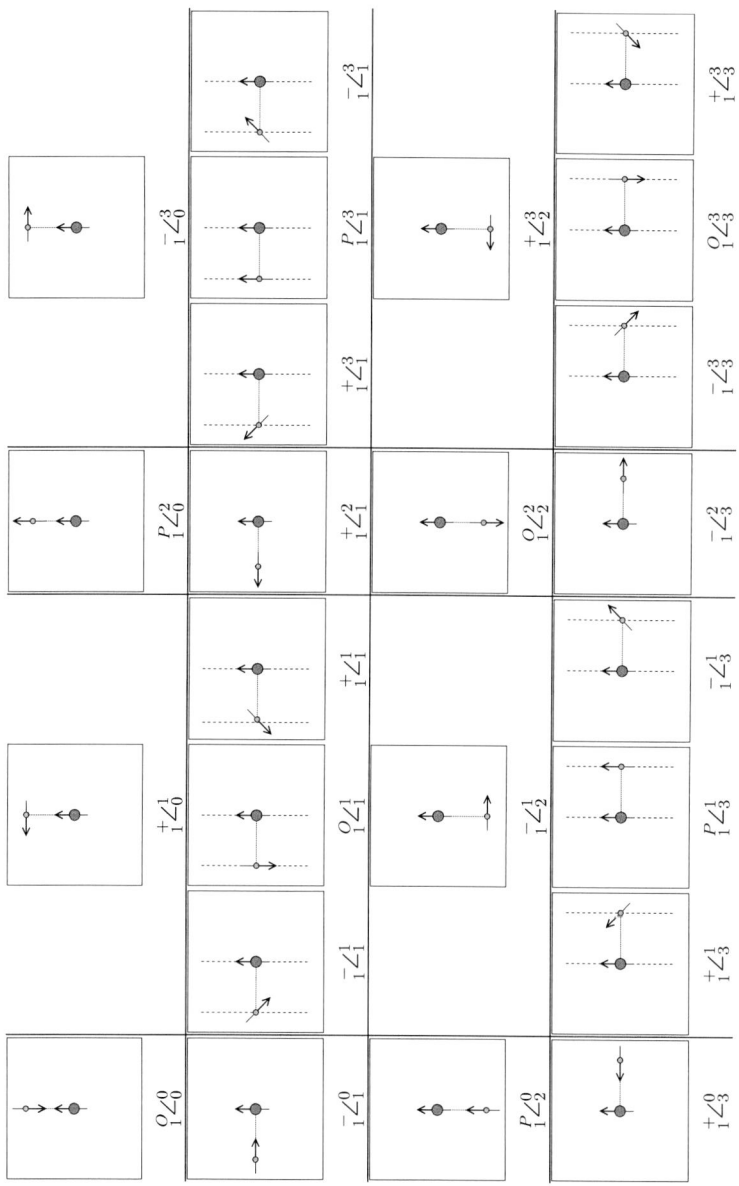

Table 4.9: An iconic representation of $\mathcal{OPRA}_1^\star$ relations $\vec{X} \; {}_1^x\angle_i^j \; \vec{Y}$. The large circle in the center of each box denotes object $\vec{X}$ and the smaller circle denotes object $\vec{Y}$.

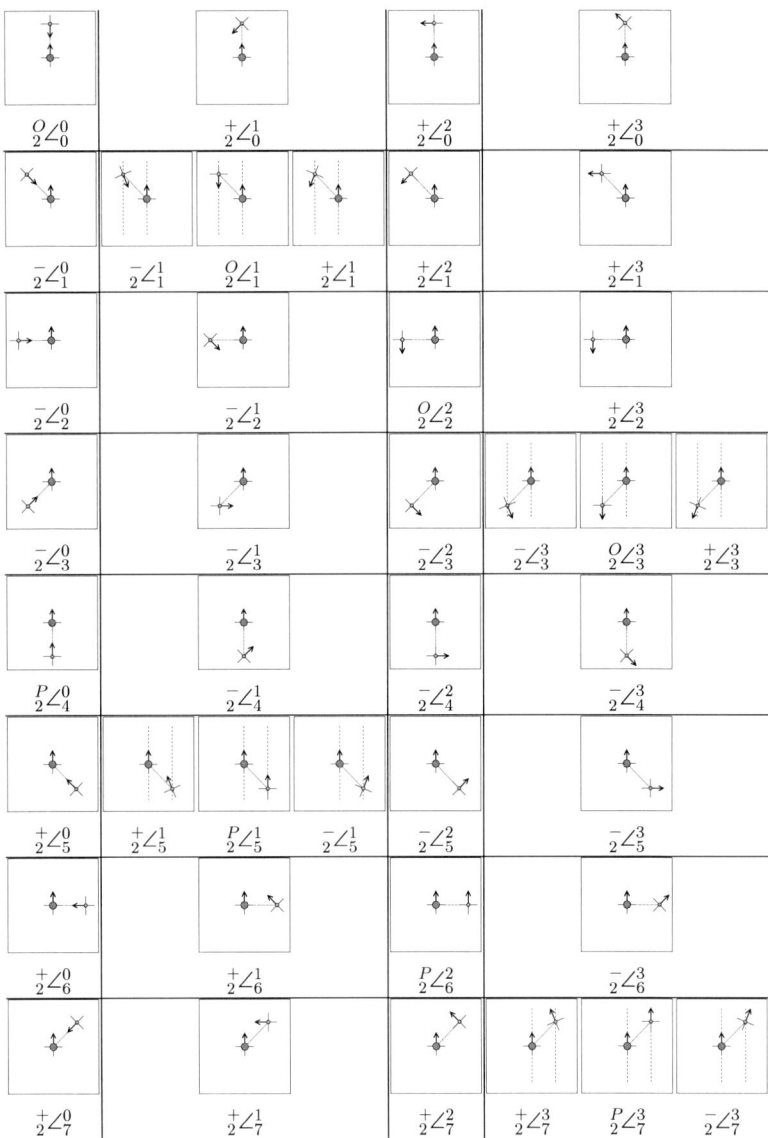

Table 4.10: Part I: An iconic representation of $\mathcal{OPRA}_2^*$ relations $\vec{X} \, {}_2^{x}\angle_i^j \, \vec{Y}$ ($i = 0..7$, $j = 0..3$). The large circle in the center of each box denotes object $\vec{X}$ and the smaller circle denotes object $\vec{Y}$.

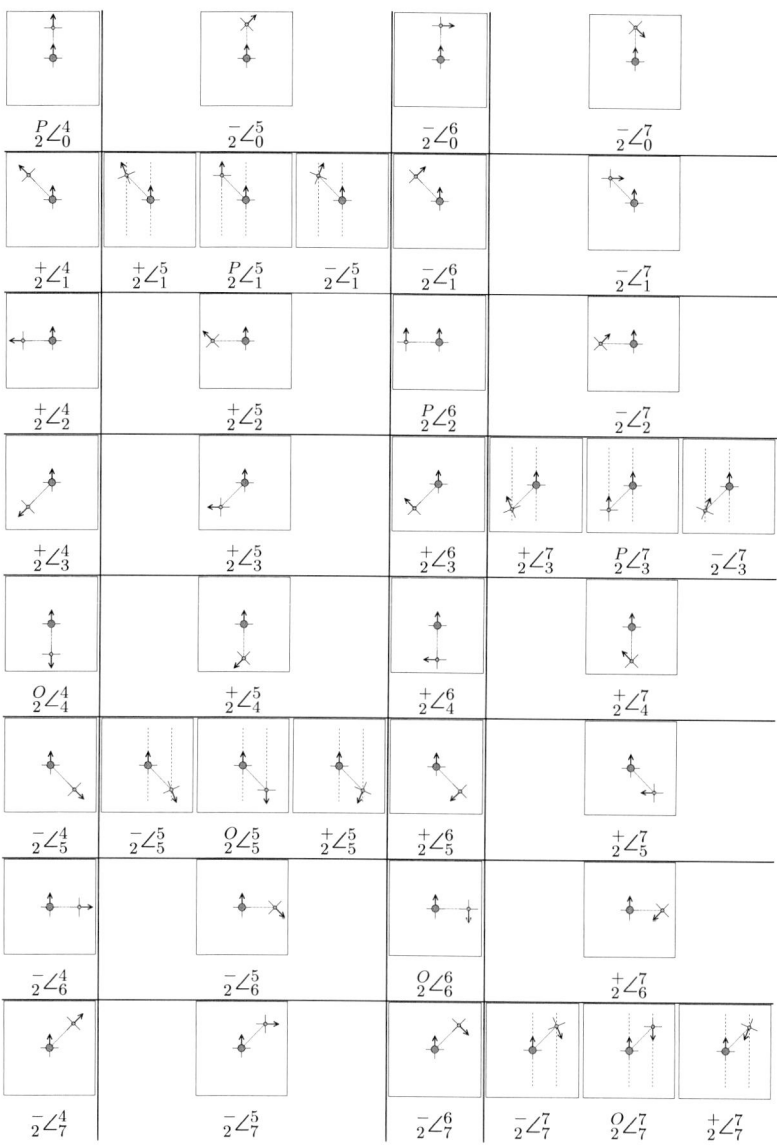

Table 4.11: Part II: An iconic representation of $\mathcal{OPRA}_2^\star$ relations $\vec{X}\ {}_2^x\angle_i^j\ \vec{Y}$ ($i = 0..7$, $j = 4..7$). The large circle in the center of each box denotes object $\vec{X}$ and the smaller circle denotes object $\vec{Y}$.

Chapter 5

Agent Control Based on Qualitative Calculi

We now investigate how qualitative orientation calculi can be applied to high-level agent control. As a basis, we use the Oriented Point Relation Algebra extended with alignment ($\mathcal{OPRA}_m^\star$). Because neighborhood-based reasoning is an abstract means for representing arbitrary dynamics of the objects represented, this concept will serve as a foundation for our approach to navigate agents by means of qualitative spatial calculi.

In the idea of conceptual neighborhood the explicit representation of actions causing changes is not contained. So, we take a closer look at the conceptual neighborhood structure and evaluate transitions regarding object properties which might influence potential changes. Based on these findings we define the *action-augmented conceptual neighborhood* for $\mathcal{OPRA}_m^\star$ relations.

The world model of an agent plays a central role in performing reasonable actions in its environment. If such a world model is strictly qualitative the problem arises whether the knowledge gathered by a single agent or shared by several agents contains conflicting knowledge. When interpreting the world model as a constraint network the complete world model turns inconsistent if two relations are in conflict. We apply conceptual neighborhoods as a means for defining distance measures so that a minimal consistent world model can be given based on an inconsistent set of relations.

5.1 Action-Augmented Conceptual Neighborhood

In the last chapter we developed the $\mathcal{OPRA}_m^\star$ calculus representing static orientation aspects. We also presented the neighborhood structure representing arbitrary dynamics of the objects represented. Conceptual neighborhood has been introduced as a means of describing possible changes of spatial relations which, for example, allows action planning at a high level of abstraction. Many of these changes are not applicable at all or are most unlikely to occur considering agents or robots in the real world. So, if two objects are in relation r then the conceptual neighborhood only defines that for any $r' \in \text{cn}(r)$ there exists some action causing a transition from r to r'. However, taking object properties into account prunes the number of neighbors which might occur in a specific situation compared to the original, i.e. the unconstrained view on the conceptual neighborhood graph.

Considering specific scenarios reveals that the concrete neighborhood structure depends very much on application-specific parameters, such as what kind of continuous transformations have to be considered for the objects involved (e.g. locomotion, deformation), whether objects can be transformed simultaneously, or whether two objects can occupy the same space or not.

In the neighboring relation the actions causing the transitions are not represented at all. In order to make our representation sufficient for agent control we need to know by what kind of action a specific change is caused. Deriving a minimal path from a start state to a goal state in the conceptual neighborhood graph ($\mathcal{CNG}$) is not sufficient, because it only represents that there exists some action that could cause this change.

We will analyze the conceptual neighborhood structures of $\mathcal{OPRA}_m^\star$ as they arise under different conditions in the context of robot navigation. We represent the results in a so-called *action-augmented conceptual neighborhood graph* ($\mathcal{ACNG}$) for $\mathcal{OPRA}_m^\star$, not only representing all potential neighborhood transitions between relations, but also considering the application-specific properties. Within an $\mathcal{ACNG}$ the path from one relation to another then also represents the basic commands needed for controlling a robot.

This approach is comparable to the causal layer in the Spatial Semantic Hierarchy (cf. Sec. 2.2.5). The causal layer links views, i.e. distinctive states in the world, by continuous behaviors of the control layer under the premise of successful execution of the behaviors. The views can be compared to relations and the behaviors to actions.

5.1.1 Continuous Transformation and Robot Navigation

Solving navigation tasks involves reasoning about paths as well as reasoning about configurations of objects or landmarks perceived along the way and, thus, requires the representation of orientation and distance information (Kuipers, 1977; Röfer, 1999). Conceptual neighborhoods and neighborhood-based reasoning are suitable models for how the world could evolve in terms of transitions between qualitative relations. We investigate continuous transformations regarding qualitative orientation calculi and discuss the concept in the context of robot motion capabilities and other relevant properties of the objects involved. Based on these, we will derive different neighborhood structures for $\mathcal{OPRA}_m^\star$.

The term *continuous transformation* is a central concept in the definition of conceptual neighborhood. Detailed investigations on different aspects of continuity have been presented in Bennett & Galton (2004), Davis (2001), Galton (2000b), Galton (2000a), and Muller (1998a). The definition of conceptual neighborhood originates from work on time intervals and, therefore, only the continuous transformations 'shortening', 'lengthening', and 'shifting' of intervals were considered. When transferring conceptual neighborhood to spatial relations, only vague discriminations were made between different types of transformations, for example, between transformations in size or transformations in position, although different types of neighborhoods were already mentioned in Freksa (1992b).

For navigation and action planning it is crucial that the $\mathcal{CNG}$s reflect the properties and capabilities of the agent so that neighborhood induces direct reachability in the physical world. Overall, three main aspects affect the neighborhood structure for a given spatial calculus in the context of robot navigation:

- the robot kinematics (motion capabilities)

- whether the objects may move simultaneously

- whether objects may coincide in position or not (superposition)

Restrictions in motion capabilities and number of objects moving will affect which relations are connected in the $\mathcal{ACNG}$. To give an example, let us assume that $\mathcal{OPRA}_2^\star$ relation $\vec{A}\,{}_2\angle_7^O\,\vec{B}$ holds between an agent A and some static object B. The orientations of the o-points correspond to the intrinsic fronts of both objects (cf. Fig. 5.1). If our robot is equipped with an omnidrive allowing it to drive sideways, it can reach configuration $\vec{A}\,{}_2\angle_0^P\,\vec{B}$ directly by moving to the right. In the following we denote the change from one relation to another relation by $\rightsquigarrow$. A robot provided with a differential drive has to traverse other configurations before reaching the desired configuration, for example:

$$\vec{A}\,{}_2\angle_7^O\,\vec{B} \rightsquigarrow \vec{A}\,{}_2\angle_7^+\,\vec{B} \rightsquigarrow \vec{A}\,{}_2\angle_7^0\,\vec{B} \rightsquigarrow \vec{A}\,{}_2\angle_7^+\,\vec{B} \rightsquigarrow \vec{A}\,{}_2\angle_0^+\,\vec{B} \rightsquigarrow \vec{A}\,{}_2\angle_0^O\,\vec{B}\,.$$

If the related objects cannot take the same position (no superposition), for instance, because they are both solid physical objects, then relations which represent such configurations are not feasible and thus are missing in the $\mathcal{ACNG}$. To simplify matters, we will talk about solid and non-solid objects in the remainder of the thesis, though the reasons for not allowing superposition can be different. One example for regarding potential neighborhood transitions to 'same' relations[1] for extended solid objects is the detection of potential collisions. Although objects cannot superpose, transitions to 'same' relations are allowed, but instead of interpreting it with physical superposition it is interpreted as collision between both objects; in other words, if there is a transition from a relation to a 'same' relation with a specific action, this action might lead to a collision.

In the following, we will systematically derive the neighborhood structure for the $\mathcal{OPRA}_m^\star$ calculus starting out with simple robot kinematics and going on to more

---

[1]'Same' relations denote relations between objects where point positions coincide, but the orientation might differ. The remaining relations are called non-'same' relations.

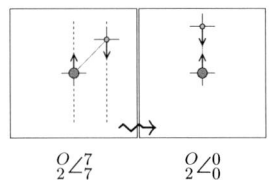

$$\substack{O \\ 2}\angle^{7}_{7} \qquad \substack{O \\ 2}\angle^{0}_{0}$$

(a) Agent $\vec{B}$ with omni-directional drive (able to move sidewards).

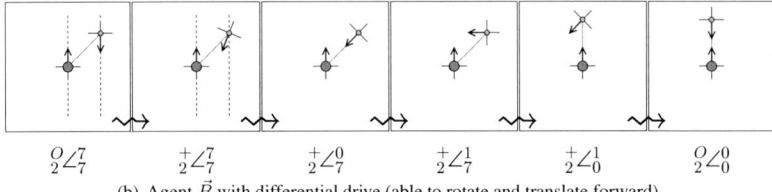

$$\substack{O \\ 2}\angle^{7}_{7} \quad \substack{+ \\ 2}\angle^{7}_{7} \quad \substack{+ \\ 2}\angle^{0}_{7} \quad \substack{+ \\ 2}\angle^{1}_{7} \quad \substack{+ \\ 2}\angle^{1}_{0} \quad \substack{O \\ 2}\angle^{0}_{0}$$

(b) Agent $\vec{B}$ with differential drive (able to rotate and translate forward).

Figure 5.1: Possible conceptual neighborhood structures regarding different motion capabilities of agent B with respect to a static object A. Direct transition is possible from $\substack{O \\ 2}\angle^{7}_{7}$ to $\substack{O \\ 2}\angle^{0}_{0}$ if agent B is able to move sidewards (a), whereas several neighborhood transitions are necessary otherwise (b).

complex motion behavior. For representing conceptual neighbors of a relation regarding specific actions we introduce a refined neighborhood function

$$\text{acn}\bigl(\substack{x \\ m}\angle^{j}_{i} , a_1, a_2 \bigr) \;=\; \{r| \quad r \text{ is possible if object } \vec{O}_1 \text{ performs action } a_1$$
$$\text{and object } \vec{O}_2 \text{ performs action } a_2 \}.$$

The parameter $\substack{x \\ m}\angle^{j}_{i}$ is a valid $\mathcal{OPRA}^{\star}_{m}$ relation representing the current relation between two objects $\vec{O}_1$ and $\vec{O}_2$ and $a_1 \in \mathcal{A}_1$ is the action performed by $\vec{O}_1$ and and $a_2 \in \mathcal{A}_2$ is the action performed by $\vec{O}_2$. $\mathcal{A}_1$ and $\mathcal{A}_2$ are the sets of possible actions the agents are able to perform. $\text{acn}(.)$ returns the set of neighboring relations regarding actions a_1 and a_2. This function is also defined for 'same' relations: $\text{acn}\bigl(\substack{x \\ m}\angle s , a_1, a_2 \bigr)$. Considering random actions ($\top$) which deliver arbitrary motion behavior for both objects $\text{acn}(r, \top, \top)$ is equal to $\text{cn}(r)$.

We distinguish the following primitive actions assuming that motion is performed relative to the intrinsic front of the object (if not specified otherwise); thus, a robot is represented by the orientation of the corresponding o-point. As no distance is represented in the calculus applied, we assume the actions to be performed until any change takes place regarding the representation chosen. In certain circumstances, for example, if an agent moves forward and the related object is in his straight back, no change will occur.

The most primitive behavior of objects is not to move at all (Stable). Next, we distinguish rotation on the spot to the right (Right) and to the left (Left). Further-more, objects are able to move straight to the front (Fwd) and straight back (Bwd). Compared to current robot systems these action primitives are the most basic motion capabilities inherent to any wheel-based robot system. In addition, there are an arbi-trary number of complex motion patterns which can be distinguished for other types of robots. In this work we will consider only two complex types of motion. First, straight motion to the side, i.e. motion perpendicular to the intrinsic front of the mov-ing object (SideR/SideL), and second, circular motion around a specific center point. Other complex motion patterns might be approximated by the primitives above. For example, if it is necessary to move forward and turn left afterwards to reach a specific configuration in terms of our action primitives, the agent may also reach this config-uration by moving forward and simultaneously turning left. Summarized we consider the following action primitives:

Stable	: no movement, object is stable
Right	: rotation to the right on the spot
Left	: rotation to the left on the spot
Fwd	: straight forward motion
Bwd	: straight backward motion
SideR/SideL	: sidewards motion, i.e. $90°$ regarding the intrinsic front to the right or left
RotR(.)/RotL(.)	: circular rotation around a specified center point to the right or left

We will investigate the following cases with respect to the action primitives above:

1. one object moving, rotation only,
2. two objects moving, rotation only,
3. one object moving, translation (forward/backward) only,
4. two objects moving, translation only, and
5. complex motion patterns.

5.1.2 Single Rotating Object

Imagine a robot R represented by the oriented point $\vec{R}$ standing in a room together with a stable object with a fixed intrinsic front, for example, a locker ($\vec{L}$). Rotating on the spot will lead to a change in relative position of the locker compared to the robot's own intrinsic front, but the robot's relative position to the locker does not change. Therefore, considering the $\mathcal{OPRA}_m^*$ relation representing the situation ($\vec{R} \ _m^x\angle_i^j \ \vec{L}$) only changes in orientation i or the alignment x need to be considered. If $i = j$ or $i = j + 2m$ does not hold turning left results in a decrease of i by one, and a right turn in an increase by one. If $i = j$ and i is even all traversed relations are predefined in alignment (cf. Fig. 5.2). If $i = j$ and i is odd a right turn leads from ${}_m^+\angle_i^i$ over ${}_m^O\angle_i^i$ to ${}_m^-\angle_i^i$. In case of $i = j + 2m$ and i is odd a right turn leads from ${}_m^-\angle_i^{i+2m}$ over ${}_m^P\angle_i^{i+2m}$ to ${}_m^+\angle_i^{i+2m}$. Reversing the roles of $\vec{L}$ and $\vec{R}$ entails the same changes in j and the inverse changes in alignment. (cf. Fig. 5.3). Thus, we can give the action-augmented neighborhood for one object rotating on the spot:

$$\text{acn}({}_m^x\angle_i^j,\text{Right},\text{Stable}) = \begin{cases} {}_m^{x\oplus 1}\angle_i^j & \text{if } i = j \wedge i \text{ odd} \wedge x \in \{+, O\} \\ {}_m^{x\oplus 1}\angle_i^j & \text{if } i = j + 2m \wedge i \text{ odd} \wedge x \in \{-, P\} \\ {}_m^y\angle_{i+1}^j & \text{else, with } y \in \text{align}({}_m\angle_i^j). \end{cases}$$

$$\text{acn}({}_m^x\angle_i^j,\text{Left},\text{Stable}) = \begin{cases} {}_m^{x\ominus 1}\angle_i^j & \text{if } i = j \wedge i \text{ odd} \wedge x \in \{-, O\} \\ {}_m^{x\ominus 1}\angle_i^j & \text{if } i = j + 2m \wedge i \text{ odd} \wedge x \in \{+, P\} \\ {}_m^y\angle_{i-1}^j & \text{else, with } y \in \text{align}({}_m\angle_i^j). \end{cases}$$

$$\text{acn}({}_m^x\angle_i^j,\text{Stable},\text{Right}) = \begin{cases} {}_m^{x\ominus 1}\angle_i^j & \text{if } i = j \wedge i \text{ odd} \wedge x \in \{-, O\} \\ {}_m^{x\ominus 1}\angle_i^j & \text{if } i = j + 2m \wedge i \text{ odd} \wedge x \in \{+, P\} \\ {}_m^y\angle_i^{j+1} & \text{else, with } y \in \text{align}({}_m\angle_i^j). \end{cases}$$

$$\text{acn}({}_m^x\angle_i^j,\text{Stable},\text{Left}) = \begin{cases} {}_m^{x\oplus 1}\angle_i^j & \text{if } i = j \wedge i \text{ odd} \wedge x \in \{+, O\} \\ {}_m^{x\oplus 1}\angle_i^j & \text{if } i = j + 2m \wedge i \text{ odd} \wedge x \in \{-, P\} \\ {}_m^y\angle_i^{j-1} & \text{else, with } y \in \text{align}({}_m\angle_i^j). \end{cases}$$

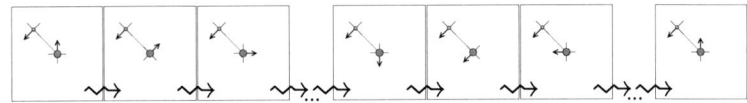

Figure 5.2: Exemplary part of the neighborhood structure if the first object is rotating to the right, i.e. the one in the center, and the other object is not moving. Note, in contrast to the regular $\mathcal{OPRA}_m^*$ icons we rotated the centered object.

If we allow both objects to occupy the same location, we also get a general representation for the neighborhood relation between 'same' relations:

$$\text{acn}({}_m^x\angle s,\text{Right},\text{Stable}) \ = \ {}_m^y\angle s + 1 \quad \text{with } y \in \text{align}({}_m\angle s)$$
$$\text{acn}({}_m^x\angle s,\text{Left},\text{Stable}) \ = \ {}_m^y\angle s - 1 \quad \text{with } y \in \text{align}({}_m\angle s)$$
$$\text{acn}({}_m^x\angle s,\text{Stable},\text{Right}) \ = \ {}_m^y\angle s - 1 \quad \text{with } y \in \text{align}({}_m\angle s)$$
$$\text{acn}({}_m^x\angle s,\text{Stable},\text{Left}) \ = \ {}_m^y\angle s + 1 \quad \text{with } y \in \text{align}({}_m\angle s).$$

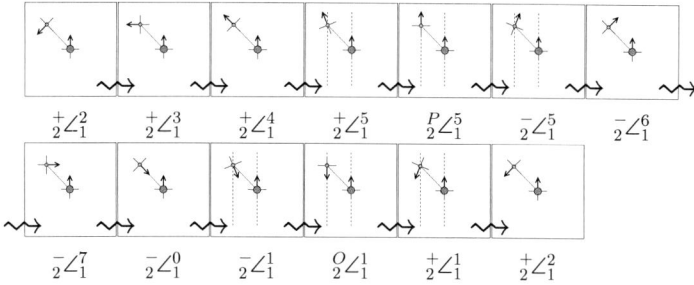

Figure 5.3: Exemplary part of the neighborhood structure if the first object is not moving and the other object is rotating to the right starting from $_2^+\angle_1^2$.

5.1.3 Both Objects Rotating Simultaneously

If both objects are allowed to rotate simultaneously, additional neighborhood transitions are possible. Although our considerations are based on discrete time steps, we assume that any change in the relation between two agents is perceived, because we are interested in the effect if both actions happen simultaneously. For determination of the additional neighborhood relations we need to consider the speed of rotation, although not represented in the calculus. If both objects rotate simultaneously on the spot, we need to consider three cases regarding $_m^x\angle_i^j$:

1. $\vec{A}$ rotates faster than $\vec{B}$,
2. $\vec{A}$ and $\vec{B}$ rotate with the same speed, and
3. $\vec{A}$ rotates slower than $\vec{B}$.

For example, let us assume $\vec{A}\ _2^O\angle_0^0\ \vec{B}$ with both objects rotating to the right. We illustrate potential results in Figure 5.4. As both objects rotate to the right, both zero values increase in all cases. In the first case, we end in $_2^-\angle_1^1$, because the traversed angle by $\vec{A}$ is greater than the angle traversed by $\vec{B}$. In the second case, the angles rotated by $\vec{A}$ and $\vec{B}$ are equal and so, the alignment stays unchanged ($_2^O\angle_1^1$). In the third case, the angle is lower and so, we end in $_2^-\angle_1^1$. We can subsume this result by $\text{acn}(\ _2^x\angle_i^1 ,\text{Right},\text{Right}) = \{\ _2^y\angle_{i+1}^{i+1}\ |y \in \text{align}(\ _m\angle_i^i)\}$. We can generalize this result to any $_m^x\angle_i^i$ with i denoting a linear region:

$$\text{acn}(\ _m^x\angle_i^i ,\text{Right},\text{Right}) = \{\ _m^y\angle_{i+1}^{i+1}\ |y \in \text{align}(\ _m\angle_i^i)\}\ .$$

For $_m^x\angle_i^i$ with i denoting planar regions we obtain additional neighborhood relations. For these cases three different alignments are possible: negative, opposite-parallel, and positive. Let us consider $_2^x\angle_1^1$ as example for the general case $_m^x\angle_i^i$. In the following y always denotes a valid alignment, i.e. $y \in \text{align}(\ _m\angle_i^j)$. If $x = O$

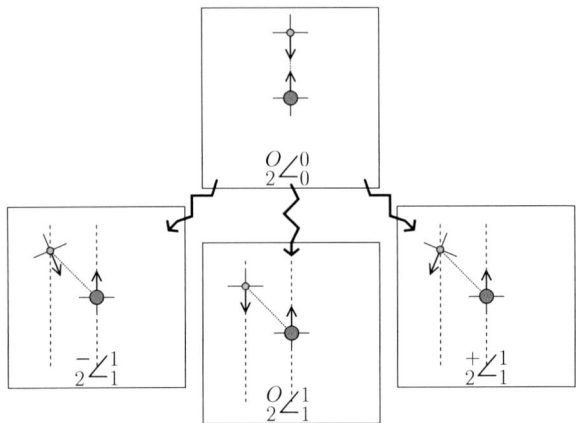

Figure 5.4: The action neighborhood for $_2\angle^0_0$ if both objects rotate to the right on the spot. If $\vec{A}$ rotates faster than $\vec{B}$, the result is $_2^-\angle^1_1$, if both agents rotate with the same speed $_2^O\angle^1_1$, and if $\vec{A}$ rotates slower than $\vec{B}$, the result is $_2^+\angle^1_1$.

we result in $_2^-\angle^1_2$, if rotation velocity of $\vec{A}$ is greater than rotation velocity of $\vec{B}$. If rotation velocities of $\vec{A}$ and $\vec{B}$ are equal, we end in $_m^O\angle^2_2$. If rotation velocity of $\vec{A}$ is lower than rotation velocity of $\vec{B}$, we get $_2^+\angle^1_2$. We illustrate this example in Figure 5.5. The results for $_2^-\angle^1_1$ are: $_2^-\angle^1_2$, $_2^O\angle^2_2$, and $_2^O\angle^1_1$ (cf. Figure 5.6), and the results for $_2^+\angle^1_1$ are: $_2^O\angle^1_1$, $_2^O\angle^2_2$, and $_2^+\angle^2_2$ (cf. Figure 5.7).

The action-augmented neighborhood relation is analogous for all $_m^x\angle^i_i$ with i denoting planar regions, therefore the results can be generalized regarding m:

$$
\begin{aligned}
\mathrm{acn}(\,_m^-\angle^i_i\,,\texttt{Right},\texttt{Right}) &= \{\,_m^{x\ominus1}\angle^i_i \mid x = -\} \\
&\cup \{\,_m^y\angle^{i+1}_{i+1} \mid y \text{ is a valid alignment}\} \\
&\cup \{\,_m^y\angle^i_{i+1} \mid y \text{ is a valid alignment}\} \\
\mathrm{acn}(\,_m^O\angle^i_i\,,\texttt{Right},\texttt{Right}) &= \{\,_m^y\angle^i_{i+1} \mid y \text{ is a valid alignment}\} \\
&\cup \{\,_m^y\angle^{i+1}_{i+1} \mid y \text{ is a valid alignment}\} \\
&\cup \{\,_m^y\angle^{i+1}_i \mid y \text{ is a valid alignment}\} \\
\mathrm{acn}(\,_m^+\angle^i_i\,,\texttt{Right},\texttt{Right}) &= \{\,_m^{x\oplus1}\angle^i_i \mid x = +\} \\
&\cup \{\,_m^y\angle^{i+1}_{i+1} \mid y \text{ is a valid alignment}\} \\
&\cup \{\,_m^y\angle^{i+1}_i \mid y \text{ is a valid alignment}\} \,.
\end{aligned}
$$

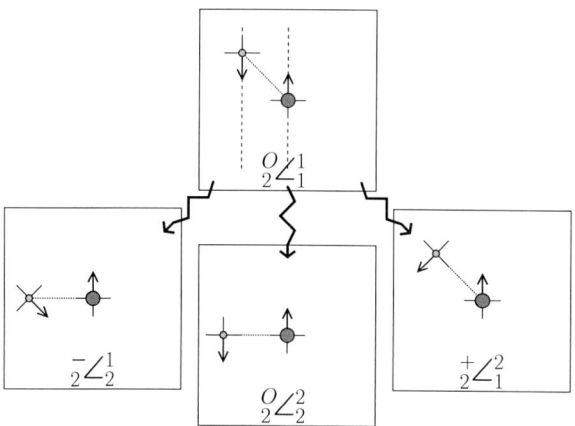

Figure 5.5: The action neighborhood for $\frac{O}{2}\angle_1^1$ if both objects rotate to the right on the spot. If $\vec{A}$ rotates faster than $\vec{B}$, the result is $\frac{-}{2}\angle_2^1$, if both agents rotate with the same speed $\frac{O}{2}\angle_2^2$, and if $\vec{A}$ rotates slower than $\vec{B}$, the result is $\frac{+}{2}\angle_1^2$.

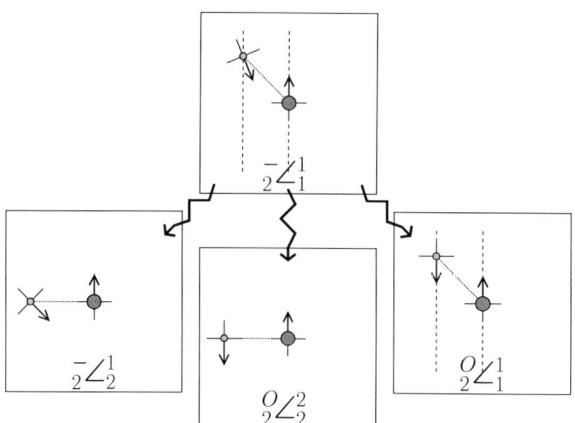

Figure 5.6: The action neighborhood for $\frac{-}{2}\angle_1^1$ if both objects rotate to the right on the spot. If $\vec{A}$ rotates faster than $\vec{B}$, the result is $\frac{-}{2}\angle_2^1$, if both agents rotate with the same speed $\frac{O}{2}\angle_2^2$, and if $\vec{A}$ rotates slower than $\vec{B}$, the result is $\frac{O}{2}\angle_1^1$.

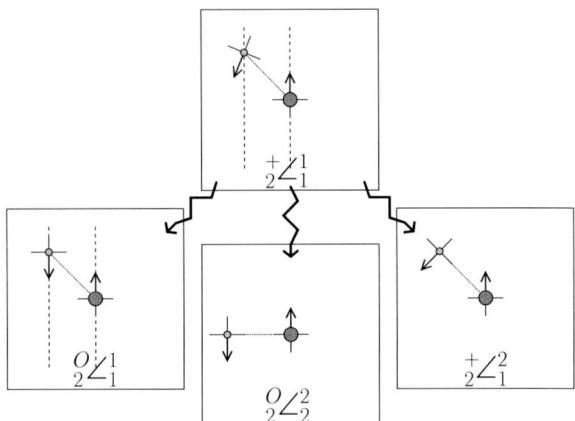

Figure 5.7: The action neighborhood for $\overset{+}{2}\angle^1_1$ if both objects rotate to the right on the spot. If $\vec{A}$ rotates faster than $\vec{B}$, the result is $\overset{O}{2}\angle^1_1$, if both agents rotate with the same speed $\overset{O}{2}\angle^2_2$, and if $\vec{A}$ rotates slower than $\vec{B}$, the result is $\overset{+}{2}\angle^2_1$.

These considerations are valid for all relations with $i = j$ denoting planar regions. For the symmetric cases with $i = 2m + j$ also denoting planar regions, the neighborhood structure can be determined analogously. For all other cases, i.e. $i \neq j$ or $i \neq 2m + j$, the neighborhood relation is easy to derive. All problematic cases, i.e. where alignment may change, have already been considered above. If i and j denote linear regions, i and j must increase, i.e. $\overset{y}{m}\angle^{j+1}_{i+1}$ with y is a valid alignment. If, for example, i denotes a linear region and or j a planar region, i must change, and j may change, i.e. $\overset{y}{m}\angle^{j}_{i+1}$ or $\overset{y}{m}\angle^{j+1}_{i+1}$. The case with i and j interchanged behaves analogously. If i and j both denote a planar region, either i changes, j changes, or both change ($\overset{y}{m}\angle^{j}_{i+1}$, $\overset{y}{m}\angle^{j+1}_{i}$, or $\overset{y}{m}\angle^{j+1}_{i+1}$).

For the other rotation options, i.e. both objects rotate left or $\vec{A}$ and $\vec{B}$ rotate in opposite directions, the action-augmented neighborhood can be derived in the same way.

'Same' relations are also dependent on the difference between the rotation velocities if both objects rotate in the same direction. Starting from $\overset{x}{m}\angle s$, assuming $\vec{A}$ rotates faster to the right than $\vec{B}$ results in $\overset{y}{m}\angle s + 1$, the same result as if only $\vec{A}$ rotates. If $\vec{A}$ rotates slower we yield $\overset{y}{m}\angle s - 1$. For left rotation we obtain the inverse changes. If both rotate with the same speed to the same side no change at all occurs. If the objects rotate to different directions it is only decisive to which side $\vec{A}$ rotates. If $\vec{A}$ rotates right, $\overset{y}{m}\angle s + 1$ follows and if $\vec{A}$ rotates left, $\overset{y}{m}\angle s - 1$ follows. We summarize the action-augmented neighborhood structure for 'same' relations regarding rotation operations below:

$$\begin{aligned}
\text{acn}(\,{}^x_m\angle s\,,\text{Right},\text{Right}) &= \\
\text{acn}(\,{}^x_m\angle s\,,\text{Left},\text{Left}) &= \{\,{}^y_m\angle s - 1\,,\,{}^y_m\angle s + 1\,|\,y \in \text{align}(\,m\angle^j_i\,)\} \\
\text{acn}(\,{}^x_m\angle s\,,\text{Right},\text{Left}) &= \text{acn}(\,{}^x_m\angle s\,,\text{Right},\text{Stable}) \\
\text{acn}(\,{}^x_m\angle s\,,\text{Left},\text{Right}) &= \text{acn}(\,{}^x_m\angle s\,,\text{Left},\text{Stable})
\end{aligned}$$

5.1.4 Translating Single Solid Objects

We now take a look at possible neighborhood transitions if only straight translation is possible and superposition of objects is not possible. Just allowing translation means that our exemplary agent can only move forward in the direction it is facing or backwards in the opposite direction. Here, we consider only solid objects, i.e. point positions must not coincide, and thus, 'same' relations are neglected here. We will illustrate these in the following section. Additionally, in our considerations only one of the two objects related is allowed to move. We consider both objects moving in Section 5.1.6.

Translations are much more complex to analyze for $\mathcal{OPRA}^\star_m$ than rotations. Therefore, we will restrict ourselves to $m = 2$ in our examples. Regarding finer granularities, the action-augmented neighborhood relations must be derived based on similar considerations.

We first look at the consequences of moving either $\vec{A}$ or $\vec{B}$ individually. Let us assume $\vec{B}$ is left behind of $\vec{A}$ and $\vec{B}$ is moving forward, i.e. $\vec{B}$ wants to move past $\vec{A}$. According to the $\mathcal{OPRA}^\star_2$ representation we have three different relations as start configuration: $\vec{A}\,{}^P_2\angle^7_3\,\vec{B}$, $\vec{A}\,{}^-_2\angle^7_3\,\vec{B}$, and $\vec{A}\,{}^+_2\angle^7_3\,\vec{B}$.

First, we assume relation $\vec{A}\,{}^P_2\angle^7_3\,\vec{B}$ as given. In Fig. 5.8 we show the corresponding neighborhood transitions. As no turning operation is executed the objects stay in parallel alignment and $\vec{B}$ moves in this specific case from the left back of $\vec{A}$ ($\vec{A}\,{}^P_2\angle^7_3\,\vec{B}$), passing alongside left of $\vec{A}$ ($\vec{A}\,{}^P_2\angle^6_2\,\vec{B}$), to the left front $\vec{A}\,{}^P_2\angle^5_1\,\vec{B}$. Next we assume $\vec{A}\,{}^-_2\angle^7_3\,\vec{B}$ as start configuration (cf. Fig. 5.9). Again, as no turning operation is performed the alignment is fixed to $-$. Because $\vec{B}$ is negatively aligned towards $\vec{A}$, $\vec{B}$ moves from the left towards $\vec{A}$ ($\,{}^-_2\angle^7_3\, \leadsto\, {}^-_2\angle^7_2\, \leadsto\, {}^-_2\angle^7_1\,$) and will pass the front of $\vec{A}$ from front left to front right ($\,{}^-_2\angle^6_1\, \leadsto\, {}^-_2\angle^5_1\, \leadsto\, {}^-_2\angle^5_0\, \leadsto\, {}^-_2\angle^5_7\,$). Finally, we take a look at $\vec{A}\,{}^+_2\angle^7_3\,\vec{B}$ (cf. Fig. 5.10). Due to the positive alignment of the objects, $\vec{B}$ moves away from $\vec{A}$. So, $\vec{B}$ passes $\vec{A}$ at its right side and afterwards $\vec{A}$ is passed on its left side by $\vec{B}$. But $\vec{B}$ will not cross the front of $\vec{A}$.

It is important to note, that in the case of $\vec{A}$ and $\vec{B}$ being negatively aligned, $\vec{B}$ passes the perpendicular of $\vec{A}$, and afterwards $\vec{A}$ is passed by the perpendicular of $\vec{B}$ (cf. $\,{}^-_2\angle^7_2\,$ and $\,{}^-_2\angle^6_1\,$ in Fig. 5.9). If both are aligned positively it is the other way round (cf. $\,{}^+_2\angle^6_3\,$ and $\,{}^+_2\angle^5_2\,$ in Fig. 5.10). If the objects are aligned in parallel it happens simultaneously (cf. $\,{}^P_2\angle^6_2\,$ in Fig. 5.8).

It is obvious from the examples that forward motion of $\vec{B}$ induces backward motion of $\vec{A}$ and vice versa (e.g. Fig. 5.8). Cases with $\vec{A}$ and $\vec{B}$ interchanged, as well as cases considering the objects to be aligned opposite-parallel are symmetric. If objects are aligned opposite-parallel they will pass each other on the same side, e.g. $\vec{A}$ right of $\vec{B}$ and $\vec{B}$ right of $\vec{A}$ instead of left/right as in the example above. Therefore, we do not go into detail about such examples here.

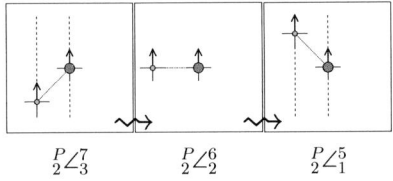

$$\textstyle\frac{P}{2}\angle_3^7 \qquad \frac{P}{2}\angle_2^6 \qquad \frac{P}{2}\angle_1^5$$

Figure 5.8: B moving forward (A moving backward) starting from $\frac{P}{2}\angle_3^7$.

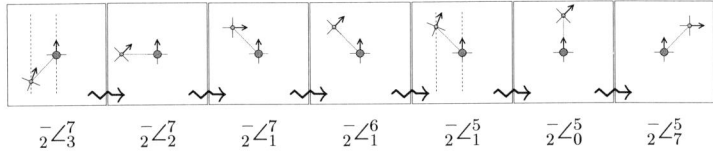

$$\textstyle\frac{-}{2}\angle_3^7 \quad \frac{-}{2}\angle_2^7 \quad \frac{-}{2}\angle_1^7 \quad \frac{-}{2}\angle_1^6 \quad \frac{-}{2}\angle_1^5 \quad \frac{-}{2}\angle_0^5 \quad \frac{-}{2}\angle_7^5$$

Figure 5.9: B moving forward starting from $\frac{-}{2}\angle_3^7$.

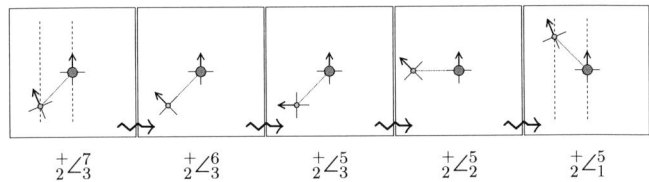

$$\textstyle\frac{+}{2}\angle_3^7 \qquad \frac{+}{2}\angle_3^6 \qquad \frac{+}{2}\angle_3^5 \qquad \frac{+}{2}\angle_2^5 \qquad \frac{+}{2}\angle_1^5$$

Figure 5.10: B moving forward (A moving backward) starting from $\frac{+}{2}\angle_3^7$.

Compared to $\mathcal{OPRA}_m$ the effects of actions in the action-augmented neighborhood of the $\mathcal{OPRA}_m^{\star}$ representation are more certain regarding forward/backward motion of a single object. Assuming the $\mathcal{OPRA}_m$ relation $\vec{A}\ _2\angle_3^7\ \vec{B}$ as starting configuration, which is a union of the three $\mathcal{OPRA}_m^{\star}$ relations from above, we cannot distinguish which object passes the others perpendicular first, and thus, whether $\vec{B}$ moves away from $\vec{A}$ or passes the front of $\vec{A}$. In planning, uncertain action effects evoke problems, because all potential outcomes need to be considered. Therefore, $\mathcal{OPRA}_m^\star$ is better suited for planning purposes than $\mathcal{OPRA}_m$.

Nevertheless, for some $\mathcal{OPRA}_m^\star$ relations the neighborhood transition is not unique considering a single forward action. As example we take a closer look at relation $_{\overline{2}}\angle_1^7$ with agent $\vec{B}$ moving forward. The relation describes a configuration where $\vec{B}$ is left front of $\vec{A}$ heading such that $\vec{B}$ passes the front of $\vec{A}$ (cf. Fig. 5.11). Three types of instantiations can be differentiated regarding the action effect of forward translation. First, the objects meet with an angle of $90°$, i.e. when $\vec{B}$ is in front of $\vec{A}$, $\vec{A}$ is perpendicular to $\vec{B}$ at the same time (cf. Fig. 5.11(a)). This results in the neighborhood sequence: $_{\overline{2}}\angle_1^7 \rightsquigarrow {}_{\overline{2}}\angle_0^6 \rightsquigarrow {}_{\overline{2}}\angle_7^5$. Second, $\vec{B}$ is turned a little more towards $\vec{A}$ such that the objects meet with an angle larger than $90°$ (cf. Fig. 5.11(b)). So, $\vec{B}$ first passes the front of $\vec{A}$ and then passes $\vec{A}$ with its right side: $_{\overline{2}}\angle_1^7 \rightsquigarrow {}_{\overline{2}}\angle_0^7 \rightsquigarrow {}_{\overline{2}}\angle_7^7 \rightsquigarrow {}_{\overline{2}}\angle_7^6 \rightsquigarrow {}_{\overline{2}}\angle_7^5$. And third, $\vec{B}$ is turned a little more away regarding $\vec{A}$ such that the objects meet with an angle less than $90°$ (cf. Fig. 5.11(c)). So, $\vec{B}$ first passes $\vec{A}$ with its right side and than the front of $\vec{A}$: $_{\overline{2}}\angle_1^7 \rightsquigarrow {}_{\overline{2}}\angle_1^6 \rightsquigarrow {}_{\overline{2}}\angle_1^5 \rightsquigarrow {}_{\overline{2}}\angle_0^5 \rightsquigarrow {}_{\overline{2}}\angle_7^5$. The resulting neighborhood structure is summarized in Figure 5.12.

Such uncertain effects of single actions – in our case different relations might be the potential result – are given for all relations $_m\angle_i^j$ with i and j being odd and $|i - j| \notin \{0, 2m\}$, because i and j represent regions and the relative angle of both objects might sum up to $\frac{2\pi}{m}$ (cf. Sec. 4.3). The exception $|i - j| \in \{0, 2m\}$ exists in $\mathcal{OPRA}_m^\star$, because the alignment extension refines these regions such that the angle between the entities is $\frac{\pi}{m}$ at maximum and the action effect of translations is certain.

All relations in $\mathcal{OPRA}_2^\star$ $_2\angle_i^j$ with uncertain effects regarding a single translation action end up in the same relation $_2\angle_{i+2}^{j+2}$, $_2\angle_{i-2}^{j-2}$ respectively, after at most three steps. So, the transition system can be called *confluent*. *Confluence* is a term in theoretical computer science describing a specific property of term rewriting systems. Assuming a transition system with a transition $\rightarrow$, it is called confluent if, and only if for all nodes n, n', n'' with $n \rightarrow n'$ and $n \rightarrow n''$ there exists a node n^x with $n' \rightarrow n^x$ and $n'' \rightarrow n^x$. This property given, in planning a confluent block ($_2\angle_i^j$ to $_2\angle_{i+2}^{j+2}$) can be substituted by a single transition augmented with the corresponding action, resulting in a transition system with only definite action effects regarding motion of single objects. Unfortunately, the confluence property does not hold for $m > 2$ if only parallel alignment is given. Further distinctions according to the angular resolution are necessary to preserve this property for finer granularities. In Section 5.1.8 we show how uncertain action effects can be disambiguated by temporal differentiation during action execution.

5.1.5 Translating Single Non-Solid Objects

We now take a look at non-solid objects. Allowing objects to coincide in point position means that transitions between same and non-'same' relations are possible. With only

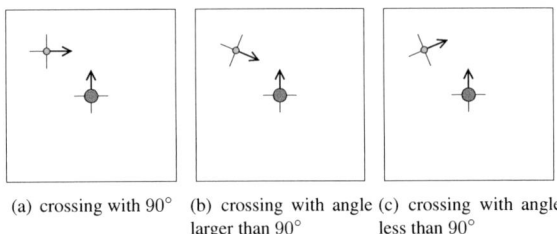

(a) crossing with 90°   (b) crossing with angle   (c) crossing with angle
                        larger than 90°   less than 90°

Figure 5.11: Three different instantiations subsumed by relation $_2\angle_1^7$

object B moving, the objects can only take the same positions for the case $\vec{A}\ {}_m^x\angle_i^0\ \vec{B}$ if B moves forward, depicted for $m = 2$ in Fig. 5.13, and for the case $\vec{A}\ {}_m^x\angle_i^4\ \vec{B}$ if B moves backward. If object A is allowed to move these cases are $\vec{A}\ {}_m^x\angle_0^j\ \vec{B}$ and $\vec{A}\ {}_m^x\angle_{2m}^j\ \vec{B}$ respectively.

In Fig. 5.14 we illustrate a configuration with two objects A and B in relation $_2\angle_3^0$. If B moves forward the objects overlap in $_2\angle7$ and will depart to $_2\angle_7^4$. It is simple to derive the general case for arbitrary m. As mentioned before, objects can only take the same positions assuming B moves forward if a relation of kind $\vec{A}\ {}_m^x\angle_i^0\ \vec{B}$ holds. When both objects superpose the heading of B points to the opposite direction it has been in before with respect to A. The direction B has been in is denoted by i and the opposite is $2m + i$. If B moves on it will have A in its back $(2m)$ and drives exactly in that region of A it has pointed to ($s = 2m + i$)

$$
\begin{aligned}
\mathrm{acn}(\ {}_m^x\angle_i^0\ ,\mathrm{Stable},\mathrm{Fwd}) &= \{\ {}_m^x\angle(2m + i)\ \} \\
\mathrm{acn}(\ {}_m^x\angle s\ ,\mathrm{Stable},\mathrm{Fwd}) &= \{\ {}_m^x\angle_s^{2m}\ \} \\
\mathrm{acn}(\ {}_m^x\angle_0^j\ ,\mathrm{Fwd},\mathrm{Stable}) &= \{\ {}_m^x\angle(2m + j)\ \} \\
\mathrm{acn}(\ {}_m^x\angle s\ ,\mathrm{Fwd},\mathrm{Stable}) &= \{\ {}_m^x\angle_{2m}^s\ \}
\end{aligned}
$$

5.1.6   Both Objects Translating

Now we allow both objects to move. In the case of *solid* objects we do not get additional neighborhood transitions, as forward motion of one object implies identical transitions as backward motion of the other object. For *non-solid* objects this is not the case. If both objects are turned towards each other, i.e. if $\vec{B}$ is on the left of $\vec{A}$, the alignment is negative, and if $\vec{B}$ is on the right of $\vec{A}$, the alignment is positive additional transitions to 'same' relations are possible. This means that under these circumstances additional transitions are possible such that the objects superpose. If, for example, 'same' relations are interpreted as collisions, this means that a collision is possible.

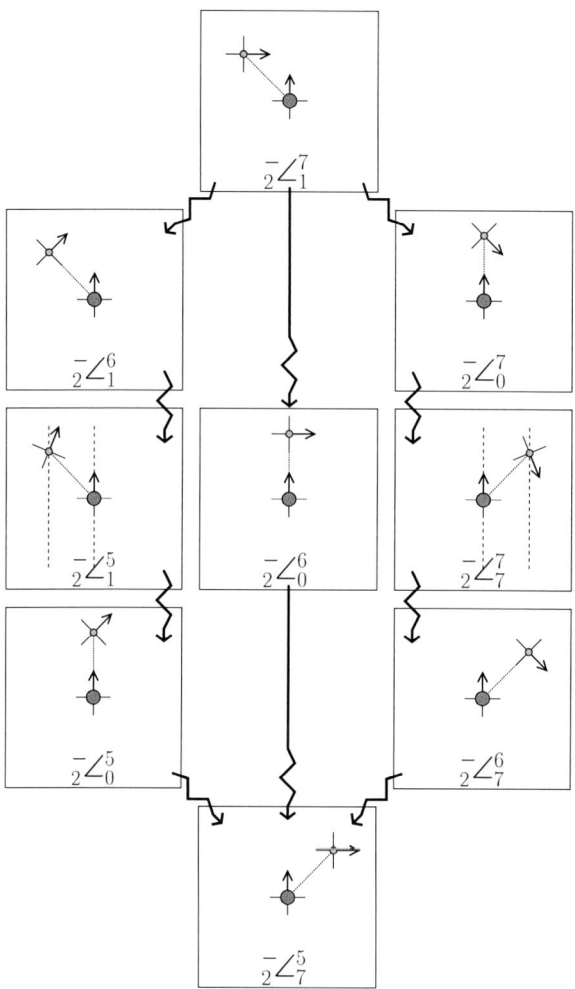

Figure 5.12: Alternative action-augmented neighborhood transitions from $_2^-\angle_1^7$ to $_2^-\angle_7^5$ if $\vec{B}$ moves straight forward. Three neighborhood transitions are possible.

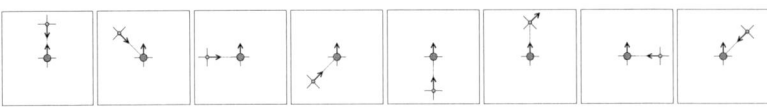

Figure 5.13: Relations representing situations in $\mathcal{OPRA}_2^*$ which might result in 'same' relations with object B moving forward.

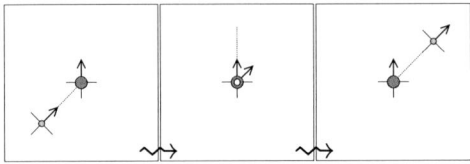

Figure 5.14: A neighborhood path starting from $_2\angle_3^0$ with B moving forward. The objects superpose in $_2\angle7$ and go on to $_2\angle_7^4$.

Interestingly, transitions between relations which bear additional transitions to 'same' relations have a special property regarding the action neighborhoods for single moving objects. If r' is a neighbor of r due to forward motion by $\vec{A}$ than r is a neighbor of r' due to forward motion by $\vec{B}$:

$$r' \in \text{acn}(r, \text{Fwd}, \text{Stable})$$
$$r \in \text{acn}(r', \text{Stable}, \text{Fwd})$$

e.g.
$$_2\angle_1^6 \in \text{acn}(\ _2\angle_1^5 , \text{Fwd}, \text{Stable})$$
$$_2\angle_1^5 \in \text{acn}(\ _2\angle_1^6 , \text{Stable}, \text{Fwd})$$

This means that forward motion of both objects interferes such that they have the opposite effect on neighborhood change. Some other relations representing configurations with the objects in parallel alignment or pointing away from each other might have this property as well, but do not lead to additional neighborhood transitions. In Fig. 5.15 and Fig. 5.16 we depict the two traces for relations which are aligned towards each other. In the first case ($_2\angle_1^5$ to $_2\angle_3^7$) the objects might end up in relation $_2\angle7$ if the objects have the 'same' relative speed and distance ratio, i.e. they need the same time to the point where their trajectories meet. Only for relation $_2\angle_1^7$ this is different, because this configuration can end up in $_2\angle_1^6$ or $_2\angle_1^5$. The reason is that the relation does not represent whether the trajectories meet with an angle smaller than $90°$ ($_2\angle_1^7$), exactly $90°$ ($_2\angle_1^6$), or larger than $90°$ ($_2\angle_1^5$) (cf. Fig. 5.11).

Similar conclusions can be drawn for the second case, from $_2^+\angle_7^3$ to $_2^+\angle_5^1$. All relations have the additional neighbor $_2^+\angle 1$ according to forward motion of both objects. Relation $_2^+\angle_7^1$ has the two additional neighbors $_2^+\angle 2$ and $_2^+\angle 3$.

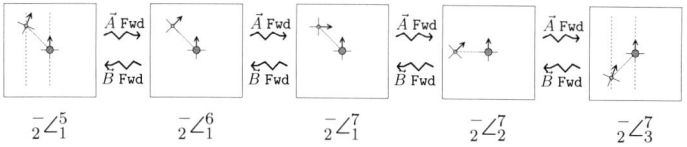

$$_2^-\angle_1^5 \qquad _2^-\angle_1^6 \qquad _2^-\angle_1^7 \qquad _2^-\angle_2^7 \qquad _2^-\angle_3^7$$

Figure 5.15: Relations which have additional action neighborhoods regarding simultaneous forward motion: $_2^-\angle_1^5$ to $_2^-\angle_3^7$

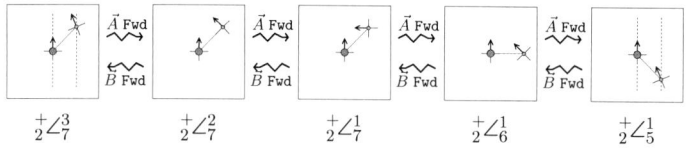

$$_2^+\angle_7^3 \qquad _2^+\angle_7^2 \qquad _2^+\angle_7^1 \qquad _2^+\angle_6^1 \qquad _2^+\angle_5^1$$

Figure 5.16: Relations which have additional action neighborhoods regarding simultaneous forward motion: $_2^+\angle_7^3$ to $_2^+\angle_5^1$.

In addition to the relations above where forward motion of one object causes the opposite effect compared to the other object moving, there are cases where the actions cause the same changes, i.e. $r \rightsquigarrow r'$ if $\vec{A}$ moves forward, $\vec{B}$ moves forward, or both move forward.

$$r \ \in \ \texttt{acn}(r', \texttt{Fwd}, \texttt{Stable}) \land \texttt{acn}(r', \texttt{Stable}, \texttt{Fwd})$$

e.g.

$$_2^+\angle_1^2 \ \in \ \texttt{acn}(_2^+\angle_1^1 , \texttt{Fwd}, \texttt{Stable}) \land \texttt{acn}(_2^+\angle_1^1 , \texttt{Stable}, \texttt{Fwd})$$

Here, the same considerations have to be taken into account as for the cases depicted in Fig. 5.15 and Fig. 5.16, if the agents perform opposite actions. In Fig. 5.17 we give an exemplary trace from $_2^+\angle_1^1$ to $_2^+\angle_3^3$.

5.1.7 Complex Motion Patterns

Obviously, there are more behavior patterns than straight translation and rotation on the spot. Many artificial agents are more or less capable of performing arbitrary trajectories. However, from our point of view the most common behaviors are motion patterns we already dealt with: straight translation and turning. Many other complex

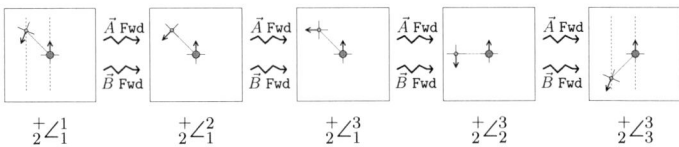

Figure 5.17: Relations which have additional action neighborhoods regarding simultaneous forward motion of one object and backward motion by the other: $_2\angle_1^1$ to $_2\angle_3^3$.

behavior patterns can be approximated by these two primitives. For example, if planning on the basis of an action-augmented neighborhood graph with translation and rotation on the spot yields forward motion and a subsequent rotation, this might also be performed in a single curved trajectory. Nevertheless, there are two types of motion we want to deal with explicitly:

- sidewards motion, and

- circular motion around a fixed center.

Sidewards Motion

Sidewards motion is straight motion perpendicular to the intrinsic front. The effects of sidewards motion can be determined by means of the action neighborhood for simple forward translation. For example, if both objects are straight heading towards each other and $\vec{B}$ moves sidewards to the right ($\texttt{acn}(\ _2\angle_0^0\ ,\texttt{SideR},\texttt{Stable})$), the neighboring relation is related to $\vec{B}$ turning $90°$ to the right and then moving forward ($\texttt{acn}(\ _2^+\angle_2^2\ ,\texttt{Fwd},\texttt{Stable})$). In $\mathcal{OPRA}_4^*$ a right turn of $90°$ is always an increase for the corresponding orientation: $i+2$ if $\vec{A}$ turns right, and $j+2$ if $\vec{B}$ turns right. A left turn results in a decrease by two. For arbitrary even m a $90°$ turn results in a change by m.

Some problems are caused by relations with $|\texttt{align}(\ m\angle_i^j\ )| > 1$, i.e. $\mathcal{OPRA}_m$ relations which have been refined to several $\mathcal{OPRA}_m^*$ relations. On the one hand, assume relation $_2\angle_0^0$ is given and $\vec{B}$ moves sidewards to the right. So, we determine $_2\angle_0^2$ with its neighbor $_2^+\angle_1^3$ for forward motion. Turning $90°$ back results in the three relations $_2^+\angle_1^1$, $_2^O\angle_1^1$, or $_2^-\angle_1^1$. Because of straight motion we have to restore the original orientation (O) and have the correct result $_2^O\angle_1^1$. We show the iconic representations for the relations in Fig. 5.18.

On the other hand, assume relation $_2^+\angle_5^7$ and $\vec{B}$ moves sidewards to the right. The $90°$ turn results in the three relations $_2^+\angle_5^1$, $_2^P\angle_5^1$, and $_2^-\angle_5^1$. Determining the Fwd action neighbors for all three relations, turning them back by $90°$, and restoring the original alignment results in the correct action neighbors for $\texttt{acn}(\ _2^+\angle_5^7\ ,\texttt{Stable},\texttt{SideR})$. We depict this case in Fig. 5.19. We can generalize the action-augmented neighbors

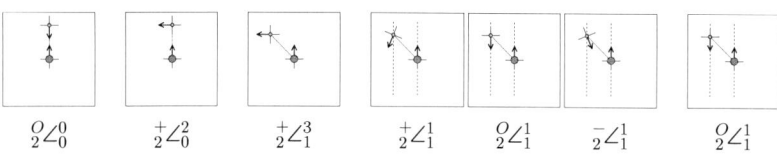

$$\begin{smallmatrix}O\\2\end{smallmatrix}\angle_0^0 \qquad \begin{smallmatrix}+\\2\end{smallmatrix}\angle_0^2 \qquad \begin{smallmatrix}+\\2\end{smallmatrix}\angle_1^3 \qquad \begin{smallmatrix}+\\2\end{smallmatrix}\angle_1^1 \qquad \begin{smallmatrix}O\\2\end{smallmatrix}\angle_1^1 \qquad \begin{smallmatrix}-\\2\end{smallmatrix}\angle_1^1 \qquad \begin{smallmatrix}O\\2\end{smallmatrix}\angle_1^1$$

Figure 5.18: Deriving action neighbors for right sidewards motion by relating to the action neighbors for forward motion: from ${}^{O}_{2}\angle^0_0$ to ${}^{+}_{2}\angle^2_0$ by rotating $\vec{B}$ $90°$ to the right, to ${}^{+}_{2}\angle^3_1$ by moving forward, to $\{\, {}^{+}_{2}\angle^1_1 \,,\, {}^{O}_{2}\angle^1_1 \,,\, {}^{-}_{2}\angle^1_1 \,\}$ by turning $\vec{B}$ $90°$ left, to ${}^{O}_{2}\angle^1_1$ by restoring the original alignment.

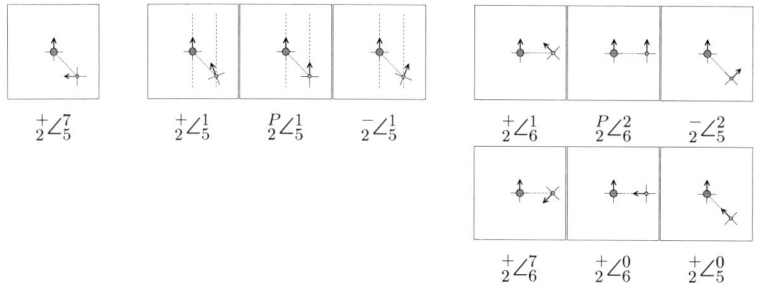

$$\begin{smallmatrix}+\\2\end{smallmatrix}\angle_5^7 \qquad \begin{smallmatrix}+\\2\end{smallmatrix}\angle_5^1 \qquad \begin{smallmatrix}P\\2\end{smallmatrix}\angle_5^1 \qquad \begin{smallmatrix}-\\2\end{smallmatrix}\angle_5^1 \qquad\qquad \begin{smallmatrix}+\\2\end{smallmatrix}\angle_6^1 \qquad \begin{smallmatrix}P\\2\end{smallmatrix}\angle_6^2 \qquad \begin{smallmatrix}-\\2\end{smallmatrix}\angle_5^2$$

$$\begin{smallmatrix}+\\2\end{smallmatrix}\angle_6^7 \qquad \begin{smallmatrix}+\\2\end{smallmatrix}\angle_6^0 \qquad \begin{smallmatrix}+\\2\end{smallmatrix}\angle_5^0$$

Figure 5.19: Deriving action neighbors for right sidewards motion by relating to the action neighbors for forward motion: from ${}^{+}_{2}\angle^7_5$ to $\{\, {}^{+}_{2}\angle^1_5 \,,\, {}^{P}_{2}\angle^1_5 \,,\, {}^{-}_{2}\angle^1_5 \,\}$ by rotating $\vec{B}$ $90°$ to the right, to $\{\, {}^{+}_{2}\angle^1_6 \,,\, {}^{P}_{2}\angle^2_6 \,,\, {}^{-}_{2}\angle^2_5 \,\}$ by moving forward, to $\{\, {}^{+}_{2}\angle^7_6 \,,\, {}^{+}_{2}\angle^0_6 \,,\, {}^{+}_{2}\angle^0_5 \,\}$ by turning $\vec{B}$ $90°$ left and restoring the original positive alignment.

for sidewards motion:

$$\mathrm{acn}(\, {}^{x}_{2}\angle^j_i \,, \mathrm{SideR}, \mathrm{Stable}) = \{\, {}^{x}_{2}\angle^{j'}_{i'} \mid {}^{y}_{2}\angle^{j'}_{i'+2} \in \mathrm{acn}(\, {}^{x}_{2}\angle^j_{i+2} \,, \mathrm{Fwd}, \mathrm{Stable})\}$$

$$\mathrm{acn}(\, {}^{x}_{2}\angle^j_i \,, \mathrm{Stable}, \mathrm{SideR}) = \{\, {}^{x}_{2}\angle^{j'}_{i'} \mid {}^{y}_{2}\angle^{j'+2}_{i'} \in \mathrm{acn}(\, {}^{x}_{2}\angle^j_{i+2} \,, \mathrm{Stable}, \mathrm{Fwd})\}$$

Because of the similarities between forward/backward translation and sidewards motion we need to consider additional action neighbors if both objects move, for example, ${}^{-}_{2}\angle^5_7$ for both moving to the right, in line with ${}^{-}_{2}\angle^7_1$ if both move forward (cf. Fig. 5.20). These neighbors can be determined according to the cases in Section 5.1.6 where both objects move forward.

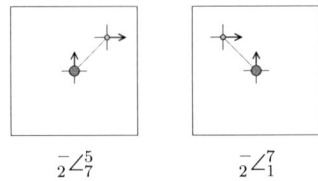

$$_2\angle_7^5 \qquad\qquad _2\angle_1^7$$

Figure 5.20: Cases where certain distance speed ratios result in different neighboring relations if both objects move: $_2\angle_7^5$ if both objects move sidewards to the right and $_2\angle_1^7$ if both objects move forward (cf. Sec. 5.1.6).

Circular Motion

Another type of complex motion we take a closer look at is circular motion. We define circular motion as motion around a center point along the boundary of a circle with a fixed diameter. For reasons of simplicity we only consider cases where the orientation line is aligned tangentially to the boundary of the circle.

Let us first consider rotation of object $\vec{A}$ on the spot. In the top row of Figure 5.21 we illustrate this case. In contrast to the general pictorial representation of the relations where the center object is stable, here, $\vec{A}$ rotates to the right. Assuming now that $\vec{B}$ instead of $\vec{A}$ moves (bottom row) the same neighborhood transitions induce circular motion with the center point in $\vec{A}$. This means that for a given sequence of qualitative perceptions the interpretation of which actions were executed is not unique if the individual motion of objects is not considered.

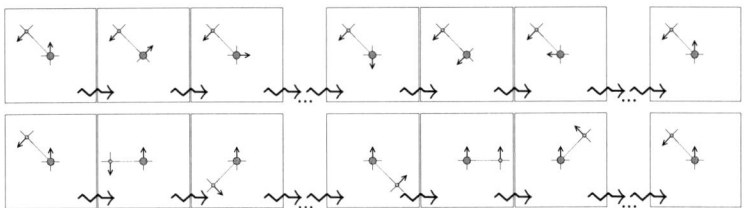

Figure 5.21: Rotation on the spot to the right by $\vec{A}$ induces circular motion of $\vec{B}$ to the left with its center in $\vec{A}$.

The action neighborhood for circular motion is strongly dependent on the relative distance between $\vec{A}$ and $\vec{B}$ to the center point of the circular motion. As distance is not part of the $\mathcal{OPRA}_m^\star$ representation we only consider linear relations here, i.e. for the case of $\frac{x}{2}\angle_i^j$ with i and j are even.

For linear relations we can extract seven different classes of center points in $m = 2$

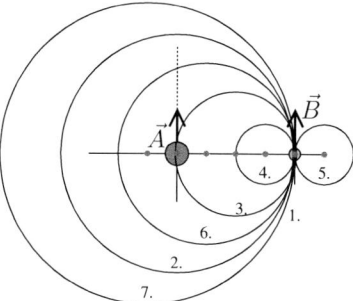

Figure 5.22: Different circular trajectories of an object $\vec{B}$ moving around $\vec{A}$ with respect to different center points.

which influence the action neighborhood if one object moves. We illustrate them in Fig. 5.22. We assume object $\vec{B}$ moves. The first center is object $\vec{B}$ itself, which we already investigated as rotation on the spot in Section 5.1.2. The second possible center is $\vec{A}$ which bears the same neighborhood structure as if $\vec{A}$ rotates on the spot (cf. Fig. 5.21). The next distinctive point is the middle point between $\vec{A}$ and $\vec{B}$ such that the neighborhood trace contains a 'same' relation. The fourth class of points is also on the line between $\vec{A}$ and $\vec{B}$ but closer to $\vec{B}$. So, $\vec{B}$ will always stay on the same side regarding $\vec{A}$ (e.g. in Fig. 5.22 on the right side of $\vec{A}$). The same holds for center points which are behind $\vec{B}$ seen from $\vec{A}$. The sixth class of points is between $\vec{A}$ and $\vec{B}$ but closer to $\vec{A}$. The characteristic of these neighborhood traces is that the moving object is already turned towards the surrounded object if the other object's front is passed, and consequently, the distance between both objects decreases. For the last category of center points, on the line behind $\vec{A}$ seen from $\vec{B}$, this is the opposite, i.e. the distance still increases if the other half plane is entered.

For relations containing planar regions several subclasses can be determined which are dependent on much finer distinctions between the relative distances of $\vec{A}$ and $\vec{B}$ to the center point. For granularities larger than two, additional classes arise if finer distance distinctions are considered. In Figure 5.23 we illustrate such a case. For center points which are behind $\vec{B}$ seen from $\vec{A}$ it makes a difference in granularity $m = 4$ how far the point is behind $\vec{B}$. Because the number of potential neighbors is very high concerning circular motion it is not reasonable to consider this type of motion in applications which use the $\mathcal{ACNG}$ for action planning or similar tasks. So, if circular motion is essentially needed and cannot be approximated by straight linear translation and rotation, from our point of view it is explicitly necessary to integrate distance in the underlying representation.

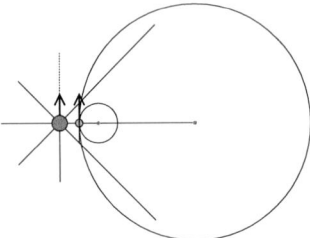

Figure 5.23: The importance of distance information regarding neighborhood traces for circular motion.

5.1.8 Temporal Disambiguation of Action-Augmented Neighborhood Transitions

In the last section we derived the action-augmented neighborhood for $\mathcal{OPRA}_m^\star$ relations. Combining orientation information ($\mathcal{OPRA}_m$) and alignment information ($\mathcal{AC}$) uncertainty of primitive action outcomes is reduced compared to plain $\mathcal{OPRA}_m$. Nevertheless, important questions in everyday life of humans or animals cannot be solved satisfactorily by only regarding single $\mathcal{ACNG}$ transitions:

- Are two moving objects going to collide or will one object pass the other object in its front or back?

- Which action should be performed to avoid a potential collision? In sports this question is sometimes posed from a different perspective. Which actions need to be taken to intercept an opponent player or the ball?

Interception Strategies: Simple Pursuit and Constant Bearing

The simplest strategy for following an object is by always facing the current position of the followed object and moving straight forward. We depict this strategy in Figure 5.24. We denote the persecuting robot or agent by $\vec{A}$ and the target object by $\vec{T}$. Regarding the $\mathcal{OPRA}_m^\star$ $\mathcal{ACNG}$ for controlling a robot that is hunting a moving target with this strategy means that $\vec{A}$ must try to preserve relation $\vec{A} \; {}_m^x\angle_0^j \; \vec{T}$ with $x \in$ align($m\angle_0^j$). If $\vec{A} \; {}_m^x\angle_i^j \; \vec{T}$ with $0 < i < 2m$ holds, i.e. $\vec{T}$ is on the left side of $\vec{A}$, the shortest path in the $\mathcal{ACNG}$ from $\vec{A} \; {}_m^x\angle_i^j \; \vec{T}$ to $\vec{A} \; {}_m^x\angle_0^j \; \vec{T}$ tells the robot to turn left. If $2m < i < 4m$ holds, i.e. $\vec{T}$ is on the right side of $\vec{A}$, the $\mathcal{ACNG}$ tells the robot to turn right. This strategy is suboptimal regarding time and distance traveled until the target is caught. A modified version of this strategy is a conservative strategy for avoiding collisions. If the agent always points behind the back of the target there will never be a collision if we assume objects with no width. For considerations regarding spatially extended objects and point-based abstractions we refer to Chapter 6, especially Section 6.6.1.

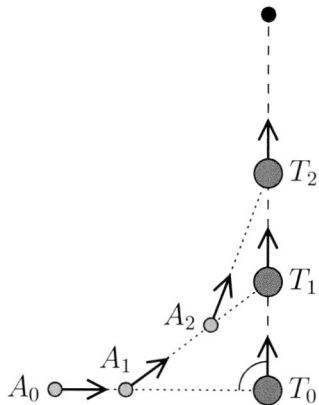

Figure 5.24: Simple Pursuit Strategy: the persecuting agent $\vec{A}$ tries to intercept $\vec{T}$ by always facing the current position of $\vec{T}$.

Another strategy for intercepting moving objects is *constant bearing*. Applying a constant bearing interception strategy an agent tries to keep a constant angle between its motion heading and the target. Additionally, the agent should move straight forward to avoid circular paths around the target. Constant Bearing is also a heuristic for detecting potential collisions under the assumption of straight motion. If one object actively changes the relative angle, for example, turning or changing speed, a collision can be prevented. If the relative angle from the heading of $\vec{A}$ to $\vec{T}$ decreases $\vec{T}$ will pass in front of $\vec{A}$. If the angle increases, $\vec{T}$ will pass in the back of $\vec{A}$. We will call the relative angle between $\vec{A}$ and $\vec{T}$ target angle α^T. Accordingly, we denote the relative angle from $\vec{T}$ to $\vec{A}$ by β^A (cf. Fig. 5.25).

Although known to seamen for ages, constant bearing was not addressed in psychology until the 1960's, for example, in Adams (1961). Investigations of humans and animals revealed that this strategy is applied in many cases to pursue and intercept moving objects, e.g. in Fajen & Warren (2004) for humans intercepting moving targets by foot, or in Olberg et al. (2000) for prey pursuit of dragonflies. In Ghose et al. (2006) constant bearing is shown to be the time optimal strategy for predictable targets, i.e. assuming straight linear motion. They also present a method with better temporal properties regarding unpredictable targets, but we will not consider this further here.

In Figure 5.25 we illustrate the general principle of constant bearing intersection. $\vec{A}$ can catch up target $\vec{T}$ in minimal time if it keeps the relative angle between its heading and $\vec{T}$ (α^T) constant for successive perceptions. The positions of the moving objects at time point t_i with $i \in \{0, 1, 2\}$ is denoted by $\vec{A_i}$ and $\vec{T_i}$ respectively. The target angle at t_i is given by α_i^T. Assuming straight motion, i.e. no action is taken to prevent a collision, the objects will collide at time point t_x in C_x. In contrast, Fig. 5.26 depicts a scene with α_i^T increasing and β_i^A decreasing for successive t_i. Therefore, we can infer that $\vec{A}$ reaches C_x before $\vec{T}$, i.e. $\vec{A}$ passes in front of $\vec{T}$.

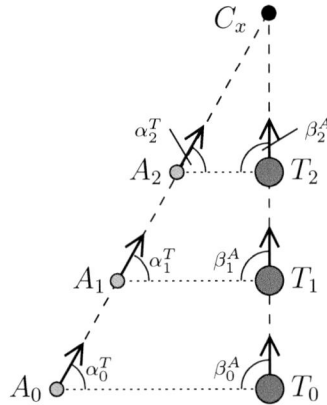

Figure 5.25: Constant Bearing: assuming straight motion of target ($\vec{T}$) the persecuting agent $\vec{A}$ can intercept $\vec{T}$ at C_x in minimal time by preserving the target angle to $\vec{T}$ (α_i^T) at successive time points t_i ($\alpha_0^T = \alpha_1^T = \alpha_2^T$).

Constant Bearing in $\mathcal{OPRA}_m^\star$ $\mathcal{ACNG}$

In terms of a qualitative orientation representation the constant bearing strategy means that the current relation to the target should be preserved for intercepting this target. The other way round, if a collision is not desired, two objects are in danger of colliding if the relation between two moving objects remains the same for successive perceptions.

We now go back to the relations which bear additional action neighbors for simultaneously translating objects compared to only a single object moving. We investigate exemplarily the trace from $_2\angle_5^1$ to $_2\angle_7^3$ (cf. Sec. 5.1.6). We assume $\vec{A}\,_2^+\angle_5^1\,\vec{B}$ given, i.e. $\vec{B}$ is right back of $\vec{A}$ and aligned towards $\vec{A}$. Their trajectories will definitely intersect if they continue moving forward, but the question is whether they collide or pass in front or back of each other.

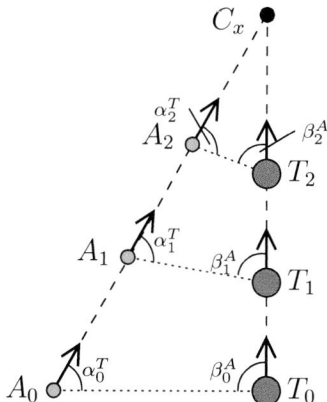

Figure 5.26: Constant Bearing: assuming straight motion the agent will be at C_x before $\vec{T}$, i.e. $\vec{A}$ passes in front of $\vec{T}$, because α_i^T increases for successive time points t_i ($\alpha_0^T < \alpha_1^T < \alpha_2^T$), and β_i^T decreases.

Regarding the principle of constant bearing a neighborhood transition in itself contains additional information for further changes. If a change from ${}_2^+\angle_5^1$ to ${}_2^+\angle_6^1$ is perceived the target angle decreased and so we can infer that the next changes will be to ${}_2^+\angle_7^1$, ${}_2^+\angle_7^2$, ${}_2^+\angle_7^3$, and finally ${}_2^+\angle_0^3$, which means that $\vec{B}$ passes in front of $\vec{A}$. If the next configuration perceived is $\vec{A}\ {}_2^+\angle_5^0\ \vec{B}$, $\vec{B}$ will pass in the back of $\vec{A}$, because the target angle increases. Thus, by perceiving only a single change we can predict that the objects will not collide. Only if no change is recognized for successive perceptions the objects are in danger of a colliding, or the agent is going to intercept the target object.

Assuming a coarse granularity like $m - 2$ it is not likely that many changes are perceived. So, one strategy for perceiving potentially more changes is increasing the granularity. But this is not always possible or reasonable, for example, because of poor sensors or restricted memory and calculating ressources. Additionally, from a cognitive perspective a very fine angular resolution is counter-intuitive.

Another strategy, also taught to student sailors and student pilots, is to construct an auxiliary line from oneself to the other object. Such a line is constructed from the position of the driver or pilot to a fixed part on the vehicle, for example, parts of the rail, so that the target vehicle is on this line. In terms of $\mathcal{OPRA}_m^\star$ this means that a line is constructed from the persecutor over an object X which is fixed on the vehicle to the target object: $\vec{P}^{PX}\ {}_1^x\angle_0^j\ \vec{T}_0$ where $x \in$ align(${}_1\angle_0^j$). For artificial agents carrying metrical sensories, such as laser range finders or camera pan-tilt units, it is easier to remember the target angle α^T without any auxiliary object. If in follow-up perceptions the target object is no longer on this line, it needs to be checked to which side it moved. Assume $\vec{T}$ is to the right of $\vec{P}$ in the beginning ($\vec{P}\ {}^x_1\angle^j_3\ \vec{T}_0$). If at some subsequent time point t_n $\vec{P}^{PX}\ {}^x_1\angle^j_1\ \vec{T}_n$ is perceived, i.e. $\vec{T}$ is on the left of the auxiliary line, the target angle decreased and so $\vec{T}$ will pass in front of $\vec{P}$. If at t_n $\vec{P}^{PX}\ {}^x_1\angle^j_3\ \vec{T}_n$ is perceived α^T increased and so $\vec{T}$ will pass behind $\vec{P}$.

What to do if a potential collision is detected?

If a potential future collision is detected the question is now: Which action should be performed to prevent a looming collision? We identified the relations ${}^+_2\angle^1_5$, ${}^+_2\angle^1_6$, ${}^+_2\angle^1_7$, ${}^+_2\angle^2_7$, and ${}^+_2\angle^3_7$ as representing some of the configurations where collisions might arise if both objects move forward. We will call these relations *collision relations*. In contrast we call relations which do not incorporate potential collisions *safe relations*. The task is now to get from a collision relation to a safe relation. With the help of the $\mathcal{ACNG}$ we can derive potential actions. To this end, we must assume that there is enough distance between both objects so that there is enough time for successful execution of the necessary action.

　　　Exemplarily we assume $\vec{A}\ {}_2\angle^1_5\ \vec{B}$ as start configuration, i.e. $\vec{B}$ is left behind of $\vec{A}$ and heading towards $\vec{A}$. A left turn of $\vec{A}$ results in ${}^P_2\angle^1_5$ which is a save relation, whereas a right turn does not help, because the resulting relation ${}^+_2\angle^1_6$ is also a collision relation. For $\vec{B}$ turning to either side results in a safe relation: ${}^P_2\angle^1_5$ if turning right and ${}^+_2\angle^0_5$ if turning left. Another option to traverse from ${}^+_2\angle^1_5$ to ${}^+_2\angle^0_5$ is by $\vec{A}$ translating forward. If both objects are already moving, this means that $\vec{A}$ needs to speed up or $\vec{B}$ needs to slow down. If $\vec{A}$ slows down or $\vec{B}$ accelerates we obtain ${}^+_2\angle^1_6$ which is still a collision relation. Nevertheless, these actions might solve the collision situation, because with the neighborhood transition from ${}^+_2\angle^1_5$ to ${}^+_2\angle^1_6$ we gain the information that the target angle decreased. If we do not get this information about neighborhood change, for example, because of coarse calculus resolution, choosing these actions is not a good idea. For other collision relations actions which lead to safe relations can be derived from the $\mathcal{ACNG}$ in a similar manner.

5.2　Dealing with Conflicting Information: Relaxing Constraint Networks

Artificial agents acting in space need to collect information about their environment to build up their world model. If qualitative representations are used it may happen that information currently perceived conflicts with information gathered previously. Conflicting knowledge may also arise if several robots share their qualitative world models. Whether or not there is conflicting knowledge in qualitative representations can be determined by encoding the knowledge as a constraint network and then checking its

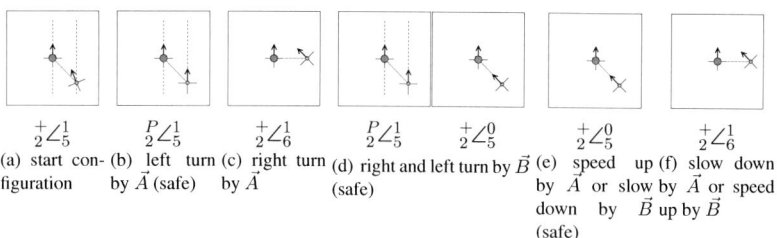

$\begin{matrix} + \\ 2 \end{matrix} \angle^1_5$ $\begin{matrix} P \\ 2 \end{matrix} \angle^1_5$ $\begin{matrix} + \\ 2 \end{matrix} \angle^1_6$ $\begin{matrix} P \\ 2 \end{matrix} \angle^1_5$ $\begin{matrix} + \\ 2 \end{matrix} \angle^0_5$ $\begin{matrix} + \\ 2 \end{matrix} \angle^0_5$ $\begin{matrix} + \\ 2 \end{matrix} \angle^1_6$

(a) start con-figuration (b) left turn by $\vec{A}$ (safe) (c) right turn by $\vec{A}$ (d) right and left turn by $\vec{B}$ (safe) (e) speed up by $\vec{A}$ or slow by $\vec{A}$ or slow down by $\vec{B}$ up by $\vec{B}$ (safe) (f) slow down by $\vec{A}$ or speed down by $\vec{B}$ up by $\vec{B}$ (safe)

Figure 5.27: Actions derived from the $\mathcal{ACNG}$ to resolve the collision relation $\begin{matrix} + \\ 2 \end{matrix} \angle^1_5$ to a safe relation.

consistency. However, if the network is found to be inconsistent it is not possible to derive which fragments caused the inconsistency. This turns the complete world model useless for further application.

As suggested in Moratz & Freksa (1998), conceptual neighborhoods offer a suitable way to deal with conflicting information. In the following, we will demonstrate this by showing how conceptual neighborhoods provide domain-specific heuristics to resolve conflicts. The distance between two relations in the neighborhood graph can be used to derive distance measures between constraint networks. This allows minimal relaxation effort required to resolve inconsistencies. We start out by illustrating the problem with a small example and by defining relaxation; we proceed by showing how conceptual neighborhood relations can be used to derive application-specific distance functions. Finally, we address the problem of determining the minimal relaxation with respect to a chosen distance function.

5.2.1 Inconsistent Information and Relaxations

Let us consider a small example involving three robots as illustrated in Figure 5.28. The robots A, B, C are solving some task as a team. All robots have a limited viewing angle (indicated by the dashed lines) which, in this case, means that A only sees B, B only sees C, and C only sees A. The robots represent information about the current situation as qualitative spatial relations in the $\mathcal{OPRA}^*_2$ calculus. Additionally, they have the ability to communicate with each other to exchange information on what they currently perceive. This results in a shared world model that includes information not available to the individual robot, for example, information about the robot that is currently outside their view. However, the combined world model will not necessarily be consistent. In our case, due to slight errors in the perception of robot B, the relations perceived by the robots are as shown in Table 5.1.

The corresponding constraint network is inconsistent as the configuration described by these three relations is not satisfiable in the domain of oriented points. For

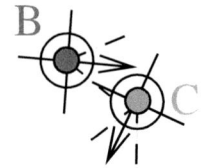

Figure 5.28: A scene with 3 robots represented in $\mathcal{OPRA}_2$.

Perceived situation	Real situation
$\vec{A} \,_2\angle_7^5\, \vec{B}$	$\vec{A} \,_2\angle_7^5\, \vec{B}$
$\vec{A} \,_2\angle_0^5\, \vec{B}$	$\vec{A} \,_2\angle_7^5\, \vec{B}$
$\vec{A} \,_2\angle_1^7\, \vec{B}$	$\vec{A} \,_2\angle_1^7\, \vec{B}$

Table 5.1: The $\mathcal{OPRA}_2^*$ relations for the real situation in Fig. 5.28 and the relations perceived by the individual robots.

instance, the composition of $\vec{A} \,_2\angle_7^5\, \vec{B}$ and $\vec{B} \,_2\angle_0^5\, \vec{C}$ results in $\vec{A} \,_2^y\angle_{5..7}^{5..7}\, \vec{C}$ with the according alignments for y, while, on the other hand, taking the converse of $\vec{C} \,_2\angle_1^7\, \vec{A}$ yields $\vec{A} \,_2^+\angle_7^1\, \vec{C}$. Since the intersection of these two results is empty, the constraint network cannot be consistent (cf. Sec. 2.3.2).

In such a situation it is desirable to relax the given constraints until a consistent constraint network is found instead of completely discarding the inconsistent information. As in our work constraints are disjunctions of base relations from a particular spatial calculus written as sets, we can use set inclusion to define what we mean by relaxation of an individual constraint:

Constraint Relaxation
    Constraint C_1 is a *relaxation* of constraint C_2 if and only if $C_2 \subseteq C_1$.

We can extend this notion to complete constraint networks over the same set of variables by defining that $CN_1 = <V, l_1>$ is a relaxation of $CN_2 = <V, l_2>$ (written $CN_2 \subseteq CN_1$) if and only if for all $v_i, v_j \in V$, $l_2(v_i, v_j) \subseteq l_1(v_i, v_j)$ holds.

5.2.2 Distance Functions Based on Conceptual Neighborhoods

We usually are not interested in arbitrary relaxations of the original network, but are looking for *minimal relaxations* with respect to the domain and task at hand. To define minimality, we need a distance function over constraint networks. As we will show, distances between relations in the conceptual neighborhood graph are well-suited as a basis to formulate such distance functions.

We define the distance d_b between two base relations $r_i, r_j \in \mathcal{BR}$ of a calculus as the length of the shortest path connecting them in the neighborhood graph $\mathcal{CNG}$. Alternatively, the distance d_b between relations can also be defined based on the action-augmented neighborhood graph with varying weights concerning different actions, for example, with turning actions having lower weights than translation actions. For our example, we choose the shortest path in the $\mathcal{ACNG}$ with only straight translation and rotation and neighborhood distance 1 for all actions:

$$d_b(r_i, r_j) = x \iff x \text{ is the length of the shortest path connecting}$$
$$r_i \text{ and } r_j \text{ in } \mathcal{CNG}$$

We extend this distance measure to constraints that are disjunctions of base relations. These are written as sets. The intuition behind this extension is that the distance should correspond to the number of times we have to apply the `relax()` operation[2] to one of the sets until the resulting set contains all the relations from the other set. This corresponds to calculating the symmetric Hausdorff distance between the two sets based on d_b. We, therefore, define the distance $d_c(S, R)$ between two sets of base relations $S, R \in 2^{\mathcal{BR}}$ as:

$$d_c(S, R) = \max\{h(S, R), h(R, S)\}$$

where

$$h(X, Y) = \max_{x \in X} \left(\min_{y \in Y} d_b(x, y) \right) .$$

How to extend this distance function for individual constraints to constraint networks over the same set of variables depends on the concrete application considered since the resulting distance function describes what we consider similar in a given context. There are several possible values one might want to minimize in a given application:

- the number of corresponding constraints that differ in constraint networks CN_1 and CN_2:

$$\text{ConstraintsChanged}(CN_1, CN_2) = |\{(v_i, v_j) \mid v_i, v_j \in V \wedge$$
$$l_1(v_i, v_j) \neq l_2(v_i, v_j)\}|$$

---

[2] $\text{relax}(S) = \left(\bigcup_{b \in S} \text{cn}(b) \right) \cup S$, i.e. $\text{relax}(S)$ defines the union of all conceptual neighbors for each individual relation from the set S (cf. Sec. 2.3.3)

- the maximal distance between corresponding constraints as given by d_c:

$$\texttt{MaxChangedDistance}(CN_1, CN_2) = \max_{v_i, v_j \in V} d_c\left(l_1(v_i, v_j), l_2(v_i, v_j)\right)$$

- the overall sum of distances between corresponding constraints as given by d_c:

$$\texttt{SumOfDistances}(CN_1, CN_2) = \sum_{v_i, v_j \in V} d_c\left(l_1(v_i, v_j), l_2(v_i, v_j)\right)$$

Such measures can be combined arbitrarily to define an overall distance function d_{CN} over the space of constraint networks over the same set of variables and the same set of relational constraints, for example, by taking the weighted sum:

$$
\begin{aligned}
d_{CN}(CN_1, CN_2) = \quad & \alpha \cdot \texttt{ConstraintsChanged}(CN_1, CN_2) \\
+ \; & \beta \cdot \texttt{MaxChangedDistance}(CN_1, CN_2) \\
+ \; & \gamma \cdot \texttt{SumOfDistances}(CN_1, CN_2)
\end{aligned}
$$

5.2.3 Minimal Relaxations

Finding the minimal relaxation corresponds to solving a combinatorial optimization problem in which the cost function is given by our distance function d_{CN}. Relaxed constraint networks are constructed by applying the `relax` function to individual constraints. This means that a constraint is replaced by the coarsest relation with distance 1 according to the distance function d_c.

Let $\mathcal{RC}_{CN}$ be the set of all constraint networks which are relaxations of a given constraint network CN that are consistent:

$$\mathcal{RC}_{CN} = \{\, N \mid CN \subseteq N \wedge N \text{ is consistent} \,\}$$

The goal of the relaxation process is to find a constraint network $CN^* \in \mathcal{RC}_{CN}$ that is closest to CN according to the chosen distance function d_{CN}. We call such a network a *minimal consistent relaxation* of CN:[3]

$$CN^* = \arg\min_{N \in \mathcal{RC}_{CN}} d_{CN}(N, CN)$$

The number of possible relaxations is n^l where n is the number of constraints (which is proportional to $|V|^2$) and l is the diameter of the constraint graph, which

---

[3]Note, that CN^* is not well-defined, as several minimal consistent relaxations may exist.

means a constraint can be relaxed at most l times. If the distance to the original network grows monotonically whenever the `relax` operator is applied to a constraint, a general algorithm similar to Dijkstra's shortest path algorithm can be used to find a minimal relaxation. Constraint networks would then be stored in a priority queue sorted by increasing distance from the original constraint network. In every step the first network is taken from the queue and checked for consistency. If it is not consistent, several new networks are generated by applying `relax` to one of the constraints of the current network. These new networks are then sorted into the queue. If the inspected network is consistent, it has to be a minimal consistent relaxation.

However, for certain distance functions it is possible to directly enumerate the relaxations in order of increasing distance without the need of keeping multiple constraint networks stored in a queue. Provided we have such an enumeration function `generateRelaxation`(N) that generates the next relaxation from the currently considered relaxation N with respect to the distance function, and we have a function `consistency`(N) that decides the consistency of network N, we can define a recursive function `mcr`(CN) that computes a minimal consistent relaxation of a given network CN as follows:

$$\text{mcr}(CN) = \begin{cases} CN & : & \text{if consistency}(CN) \\ \text{mcr(generateRelaxation}(CN)) & : & \text{otherwise} \end{cases}$$

In our example case, we are dealing with noisy sensor information. So, there might be inaccurate sensor readings which lead to a small change in the perceived relations. Therefore, we want our overall distance function d to combine MaxChangedDistance and SumOfDistances in a way that MaxChangedDistance is given precedence over SumOfDistances. This means that given two different relaxations CN_1, CN_2 of CN, MaxChangedDistance(CN_1, CN) > MaxChangedDistance(CN_2, CN) implies $d(CN_1, CN) > d(CN_2, CN)$. Only if MaxChangedDistance is the same for CN_1 and CN_2, SumOfDistances would be used to decide which one is closer to CN. Employing this distance is appropriate for our application since it prefers relaxations with multiple small changes over a few large changes while, as a second criterion, it minimizes the overall sum of changes. In applications in which few large outliers are more likely than many small changes, a combination of ConstraintsChanged and SumOfDistances would be the better choice.

For many applications a reasonable distance function gives strict precedence of one criterion over another. In principle, such distance functions can still be formulated as a weighted sum by choosing the weights accordingly. Moreover, in most cases it is possible to formulate direct enumeration algorithms.

The enumeration function actually applied to this example does not return the relaxed constraint networks themselves but, instead, generates triples consisting of the following information:

1. a list of n numbers, one for each constraint, telling how often constraint i with $0 \le i < n$ has to be relaxed,

2. the overall sum of relaxations, and

3. the maximum relaxation steps to be performed on a single constraint.

To generate the relaxed network, each constraint has to be relaxed as often as specified by the corresponding number given in the list (first element of the triple), for example, for the list [2 1 0] constraint 1 is relaxed twice, constraint 2 is relaxed once and constraint 3 is not relaxed at all. The overall sum of relaxations is three, and the maximum number of individual relaxations is two.

Coming back to our example in Figure 5.28, for simplicity we assume that our robots can either rotate on the spot or move straight in the direction they are facing and, thus, we employ the corresponding neighborhood structure as discussed in Section 5.1. This results in one of the following two possible minimal consistent relaxations:

$$
\begin{aligned}
&\vec{A} \,{}_2^-\angle_7^5\, \vec{B} \qquad\quad \vec{A} \,{}_2^-\angle_7^5\, \vec{B} \\
&\vec{B} \,{}_2^-\angle_7^5\, \vec{C} \quad \text{and} \quad \vec{B} \,{}_2^-\angle_7^6\, \vec{C} \\
&\vec{C} \,{}_2^-\angle_1^7\, \vec{A} \qquad\quad \vec{C} \,{}_2^-\angle_1^7\, \vec{A}
\end{aligned}
$$

The original situation is correctly described by the first solution, but the other would have been just as likely, given the inconsistent information. Even if the agents follow a conservative policy and only accept what holds in all minimal consistent relaxations, they still are able to determine the position of the robot not visible to them. In the example, only the exact orientation of C with respect to B cannot be determined.

Even though we can generate relaxations in order of increasing distance to the original constraint network, the huge number of possible relaxations means that only problems in which the minimal consistent relaxations are rather close to the original network can be relaxed in appropriate computation time. In our example, it is reasonable to assume that perceived relations have a neighborhood distance $d_b \le 2$ with respect to the actual relation. Therefore, if no corresponding consistent relaxation with MaxChangedDistance ≤ 2 is found, the relaxation process could stop, as something unexpected must have happened. In general, the algorithm cannot guarantee that the constraint network representing the real situation is contained, although for the example it is contained in the set of minimal relaxations. For example, let us assume a complete sensor failure results in a random value for a specific relation. Regarding the corresponding inconsistent network (CN_0), the constraint network representing the real situation (CN_{real}) might have a greater distance to CN_0 than a minimal relaxed consistent network (CN^*), i.e. $d_{CN}(CN_{real}, CN_0) > d_{CN}(CN^*, CN_0)$.

To summarize, conceptual neighborhoods can serve as a meaningful and well-defined basis for optimizing the relaxation process in constraint networks. Minimal relaxation can be defined based on minimal neighborhood distance. As a prerequisite an adequate neighborhood structure for the application at hand needs to be known.

5.3 Summary

In this chapter we considered qualitative calculi with respect to aspects of agent control.

To fulfill the needs of agent control we first considered conceptual neighborhood from a perspective to spatially navigate agents in a goal-directed manner. Second, we considered inconsistent qualitative world models and how these inconsistencies can be resolved with minimal modifications with respect to the original world model.

Conceptual neighborhood by itself is not expressive enough regarding the task of agent control. Application-specific parameters must be taken into account in addition to derive actions which lead from one relation to neighboring relations. Annotating the conceptual neighborhood graph with these parameters led to the *action-augmented conceptual neighborhood graph*. The parameters incorporated here were the agents' motion capabilities, simultaneous motion of agents and objects considered, and whether objects or landmarks may coincide in position or not. Several classes of basic motion concepts were considered, namely rotation, straight translation, straight sidewards motion, and circular motion. We systematically derived the parameter-dependent neighborhood structures and gave the corresponding neighborhood functions.

We were not able to solve all problems concerning agent navigation with the combination of relative orientation calculi and the extension of conceptual neighborhood. An important question in everyday life is whether objects may collide or whether an agent is in good position for intercepting another object. We demonstrated that these questions can be resolved by the method of constant bearing. We showed how this method is reflected in qualitative spatial calculi and how appropriate actions can be derived for the task at hand.

In addition, we considered how small errors in qualitative spatial world models result in the impracticality of relying on the complete world model based on raw sensor data. If individual relations conflict and thus, an inconsistent constraint network is given, we showed how we can derive consistent networks with minimal modifications with respect to different neighborhood-based distance functions.

Chapter 6

SailAway: Collision Free Vessel Navigation Based on Qualitative Spatial Reasoning

In this chapter we present how qualitative spatial representations and reasoning techniques can be applied to agent control. We develop a qualitative framework for a demonstrator application in the domain of vessel navigation. Alternative actions are provided by transition systems of the applicable rules to form a constraint network in which consistency corresponds to exemption from collisions. The transition systems are derived stepwise by means of the action-augmented conceptual neighborhood graph ($\mathcal{ACNG}$) of $\mathcal{OPRA}_m^*$. Constraint-based reasoning techniques are then used to find a consistent and thus collision-free solution. The result is then repropagated to determine the suitable actions for the individual vessels that will lead to this particular constellation.

6.1 Introduction

Everday life of humans is in many situations guided by regulations and recommendations. Traffic scenarios form a large domain which are governed by sets of regulations. These rule systems have in common that they are generally formulated in natural language and thus contain qualitative terms for describing spatial situations and actions which are expected to be adequate in these situations. For example, in traffic laws qualitative concepts are used to describe the situations that are governed by the law, but they are also used to describe correct, i.e. rule-compliant, behavior of agents in these situations. Especially, qualitative orientation terms like 'from the left' or 'behind' and qualitative action terms like 'turn left' constitute a fundamental part of such rule sets. In many cases no specifications are given on speed, distance, or temporal limitations. It is implicitly assumed that the actions given in regulations are *safe* for the purpose of the desired effect, i.e. if an agent is supposed to turn left to avoid a collision with another agent, the turn must be performed powerful and fast enough so that the agent does not crash into the other agent. For example, if two vessels are in head-on situation and distant from each other regarding their current speed, a small turn is sufficient. In contrast, if the agents are close to one another, a hard turn might be necessary.

Artificial cognitive agents that interact with humans must be able to process such rule sets. This entails that an agent must be able to not only localize itself in the physical space, but also to classify itself in the normative space of regulations and laws. Considering the integration of an agent in the normative space, not only spatial relations are important. Most of the rules to be followed by an agent in some situation depend on the types of agents involved in a situation. Assuming different types in a specific context might lead to different decisions what an agent is allowed to do or which behavior to show according to a rule set, i.e. a different rule has to be applied. For example, in vessel navigation the behavior of a vessel depends on the types of vessels involved in the current situation. A motor vessel has to show different behavior if it meets another motor vessel than if it meets a sailing vessel, or in games like football different behavior is expected from an attacker compared to a defender. However, since knowledge of this kind can be formalized rather easily, the crucial point for formalizing navigation rules is to formally represent spatial configurations in a suitable way, i.e. in terms of the considered rules, and to formally represent the actions prescribed by these rules. In particular, the agent must perceive its current spatial situation, identify rules that might be relevant in this spatial situation with respect to types of agents involved, and finally select appropriate, but notwithstanding rule-compliant actions.

Representations of rule-compliant behavior, of course, are not limited to navigation. Examples of rule sets guiding the behavior of agents can also be found in sports, in games, in expert recommendation systems, and so on. Rule sets need to be made explicit and be formalized at different stages when artificial agents or multi-agent systems are specified or implemented. First, rules can be used to specify the desired behavior of an artificial agent, for instance a mobile robot or an autonomous vehicle, such that an implemented system can be tested against these specifications. Rules may also be used to actively control an artificial agent, for example, when we wish to restrict possible trajectories of a mobile system. Formal encodings of rules are also crucial for implementing control systems that observe and judge the behavior of other agents. Finally, rule sets need to be formalized in order to evaluate them according to given criteria, to find gaps, inconsistencies, or deadlocks. For instance, if a rule set consists of rules describing how *two* agents have to behave in specific situations one could investigate how this rule set would perform in more complex situations involving more than two agents: is the rule set still sound in the sense that its intentions, e.g. collision avoidance, are met if all agents act in compliance with the rules? Furthermore, is the rule set complete in the sense that it covers all possible situations? In summary, we can distinguish three principal ways in which formalized rule sets can be employed:

- *Control* of artificial agents: How can we define the behavior of an agent efficiently? How can we implement rule-compliant behavior?
- *Evaluation* of rule sets: Is the rule set consistent? Is it optimal for specific tasks?
- *Judgement* of agent behavior: Is the behavior rule-compliant?

Within this case study we primarily deal with agent control based on qualitative spatial representations. For illustrating how qualitative spatial representation formalisms and reasoning techniques – in detail neighborhood-based reasoning and constraint-based reasoning – can be applied to formalize rule sets that determine actions based on spatial configurations we choose the domain of collision regulations in vessel navigation for vessels in sight of one another. We introduce our demonstrator application *SailAway* below.

The set of collision regulations (ColRegs) as presented by the International Maritime Organization is given in natural language (IMO, 1972). All rules are defined for pairs of vessels. The set of rules for dealing with pairs of vessels in sight of each other is given in detail in Appendix A. A summary of the complete rules can be found on the IMO homepage[1]. For example, Rule 14 of the ColRegs states:

When two power-driven vessels are meeting on reciprocal or nearly reciprocal courses so as to involve risk of collision each shall alter her course to starboard so that each shall pass on the port side of the other.

Qualitative representations allow us to mediate between metrical information perceivable to the agents and abstract conceptual knowledge expressed in the rule set. Each rule from such a rule set comprises some particular qualitative configurations (meet on reciprocal or nearly reciprocal courses so as to involve risk of collision) and allows specific actions for the agents involved (shall alter her course to starboard so that ...). We combine constraint- and neighborhood-based reasoning methods to infer *admissible actions* from a set of *"physically" possible actions*. Admissible actions are actions which are not only physically possible but also in compliance to the rule set at the same time. As the underlying qualitative representation we use $\mathcal{OPRA}_m^\star$ together with its composition and action-augmented neighborhood structures as derived in Section 5.1. In our application we neglect the spatial extent of the objects, as we are interested in deriving general strategies for navigation. If the objects are in immediate proximity one could model the local environment with additional relations representing the extensions of the objects.

In the remainder of this chapter, we start by introducing the overall structure of our demonstrator application. It consists of a simulator, providing the environment for our demonstration domain of vessel navigation, and a qualitative framework deriving

---

[1] http://www.imo.org/Conventions/contents.asp?doc_id=649&topic_id=257 (October 2007)

coarse actions in compliance with collision regulations in the domain. Thereafter, we present the domain and the simulator. Afterwards we describe the qualitative framework in more detail, which consists of a qualitative scene description, a formalization of the rules, and a symbolic reasoning component. We introduce how the qualitative scene description is organized, and how the rule transition systems are derived in a stepwise manner from the $\mathcal{ACNG}$. Afterwards we show how these two knowledge sources can be combined with constraint-based reasoning techniques. We close with a discussion on the experiences made with the qualitative approach to agent control within our experimental implementation.

6.2 General Overview of the Qualitative SailAway Framework

For demonstrating how qualitative spatial representations and techniques can be applied for agent control in the domain of vessel navigation we developed a qualitative framework for a demonstrator application, in the following also called *SailAway*. Though, most of the techniques applied carry over to other navigation scenarios. In Fig. 6.1 we depict the overall architecture of *SailAway*.

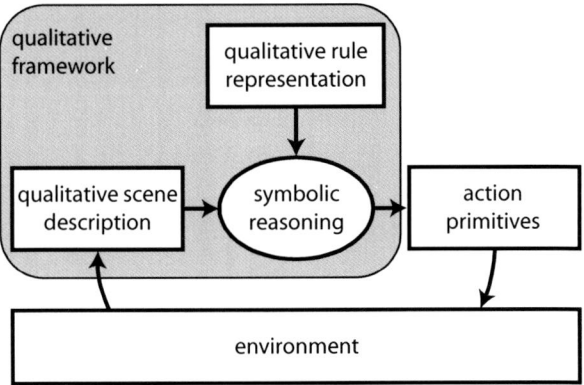

Figure 6.1: The qualitative methods underlying SailAway.

The *environment* is an open sea scenario with vessels moving around towards different targets. The environment is represented to the agent by a *qualitative scene description* that contains qualitative information about the current relative position for each pair of vessels in sight of each other in the environment. In the context of vessel navigation, position information, i.e. information about direction and distance, is essential. In particular, orientation information is required to differentiate spatial constellations as described by navigation rules. Currently, distance information only plays a subordinate role in our approach. We use such information only to distinguish those vessels that are close enough to other vessels such that they need to be considered when navigation rules are evaluated.

Navigation rules restrict the possibilities of agents to act in space. For representing possible actions and their effects in a formal model, spatial and temporal information needs to be combined. The *qualitative rule representation* encodes relevant parts of the collision regulations, i.e. how two power-driven vessels have to behave if they are in danger of collision. On the basis of rule formalizations, configurations can be classified and admissible actions for an agent can be deduced. An appropriate formalization is key to an accurate modeling of the rules and essential for empowering effective reasoning. The formalization serves as a double link; it links continuous real-world configurations to discrete classes of configurations and it links rule descriptions to symbolic representations. These rule representations are derived from the action-augmented conceptual neighborhood graph ($\mathcal{ACNG}$) as developed in Sec. 5.1. Finally, the current scene description and the rule representations which apply to the current situation are related by *symbolic reasoning*, such that an *action primitive* can be selected. The symbolic reasoning comprises the extrapolation of the current scene description based on the effect of rule-compliant actions, and the deduction of a consistent scenario in terms of constraint-based reasoning from the set of extrapolated scene descriptions. The action primitives for controlling the vessels can be derived directly from the consistent scenario. The actions are executed immediately and affect the qualitative scene description perceived by the agents.

The system is implemented as a modular architecture with several stand-alone modules communicating via TCP/IP. The module for qualifying the scene description is realized by the QSR toolbox SparQ (Wallgrün et al., 2006). For constraint solving any available tool can be interlinked. Currently, we apply the spatial inference engine of SparQ. An alternative system which has been deployed is the generic qualitative constraint solver GQR[2]. The solvers apply different heuristics for solving constraint networks.

6.2.1 The SparQ Toolbox

SparQ is a generic toolbox for representing space and reasoning about space based on qualitative spatial relations. The toolbox makes available several qualitative spatial calculi and general reasoning techniques developed in the QSR community in a single homogeneous framework. A detailed introduction to SparQ can be found in Wallgrün et al. (2006) and Dylla et al. (2006).

SparQ consists of a set of modules that logically structure the different services provided. Among the qualitative reasoning techniques offered we use the interface for mapping the continuous domain to qualitative representations (qualification), i.e. trans-

---

[2]`https://sfbtr8.informatik.uni-freiburg.de/R4LogoSpace/Resources/` GQR

ferring the quantitative vessel positions into qualitative ones, and for checking the consistency of constraint networks. The general architecture is visualized in Figure 6.2. For using SparQ within *SailAway* the calculus description of $\mathcal{OPRA}_m^*$ was derived and integrated into the system.

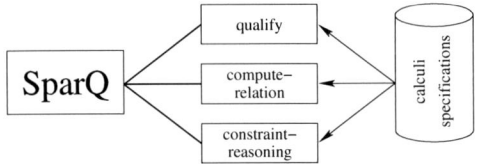

Figure 6.2: Module architecture of the SparQ toolbox.

6.3   The Domain: Collision Rules in Vessel Navigation

The domain of vessel navigation is characterized by an open water space ($\mathbb{R}^2$) with vessels moving along a given course. The collision regulations distinguish different types of vessels. Within our investigations we incorporate:

- sport vessels larger than 20 meters (SpV)
- sailing vessels (SV),
- sailing vessels currently powered by an engine (SVm),
- power driven vessels, also called motor vessels (MV), and
- vessels powered by muscular strength, e.g. rowing vessels (RV).

We have to concern that vessels are inert due to their mass such that they cannot stop or revert their motion direction within a short period. In general, the motion of standard vessels can be compared to Ackermann kinematics, i.e. no turning possibilities without any translational velocity and no side motion. Rowing vessels can be regarded as an exception as they can nearly turn on the spot due their comparatively slow speed and small inertia.

Within this application we restrict to rules concerning *vessels in sight of one another*. We neglect conditions of restricted visibility as, for example, caused by fog or heavy rain. The behavior for pairs of vessels which are in sight of each other and in danger of collision is governed by eight rules (Rule 11 - Rule 18 of ColRegs). The rules define which one is the stand-on vessel and which one is the give-way vessel. In general, three different categories of spatial arrangements can be classified where different behavior is defined:

- head-on situations (reciprocal or nearly reciprocal course)
- overtaking situations (approaching from abaft), and

- crossing situations (from port or starboard).

The behavior is not only defined by the spatial relation between the vessels, but also by the types of vessels involved. For example, two power-driven vessels which are in a head-on situation both shall turn starboard and pass at the port side of the other (cf. Fig. 6.3(a)). If a motor vessel and a sport vessel (larger than 20 meters) meet in head-on situation only the motor vessel has to turn starboard and the sport vessel shall keep course and speed (cf. Fig. 6.3(b)). In crossing situations the give-way vessel should always try to avoid crossing ahead of the other vessel to minimize risk of collision. In textbooks idealized behavior according to the individual rules for pairs of vessels is depicted by pictorial representations similar to those in Fig. 6.3. For a complete set of pictorial representations we refer to Appendix A.2.

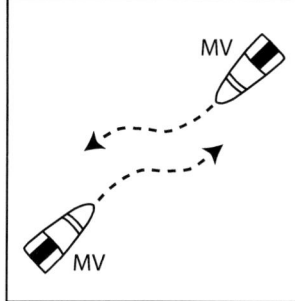 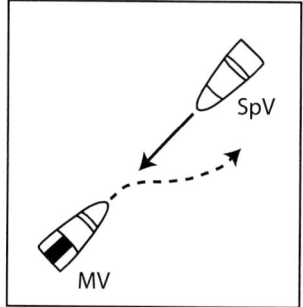

(a) Two motor vessels (MVs): both have to alter their course starboard to pass each other on port side.

(b) Motor vessel and Sport vessel (SpV): MV has to turn starboard, SpV holds course.

Figure 6.3: Exemplary rule for two different kinds of vessels (solid line: stand-on vessel, dashed line: give-way vessel).

All rules are defined for only two vessels in sight of each other. Situations with more than two vessels have to be dealt by with applying the rules for the individual pairs of vessels. It is not defined explicitly how to behave if the behaviors given by the rules contradict. Nevertheless, the vessels are allowed to behave differently compared to the rule set in order to prevent collisions, e.g. if the behavior proposed would lead to a dangerous situation with another vessel. It is not stated in which situations conflicts may arise. In general, the ColRegs propose conservative behavior, e.g. in Rule 14: "if in any doubt whether a head-on situation exists she shall assume that it does exist and act accordingly". Additionally, the give-way vessel is expected to take early and substantial action to keep well clear of the stand-on vessel.

6.4   The Simulator

The simulator provides a continuously updated environment for our qualitative framework. The software is capable of holding an arbitrary number of vessels each tagged
with a unique identifier. The actual maximum number of vessels is only delimited
by the computation power of the computer the simulator is running on. The visual
interface is shown in Figure 6.4.

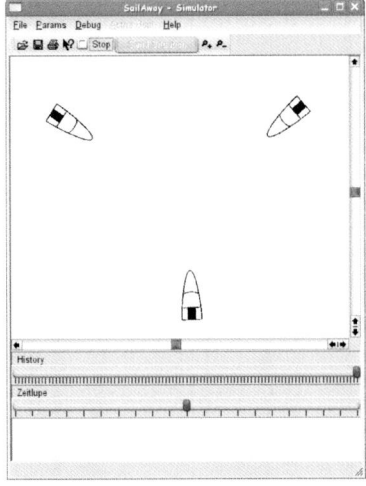

Figure 6.4: The SailAway simulator window showing a situation with three motor
vessels approaching.

Each vessel v_i moves along a circular route r^i which is defined by waypoints
$r^i = w_0^i, \ldots, w_{n_i}^i$. If the last waypoint $w_{n_i}^i$ is reached, vessel v_i heads for the first
waypoint w_0^i again. Unless no external steering command is given the vessels are
heading straight forward to the next waypoint ignoring all potential obstacles in their
way, i.e. no reactive component for collision avoidance is incorporated. The types of
available vessels corresponds to the list presented in Section 6.3. Currently, no wind
component has been implemented in the simulator. Thus, rules incorporating the direction of wind cannot be triggered.

   The vessels are moving with constant translational velocity vel_{trans} per second
($vel_{trans} > 0$) between the waypoints. Each vessel has a specific size, velocity, and
a route to follow. The unit for velocity is abstract with values around five for slow
vessels and around fifteen for fast vessels, e.g. $vel_{trans}(MV) = 15$. Currently, speed
changes are not considered. When vessels reach a waypoint they turn towards the next
waypoint with a fixed rotation speed. The rotation velocity vel_{rot} is sixty degrees per

second ($\frac{\pi}{3}[\frac{1}{s}]$).

Additionally, the vessels can be controlled by external commands. If such a command is given the vessels stop heading towards their waypoints and only act according to external commands. These steering commands have a temporary effect: the helm is put for a short period of time ($action\_time$) and afterwards the helm is put back to midships. Valid commands are keeping the helm midships (M), turning starboard (S), i.e. right, and turning port (P), i.e. left. After $action\_time$ expires the vessels move straight on until told differently. By giving a 'no process' command (NP) a vessel continues to follow its route again. According to the coarse level of actions in the $\mathcal{ACNG}$ we navigate the agents on the same coarse level. We summarize the commands:

- M: the vessel moves straight on and ignores landmarks (keep midships)

- S: the vessel turns starboard (right) with vel_{rot} for $action\_time$ and continues straight motion afterwards

- P: the vessel turns port (left) with vel_{rot} for $action\_time$ and continues straight motion afterwards

- NP: the vessel continues following its route, i.e. it heads for the next waypoint (no process)

If no distinction would be made whether vessels are in sight of each other or not, the vessels would try to avoid collisions, although they are not in any danger of a collision, because they are too far away from each other. The vessels would always have to follow some rule and would not follow their route. Thus, danger of collision is realized by a distance parameter dependent on the speed of the vessels and chosen such that there remains enough time for the vessels to apply appropriate steering commands to avoid the collision. When the distance between two vessels is smaller than this range, it needs to be evaluated whether some rule has to be applied to avoid a collision or not. For doing so, the simulator provides the metrical data of the positions and orientations of the vessels in range to the qualitative framework periodically (determined by the parameter $reasoner\_time$).

6.5 The Qualitative Framework

The qualitative framework relates the qualitative scene description and the rule representation by symbolic reasoning, i.e. neighborhood-based scene extrapolation and constraint-based reasoning, for deriving admissible actions for individual agents. Admissible actions are physically possible actions which are in compliance with the rule set.

The qualitative scene description is determined by SparQ from the metrical data provided by the simulator. The data provided consists of the center points of the vessels and a globally aligned direction vector. Transferring the description into a constraint satisfaction problem (CSP) yields a consistent constraint network with one constraining relation for each pair of vessels. For our demonstrator application we selected $\mathcal{OPRA}_m^\star$ as the qualitative calculus for abstracting from metrical details of the world. Specifically, we use $\mathcal{OPRA}_4^\star$ for our rule models as it turned out during experiments to be an adequate abstraction because it results in smooth trajectories. In contrast, models with $m = 2$ lead to square-edged behavior. Models with finer granularity, e.g. $m = 8$ generate yet smoother behavior, but are bulky due to their high number of utilized relations.

$\mathcal{OPRA}_m^\star$ is well suited for representing moving objects because of the oriented points as base entities and its variable granularity. We emphasize that $\mathcal{OPRA}_m^\star$ is not the only suitable calculus for formalizing rule systems like the collision regulations in vessel navigation. Other calculi dealing with orientation information might also be applicable, e.g. the Qualitative Trajectory Calculus (QTC). Relative orientation calculi dealing with ordinary points as basic entities are not that well suited, because the relative orientation of the moving objects must be expressed by logical interconnections.

In the first step of the symbolic reasoning process the scene description is extrapolated into the future by means of the rule formalization. The rule formalization, a subgraph of the $\mathcal{ACNG}$, delivers the result of potential actions. According to our exemplary rule where two vessels in head-on position ($_4^O\angle_0^0$) should both turn starboard, denoted by the tuple (S, S), we obtain $_4^x\angle_1^1$ with $x \in \{-, O, +\}$ depending on whether both vessels move with the same velocities or not. Doing this for all pairs of agents involved a constraint network (CN) with in most cases more than one relation per edge emerges. In the following step the extrapolated CN is checked for *scenario-consistency*, i.e. all possible atomic constraint-networks are checked for path-consistency. Each consistent atomic CN then defines potential steering commands for the vessels. If no consistent scenario can be found no global rule-compliant behavior, i.e. including all agents, is possible.

6.5.1 Logical Framework

A formalization of navigation rules relates agent types and their spatial constellations as handled by the rules. This can be compiled into a small ontology. Using a logical approach representing this information appears most adequate to provide a suitable basis for reasoning. Description logics offer a solid approach to modeling ontological information and provide also the means for formalizing spatial configurations. Agent types and configurations are represented as *concepts*, whereas spatial relations are used as *roles* to interrelate the relative positions of agents. The utilization of qualitative spatial calculi provides us with a suitable set of spatial relations that allows for linking spatial reasoning techniques to the logical framework. We employ one additional role `involves` that relates configurations to agents. For example, if we consider a configuration defined by two agents in head-on course, the role-fillers of `involves` are the specific agents in head-on course. This approach allows us to consider scene classification as ABox-reasoning in description logics: a specific configuration is realized when role fillers for `involves` can be instantiated such that the formula describing the situation is valid. In Fig. 6.5 we present an overview of the simple ontology employed in SailAway (a) and give an exemplary logical representation of the exemplary spatial configuration of agents in head-on course (b). It presents the special case of a dangerous configuration of a motor and a sport vessel in head-on collision course.

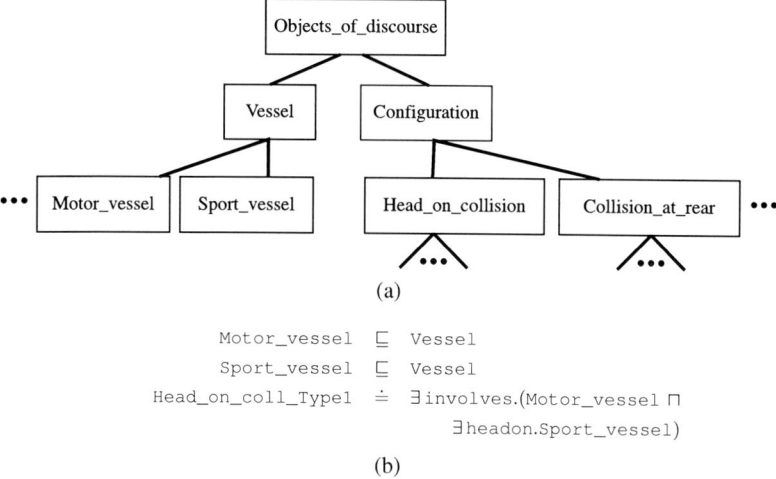

(a)

$$Motor\_vessel \sqsubseteq Vessel$$
$$Sport\_vessel \sqsubseteq Vessel$$
$$Head\_on\_coll\_Type1 \doteq \exists involves.(Motor\_vessel \sqcap$$
$$\exists headon.Sport\_vessel)$$

(b)

Figure 6.5: Overview of the ontology (a) and exemplary configuration (b).

The advantage of embedding rule formalization in a standard logic framework lies in the possibility of exploiting standard reasoning techniques. In principle, it is possible to reason about rule systems themselves (meta-level reasoning) as well as reasoning about rule-compliant actions (navigational reasoning). In any case, fundamental prerequisites are that (a) a finite set of (binary) spatial relations can describe configurations in a sufficiently precise way and that (b) the mapping from natural language to formal representations can be performed in an easy-to-use manner.

In summary, typical rule sets can be formalized using the logical framework of description logics to represent the ontology. The logical framework must incorporate a set of spatial relations that is adequate for representing the rules and for navigational reasoning. Thus, we argue for combining ontological knowledge engineering with appropriate qualitative spatial representation techniques.

6.5.2 Rule Transition Systems

Navigation rules restrict the possibilities of agents to act in space. The basic idea underlying the rule representations is to consider rule-specific *transition systems*. These transition systems can be derived from the $\mathcal{ACNG}$. In contrast to a complete $\mathcal{ACNG}$

it first contains only actions that are physically possible, i.e. executable by the agents, and second represents rule-compliant (or nearly rule-compliant) behavior of the agents. To simplify the building process of transition systems, first, a coarse model of the rule is derived (*idealized thread*). Therafter, the idealized thread is refined by means of the $\mathcal{ACNG}$ (neighborhood expansion) to determine the complete *rule transition system*.

The Idealized Thread   The starting point for defining transition systems is to identify an idealized transition sequence (the *idealized thread*), which may be considered a coarse prototypical rule-compliant plan of maneuvers from a dangerous into a safe configuration, i.e. from a start to an end configuration, containing important decision points if we observe the vessels in each point in time. Reconsider the example in Figure 6.3(a). First the vessels are head-on, then both must turn starboard. When they are not head-on anymore, they can go straight ahead (midships), and when they are just about side by side they can turn port, heading for their original course.

The rule must be triggered if two motor vessels (MV_1 and MV_2) are in head-on position, i.e. $MV_1 \; {}_4^O\!\angle_0^0 \; MV_2$ or $MV_2 \; {}_4^O\!\angle_0^0 \; MV_1$. Because of the symmetry of the two cases we restrict to the first case here. If both vessels pass each other on port side ($MV_1 \; {}_4^O\!\angle_4^4 \; MV_2$) the vessels are in a safe situation, i.e. they are in no danger of a collision anymore, and so the rule terminates.

If $MV_1 \; {}_4^O\!\angle_0^0 \; MV_2$ holds, both vessels must turn starboard. Under the assumption that both vessels travel with the same translation and rotation velocity the execution of starboard commands results in $MV_1 \; {}_4^O\!\angle_1^1 \; MV_2$. Because we defined the steering commands as safe for the purpose of the desired effect (the turn is powerful and fast enough) now both vessels can move straight on. After a while the vessels have almost passed each other ($MV_1 \; {}_4^O\!\angle_3^3 \; MV_2$) and they can start turning back towards their original course. When the vessels pass each other on port side ($MV_1 \; {}_4^O\!\angle_4^4 \; MV_2$) the rule is processed successfully and the vessels can go on to follow their route (no process). We illustrate the idealized thread in Fig. 6.6. A box defines a start configuration and a double circle a safe configuration denoting that the rule is processed and the boats are in no danger of a collision anymore.

A Complete Rule Transition System   The idealized thread is not yet a suitable formalization of rule-compliant actions, as it abstracts from alternative action effects that need to be considered: depending on the precise position of the vessels, the same action may lead to different change-overs with respect to the qualitative relations as defined by the $\mathcal{ACNG}$. In particular, we can hardly observe transitions from region to line relations as considered in $\mathcal{OPRA}_4^\star$. Additionally, as we abstract extended objects to point-like objects in our example not only linear cases, e.g. ${}_4^O\!\angle_0^0$ are interesting, but also their conceptual neighbors. Therefore, the idealized thread is extended to a transition system that also includes neighboring configurations if they are still within the scope of the traffic rule at hand. Incorporating the neighboring relations makes our formalization robust towards noise in perception and execution. For each of these

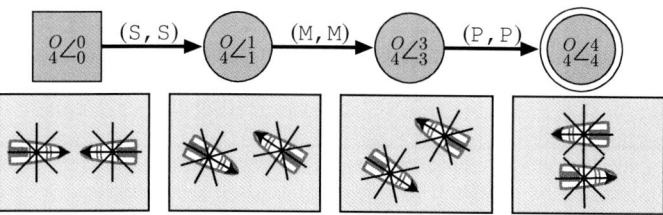

Figure 6.6: A coarse model for the rule shown in Fig. 6.3(a): If the vessels are head-on, then both must turn starboard. When they are not head-on anymore they can go straight ahead, and when they are just about side by side they can turn port, heading for their original course.

added configurations, we derive actions that lead the vessels closer to the idealized thread. Analogously, we apply this method to start and end configurations. For each rule, a specific rule transition system is derived that contains rule-compliant actions only. Transition systems may further vary if different vessel types are involved.

First, the formalization is incomplete as the relations of the idealized thread are not necessarily conceptual neighbors. For example $_4\angle_1^1$ and $_4\angle_3^3$ are not neighbors. Thus, we need to add $_4\angle_2^2$ to complete the thread.

As we consider the same type of vessel in this rule model we assume the same velocity for both in the rule transition system. But as soon as these actions are executed with different velocities or the vessels start turning at different time points, the effects of executing the actions do not necessarily lead to perceiving the relation predicted on the idealized assumption. If for example $_4\angle_3^3$ holds both vessels should turn port. Already in the case of slight differences in velocity we cannot expect the prototypical effect resulting in relation $_4\angle_4^4$, it is more likely that $_4\angle_4^{-3}$ or $_4\angle_3^{+4}$ holds. Assuming a velocity being *just about the same* for both vessels we expect the resulting perceived relation r after the vessels executed their actions (a_1, a_2) has a maximal neighboring distance of one from the prototypical result r_p, i.e. $r \in \text{cn}(r_p)$ in our model. For models concerning different types of vessels with different prototypical assumptions on velocity we need to generalize: If the velocity proportion between two vessels is just about the same as assumed in the prototypical model, $r \in \text{cn}(r_p)$ holds.

So, relations neighboring to the ones in the coarse model need also to be part of the fine-grained model. We call this method *neighborhood expansion* based on the action-augmented neighborhood graph ($\mathcal{ACNG}$). The $\mathcal{ACNG}$ contains the relation transitions corresponding to actions and their outcome. Figure 6.7 shows the fine rule model derived from the coarse model in Figure 6.6. The prototypical behavior is highlighted by the (red) shaded boxes. For each of the relations added, we derive admissible actions that lead the vessels closer to the idealized thread. Given two vessels V_1 and V_2 are in relation r_i the edge between relation r_i and r_j in the rule transition system is labeled with an action pair (a_1, a_2) with a_1 is performed by V_1 and a_2 by V_2. r_j denotes the prototypical effect of the actions executed in r_i derived from the $\mathcal{ACNG}$ of $\mathcal{OPRA}^*_m$. Unfortunately, we cannot apply the $\mathcal{ACNG}$ as derived in Section 5.1 naively. The problem is that we only derived a detailed neighborhood structure for rotation on the spot, but not a detailed structure for circular motion (cf. Sec. 5.1.7). Therefore, we approximated the effects of the vessels' actions by combinations of translation and rotatation. Currently, no automatic method is available for this process. So, the admissible actions must be selected by hand.

Rule 14 defines the rule applicable if two vessels are on "reciprocal or nearly reciprocal course". Hence, not only $_4\angle_0^0$ is a start configuration, but also all relations directly neighbored. This contains all relations $_4^x\angle_{15..1}^{15..1}$ with $x \in \{-, O, +\}^3$. Relations $_4^-\angle_1^{15}$ and $_4^-\angle_{15}^1$ represent situations where the trajectories will definitely intersect. The remaining start relations, apart from $_4^-\angle_{15}^{15}$, represent situations where a slight turning action might lead to a dangerous situation. Such additional start states may not only arise if vessels perform steering actions, but also due to certain velocity differences. The only exception is $_4^-\angle_{15}^{15}$ which represents vessels moving away from each other. It is unreasonable to follow the rule here, because the relation represents safe situations and both vessels turning starboard results in a potential collision situation. Given a potential collision both vessels must turn starboard. However, in case of $_4^O\angle_{15}^{15}$ and $_4^+\angle_{15}^{15}$ a turn to port seems more reasonable but is not in compliance with the rules. In relation $_4^-\angle_1^1$ it is still necessary to turn starboard, whereas for $_4^O\angle_1^1$ and $_4^+\angle_1^1$ it is sufficient to move straight for not being in danger of collision.

For relations $_4^O\angle_2^2$ and $_4^O\angle_3^3$ we add the neighboring relations as well. Here, the vessels should continue straight motion according to the actions in the idealized thread. Only in case of $_4^+\angle_3^3$ it is already safe for both vessels to turn port, i.e. turning towards the original course. But it is also an alternative to move straight on or even to turn starboard.

Finally, the neighboring relations for the end configuration $_4^O\angle_4^4$ are added. $_4^-\angle_4^3$ and $_4^+\angle_3^4$ are no end configurations as not both vessels have passed at each others portside. Again, the vessels may choose from the alternatives moving straight on or turning port towards the original course. Relations $_4^-\angle_5^{3..5}$, $_4^-\angle_{3..5}^5$, and $_4^O\angle_5^5$ are defined as end configurations, i.e. the rule has been successfully applied in the given start configuration. If a relation not defined within the rule model is perceived processing is also terminated, but the rule is not seen as being applied correctly, because something unexpected happened during execution, e.g. one of the agent did not act in accordance to the rules.

For keeping the fine-grained rule model clear and simple we presented a very conservative and strict variant regarding the idealized thread, i.e. only a few action alternatives are defined. We applied different models with varying number of alternatives in each relation, if in compliance with the rules. For example, in $_4^O\angle_3^3$ it is also save

---

[3]The reader might argue, that some physical situations represented by start relations, e.g. $_4^-\angle_1^{15}$ is no "nearly reciprocal" course anymore. This can be improved with finer granularity of $\mathcal{OPRA}^*_m$.

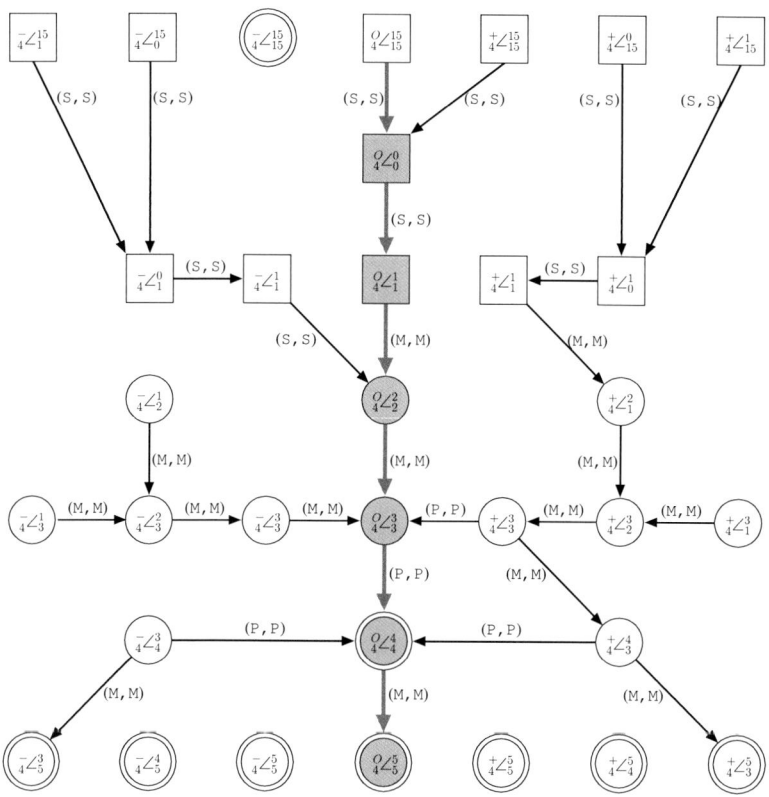

Figure 6.7: The fine model for the coarse rule model in Fig. 6.6.

if both vessels keep midships or turn starboard. We also considered rule transition systems with additional more fine-grained action alternatives. For example, in configuration $^+_4\angle^1_1$ it may be safe as well to turn "a little to port" without running into a collision.

6.5.3 (Global) Constraint-Based Rule Integration

Transition systems formalize rule-compliant actions for pairs of agents and hence allow a pair of agents to avoid collisions by performing the actions linked to their current relation. But this procedure may not suffice in situations involving *more than two vessels* governed by multiple rules. Therefore, we apply constraint-based reasoning methods to check whether actions according to the two-vessel transition systems are compatible from a global point of view as well. Additionally, constraint-based reasoning enables us to select a globally admissible action when a transition system allows alternative actions.

By checking for compatibility we can consistently integrate rules that pose constraints on the configuration of objects. Given qualitative rule representations that locally constrain the configurations of objects, then a configuration is globally consistent with respect to the rules if the combined constraint network is satisfiable. CSP-based qualitative reasoning offers a sound reasoning method for testing compatibility of configuration descriptions. For this, we generate a constraint network (CN) that encodes all spatial relations between vessel positions that may result from admissible actions applied to the current configuration. Afterwards, we check the CN for consistent scenarios, i.e. only atomic relations are assigned to the constraints between pairs of vessels, in order to deduce a single admissible action to execute.

Example 1: Consistent In Fig. 6.8 we depict an example with three motor vessels (A, B, and C). In the remainder of this thesis we abandon the vector notation and write O instead $\vec{O}$, because we only deal with o-points and no normal points anymore. The relations of the qualitative scene description are: $A\ ^+_4\angle^1_{15}\ B$, $B\ ^+_4\angle^1_{15}\ C$, and $A\ ^+_4\angle^{15}_3\ C$. The pair (A, B) and the pair (B, C) are in a head-on situation and so, both vessels should turn starboard. In contrast, A and C are in a crossing situation with C perceives A on its starboard side, and so C must turn starboard and A must keep its course (Rule 15 of ColRegs).

In Fig. 6.9(a) we depict the current scene description in terms of a constraint network and the extrapolated network regarding the transition systems. The objects in the current scene are depicted by A, B, and C, the objects of the extrapolated scene are denoted by A^+, B^+, and C^+. If possible, a solution of the extrapolated constraint network is computed, identifying globally consistent spatial relations among the agents. In other words, if a solution exists, the individual rules for pairs of objects are compatible. The result is then repropagated to determine the suitable actions for the individual vessels that will lead to this particular constellation. In Fig. 6.9(b) we depict one possible solution of our scenario. The resulting trajectories are illustrated in Fig. 6.10. This

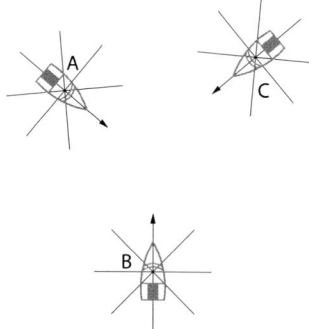

Figure 6.8: A situation with three motor vessels: $A \ {}_4^+\angle_{15}^1 \ B$, $B \ {}_4^+\angle_{15}^1 \ C$, and $A \ {}_4^+\angle_3^{15} \ C$.

process ensures that the selected actions are admissible with respect to the individual rules (by construction of the constraint network) and with respect to the global scene (by global constraint satisfaction).

Example 2: Inconsistent   In Fig. 6.11 we depict a second example with two motor vessels and one sport vessel. In relation to motor vessels sport vessels are always stand-on vessels an thus, must keep their course. Reciprocally, the motor vessels have to give way, and thus, they must pass behind the sport vessel. If two motor vessels meet in a crossing situation, the vessel which has the other on her own starboard must keep clear (ColRegs Rule 15). These rules are not compatible, as on the one hand, motor vessel C must turn starboard regarding A and on the other hand she must turn port regarding B. So, this example yields an inconsistent extrapolated constraint network. In Fig. 6.12(a) we depict the current scene description in terms of a constraint network and in Fig. 6.12(b) the result as derived by SparQ.

6.6   Discussion

We investigated the applicability of qualitative reasoning techniques to a real-world application scenario. Our investigation confirmed previous research in that qualitative representations enable mediation between real-world metric information and conceptual knowledge as used in communication. It provides effective means to compile rules into formal representations. On the basis of a qualitative abstraction, symbolic reasoning is applicable. It turned out that we need to combine different reasoning techniques to obtain an effective approach. Constraint-based reasoning appears valuable to

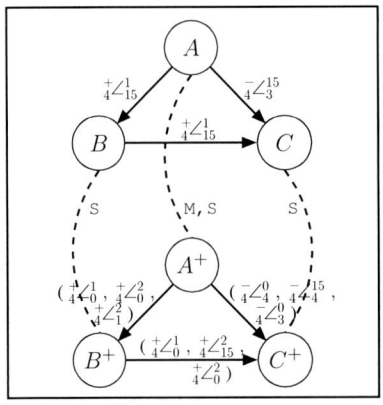

(a) Deriving a CSP network by the rule models (A^+, B^+, and C^+) from the original configuration (A, B, and C)

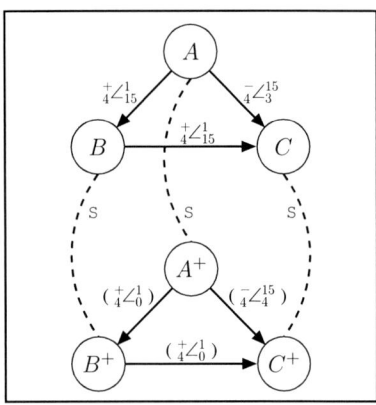

(b) Consistent scenario deduced from (a)

Figure 6.9: Reasoning with CSPs for rule-compliant actions of vessels A, B, and C.

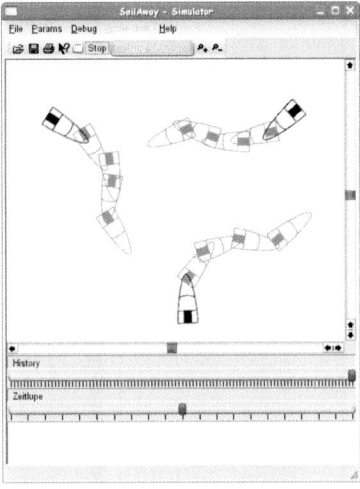

Figure 6.10: The resulting trajectories for three motor vessels (cf. Fig. 6.9)

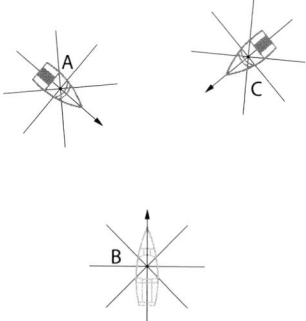

Figure 6.11: An exemplary configuration of three vessels: $A \, {}^{+}_{4}\angle^{1}_{15} \, B$, $B \, {}^{+}_{4}\angle^{1}_{15} \, C$, and $A \, {}^{+}_{4}\angle^{15}_{3} \, C$.

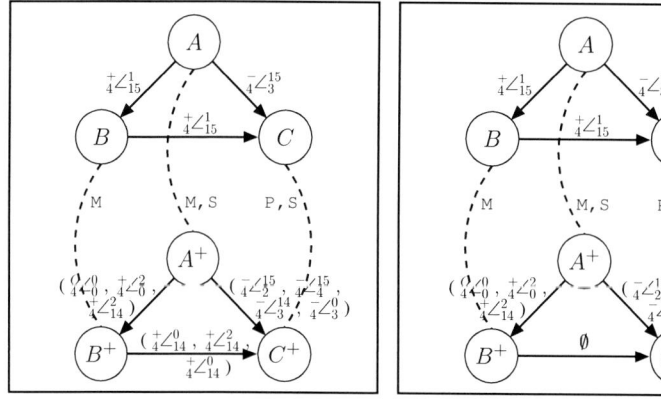

(a) CSP network derived by rule transition systems.   (b) The network is inconsistent.

Figure 6.12: Reasoning with CSPs for rule-compliant actions of vessels A, B, and C. Because the constraint network, derived by means of the rule transition systems, is inconsistent, no global admissible actions exist.

integrate local knowledge to survey knowledge, whereas a causal view on conceptual neighborhood allows us to handle prototypical information, in the given case information about motion based on a set of coarse action primitives. Most notably, a qualitative representation provides a single substrate in terms of syntax, semantics, and reasoning methods that allows for a tight integration of all components in an agent control application.

With our experimental application *SailAway* we demonstrated that a combination of purely qualitative methods and a set of coarse actions are a sufficient and an effective model of collision regulations in vessel navigation. So, rule transition systems based on action-augmented conceptual neighborhood are a reasonable formalization of natural language regulations similar to our domain. In empirical validation we observe that all vessels move according to the rules whenever globally compliant actions exist. By choosing a scenario-consistent network, the actions that lead to this particular scenario are the admissible actions for the individual agents. Furthermore, globally inconsistent configurations are detected. In such situations an agent has no admissible action it can choose (cf. Example 2).

With the *SailAway* demonstrator we have shown that a qualitative framework is applicable in the context of agent control. Furthermore, we found configurations where rules are not compatible from a global perspective. This is a part of rule set evaluation, with the result that in some more complex configurations local rules cannot be applied naively. Other strategies as ignoring one or more rules, or hierarchization, e.g. based on speed or distance, must be applied to resolve such conflicts. So far, we have not applied the qualitative framework to judge agent behavior with respect to the rule set given. The problem lies in the evaluation of the behavior of the other objects with respect to the own behavior within a coarse representation of relative orientation.

In the remainder of this section we discuss some of our experiences with *SailAway* in more detail. We will consider why collisions still occur in some situations, and consider different granularities of $\mathcal{OPRA}_m$. Furthermore, we elaborate on our decisions to select specific parameter values.

6.6.1 Collisions

The qualitative modeling based on $\mathcal{OPRA}_4$ has proofed reasonable in the experiments. However, since we abstract from distance information beyond pure detection of proximity, underlying motion primitives would be required to consider distances in real-world application such that stronger rudder movements are used in the immediate proximity of other vessels. Then, proximity must be evaluated with respect to distance and speed of the agents involved. Since we have only realized non-adaptive action primitives, in rare cases our application may not be able to prevent collisions, if due to a maneuver a new vessel comes into immediate proximity. In these cases the coarse non-adaptive actions are not necessarily safe for the purpose of the desired effect anymore. Additional collisions may occur by reason of dealing with point abstractions of physically extended objects. For example, assume that two vessels are in relation

${}_4^-\angle_{15}^{15}$, but that they are physically "close" to ${}_4^O\angle_0^0$. We depict such a situation in Fig. 6.13(a). Under the premise of determining the relative orientation on the basis of the center point of the vessels and acting according to the rules we were not able to sort out these cases with the given granularity. If we allow both vessels to turn port against the rules the problem can be solved. We did not investigate how this exception affects the global context. Another approach to improve collision behavior is to model the local environment with additional points representing the extensions of the objects if they are in immediate proximity. One option would be to utilize points on the vessels' boundaries to the sides to resolve such situations. In Fig. 6.13(b) we illustrate what this might look like.

Overall, we can conclude that agents in the environment show behavior according to the rules, although, the agents in *SailAway* do not behave completely collision-free. In the following, we will discuss on implications of parameter values and dependencies between them.

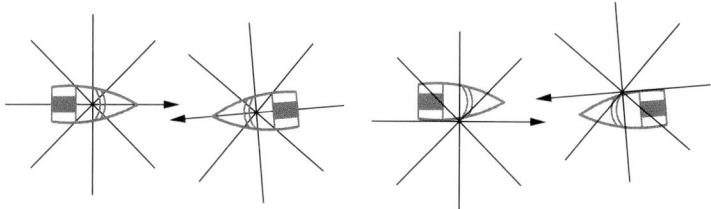

(a) Relation determined with center points: (b) Relation determined with boundary points:
${}_4^-\angle_{15}^{15}$ ${}_4^-\angle_1^1$

Figure 6.13: Two vessels on collision course if both vessels move straight on.

6.6.2   Different Granularities

In addition, we experimented with different granularities. It turned out that smoother behavior can be modelled with finer granularities. For example with $m = 2$ the front-left of the agent can only be seen as a whole, i.e. is represented by a single base relation, resulting in wide evasion behavior in some cases. With $m = 4$ two different planar regions (and one linear region), and with $m = 8$ four different planar regions (and three linear regions) can be differentiated such that finer distinctions in control commands can be made. This results in smoother behavior, and in more efficient behavior due to less rotation. For example, if two vessels are in relation ${}_4^+\angle_3^3$ it is already safe turning towards the actual waypoint (cf. transition system in Fig. 6.7). In contrast, in $m = 2$ this is subsumed by ${}_2^+\angle_1^1$ containing situations where this behavior is not safe.

Taking a closer look at the ColRegs we find evidence that granularity $m = 8$ (or a multiple) is a reasonable choice. For example, Rule 13 states: *A vessel shall be deemed to be overtaking when coming up with another vessel from a direction more than 22.5 degrees abaft her beam, that is, in such a position with reference to the vessel she is overtaking, that at night she would be able to see only the sternlight of that vessel but neither of her sidelights.* Furthermore, the position lights of vessels are visible to other vessels in distinct angular ranges (cf. IMO, 1972, Part C - Rule 21 and Annex I). The red port light of a vessel $\vec{A}$ is visible to a vessel $\vec{B}$ between zero degrees and 112.5 degrees ($\vec{A}\ {}^{x}_{8}\angle^{j}_{1..10}\ \vec{B}$). The green starboard light is visible between 247.5 degrees and 360 degrees ($\vec{A}\ {}^{x}_{8}\angle^{j}_{22..31}\ \vec{B}$). The stern light is visible in the range of 135 degrees ($112.5° - 247.5°$) regarding the back of a vessel ($\vec{A}\ {}^{x}_{8}\angle^{j}_{11..21}\ \vec{B}$).

Unfortunately, at the moment we must derive the rule transition models by hand, which is a task with growing complexity regarding the granularity of the calculus. So, $m = 4$ turned out to be a good compromise between smooth behavior and complexity of model building.

6.6.3 Improvement of Parameter Settings

In general, the question of granularity or resolution of an underlying representation must be considered with respect to other system parameters.

We consider system settings improvable, if the neighborhood distance[4] between two successive perceptions of single relations (r_i, r_{i+1}) is (in general) too large, i.e. $d_b(r_i, r_{i+1}) > N$ where N is a task-specific value. For example, if $d_b(r_i, r_{i+1}) = 2m$ with $r_i, r_{i+1} \in \mathcal{OPRA}^*_m$ we cannot determine at which side the objects passed each other (behavior judgement). With at least one perception in between and the assumption of straight motion we could clarify this question. This is like closing the eyes between two perceptions. So, the interval between two perceptions can be considered too long. Regarding perception of artificial agents, the minimal duration of a perception cycle and the maximum resolution are restricted by the hardware.

Considering the question for an adequate granularity in the context of agent control yields additional aspects. In the transition systems we encoded the prototypical result of actions for all situations subsumed by the relations given. If the agents now pass through a number of relations until the next perception is made, the action chosen in the original configuration might not be adequate for relations in between. So, the resolution chosen for representation is too fine, because "too much happens" between two perceptions. The result of these considerations, i.e. the resolution chosen, only holds for objects within a certain distance range, because close objects traverse an angular sector faster than a distant object with the same speed. From this follows that assuming different distance classes the associated rule transition systems must be customized, e.g. by choosing different granularities or different action primitives.

Several reasons can be given if no change occurs regarding a qualitative representation, i.e. $d_b(r_i, r_{i+1}) = 0$. First, really nothing happens in the environment (stable

---

[4]Neighborhood distance between two relations r_i and r_j is defined by $d_b(r_i, r_j)$ (cf. Section 5.2.2).

environment); second, nothing happens in a specific spatial aspect, e.g. when dealing with orientation, one object is moving straight away from the other one, maintaining the orientation with respect to that object; and third, the reasoning cycle might be chosen too short regarding granularity. If perceptions take place every few milliseconds for an angular resolution of ninety degrees, it is most unlikely that change occurs for two randomly chosen successive perceptions. Vice versa, the granularity might be too coarse regarding a fixed perception cycle. Because $\mathcal{OPRA}_m^{\star}$ contains linear regions between planar regions we adjusted our parameters that in general $d_b(r_i, r_{i+1}) \leq 2$ holds for successive perceptions.

6.6.4 Asymmetry in Perception and Reasoning Cycle

In the context of agent control the qualitative rule representation must be considered in combination with the actions executed. If two objects rotate (in the same direction) with equivalent angular speed around a center point the relative orientation between both objects does not change (e.g. cf. "circular trajectories" in van de Weghe, 2004). Consider two motor vessels in relation $_4\angle_3^3$ with just about the same speed. According to the rule representation both vessels turn port. Considering the argument above, the relation between both vessels may not change and so the commands to turn port are given again. This may result in a circular movement of both vessels for a while. Hence, we choose different values for $action\_time$ (the duration of actions) and $reasoner\_time$ (the period until a new action is derived) with the characteristic $action\_time < reasoner\_time^5$. Given according turning commands for two vessels with such a parameter setting the vessels move straight on for $(reasoner\_time - action\_time)$ after the rotation is performed. Due to this asymmetry we did not observe circular motion behavior as described above.

6.6.5 Outlook

Currently, we only make use of comparatively simple reasoning techniques as we only aim at determining *some* action that is both locally and globally compliant with the rules. However, situations involving multiple vessels can arise where no globally admissible actions exist. In future work we aim at introducing a planning component that can look ahead and thus allows avoiding deadlocks.

Furthermore, since we are interested in cognitive agents, we will modify our approach such that representation and reasoning processes occur at the level of the individual agents with partial knowledge, rather than at the level of a control system with a bird's eye view.

Currently, no automatic methods are known for dissolving situations with no admissible actions. Neighborhood relaxation as used for dealing with inconsistent world models (cf. Sec. 5.2) seems a worthwhile starting point for the development of such an

---

[5]The actual values chosen are $action\_time = 500ms$ and $reasoner\_time = 750ms$.

automatic method. With an adequate distance function minimal consistent networks can be determined. The result may provide information about how agents should behave, violating a minimal number of rules, or how the coarse action prototypes should be adapted. Another approach may be based on the hierarchization of the rules regarding the types of vessels or the distance between the vessels.

Chapter 7

Conclusion

In this chapter we summarize the results and contributions of this dissertation. Furthermore, we relate these results to possible future research directions.

7.1 Results

In recent years more and more agent systems have found their way into everyday life. They help people in diverse tasks such as driver assistance or housekeeping. This requires interaction and communication with humans or other agents. In interacting with people, certain regulations for interaction must be kept, for example, right-of-way rules in traffic scenarios. Agents must be aware of such rules and additionally, must be able to process the rules appropriately. These rules have in common that they are usually formulated in natural language and, thus, make extensive use of qualitative terms for describing the situations governed, and also for properties of the agents involved.

In this thesis we have considered the question whether qualitative spatial representations and reasoning techniques are suitable for agent navigation and whether explicit metric knowledge is necessary for this task. The problem needs to be considered from two sides. First, we need to contemplate what is an adequate representation regarding agent navigation purposes and how we can reason with this representation. And second, we need to determine what actions an agent must perform to keep conditions given by a set of regulations.

As example scenario in this thesis we have chosen the domain of right-of-way rules of vessel navigation. We have shown that qualitative knowledge about relative orientation is sufficient for dealing with this task. A great variety of relative orientation representations are known that can serve as a means for rule formalization. It is a crucial task to select an adequate calculus for the task at hand. For agent developers not familiar with qualitative spatial calculi the task is challenging and laborious, especially if several calculi must be tested. Therefore, we developed an *umbrella calculus* $\mathcal{OPRA}_m^\star$ on the basis of $\mathcal{OPRA}_m$, that comprises a great number of specialized orientation calculi is desirable.

We have shown that $\mathcal{OPRA}_m$, a calculus based on oriented points (o-points), provides an adequate basis. We have derived mappings from specialized calculi, such as the FlipFlop Calculus, the Double Cross Calculus, and the Qualitative Trajectory Calculus (QTC), to sets of $\mathcal{OPRA}_m$ relations. We have applied these mappings to three different tasks:

- as mediator between different calculi
- for derivation of composition tables
- for derivation of conceptual neighborhood structures

We have shown that composition of $\mathcal{OPRA}_m$ relations is not closed under constraints, and thus, scenario-consistency is only an approximation for global consistency. By post-processing a scenario-consistent network with the constructive operations *orientation rotation* and *projection*, we can find inconsistencies in configurations with four o-points that are considered scenario-consistent. Furthermore, we have found inconsistent configurations with more than four o-points that are scenario-consistent. Whether inconsistent configurations with an arbitrary number of points can be detected remains an open question. With the proposed methods (constraint-based reasoning combined with constructive operations) we are able to derive composition tables and neighborhood structures of several calculi that are presented in the literature, namely the FlipFlop Calculus, the Single Cross Calculus, the Double Cross Calculus, the QTC, and the $\mathcal{DRA}_f$. Whether this works for relative orientation representations in general, remains an open question. So far, verification of the results regarding the calculi named above indicates that this is the case for any qualitative orientation calculus. Nevertheless, developers who need to define a new orientation calculus for their purposes do not necessarily need to derive composition and neighborhood structures from scratch. Instead, they can derive prototypes of composition and neighborhood structures by means of a mapping to a set of $\mathcal{OPRA}_m$ relations.

Relative orientation information is fundamental regarding agent navigation tasks. Although in many situations it is necessary to know whether two agents move in parallel, move away from each other, or move towards each other to navigate agents reasonably, e.g. for preventing collisions, current relative orientation calculi are not capable of representing this kind of knowledge, called *alignment knowledge*, in an adequate manner. To meet these concerns we have defined the *Alignment Calculus* (*$\mathcal{AC}$*) and have derived the composition operation, the converse operation, and the neighborhood structure. Because $\mathcal{OPRA}_m$ already comprises a great number of other orientation calculi, we have chosen to refine this calculus with alignment knowledge. Out of the $(4m)^2 + 4m$ $\mathcal{OPRA}_m$ relations for a specific granularity only the alignment of $4m$ relations is ambiguous. Each of these relations refines to three new relations with different alignment. So, the overall number of $\mathcal{OPRA}_m^\star$ relations for a specific granularity m is $(4m)^2 + (3 * 4m)$. Because naive composition based on the individual composition tables is not optimal, we investigated the geometric constraints of $\mathcal{OPRA}_m^\star$ relations and represented them as linear inequalities. By solving these linear inequalities using Fourier-Motzkin elimination, we are able to eliminate infeasible relations from the composition solutions. Additionally, we have derived the neighborhood structure of $\mathcal{OPRA}_m^\star$ systematically by considering neighborhood changes of the compound calculus based on the individual components.

We propose $\mathcal{OPRA}_m^\star$ as umbrella calculus for relative orientation, because it is the most expressive and powerful calculus currently available for representing and reasoning with relative orientation and moving objects. Additionally, $\mathcal{OPRA}_m^\star$ is capable to serve as a mediator between several other specialized orientation calculi. Thus, at present $\mathcal{OPRA}_m^\star$ is the best choice to formalize domains which rely on orientation knowledge.

Conceptual neighborhood is a means for describing possible changes of spatial relations over time, i.e. it provides a dynamic view on a static representation. Unfortunately, conceptual neighborhood only gives an undifferentiated view on spatial change, not specifying what physical action causes a specific change. Taking into account properties and capabilities of the agents and objects involved, many of the transitions are unlikely to occur or even impossible. For example, if a robot is able to move forward but not backward, a transition from r to r' is possible, but not directly from r' to r because the robot would need to turn first. Thus, conceptual neighborhood in its original definition is not sufficient from an agent control perspective. We have proposed the extended concept of *action-augmented conceptual neighborhood* considering application-specific properties and capabilities of the objects involved. Until now, we have taken into account three different aspects regarding robot navigation:

- motion capabilities of the objects involved,
- whether simultaneous motion of objects is possible, and
- whether objects may coincide in position.

Considering these aspects together with basic motion concepts, for example, rotation or straight translation, we are able to determine potential future configurations of moving agents much more precisely. The action-augmented conceptual neighborhood graph ($\mathcal{ACNG}$) is better suited for generating agent behavior than the original and undifferentiated neighborhood structure.

The question whether two moving objects will collide cannot be answered sufficiently by only considering $\mathcal{OPRA}_m^\star$ and its augmented neighborhood structure. Naively, we also need distance and velocity information to answer this kind of question. Constant bearing is a method known to seamen for ages to approximate potential collisions without knowing distance or speed. If two moving objects are heading towards each other and if the relative angle between them remains constant, a potential collision situation is given. In terms of qualitative representations of relative orientation, two moving objects are in danger of collision if the orientation relation between them remains the same for successive perceptions. We demonstrated that if a collision situation is detected the $\mathcal{ACNG}$ provides reasonable actions for preventing a collision.

Overall, we have shown that orientation knowledge is sufficient to represent collision avoidance regulations.

If the spatial part of a robot's world model is represented qualitatively, we need to consider perception errors, for example, due to imprecise sensors or sensor failure. Errors may also arise if several robots share their qualitative world model. Such mistakes might lead to inconsistencies in the world model, and thus, the qualitative world model is infeasible for deriving additional knowledge by constraint reasoning. We have defined three neighborhood-based distance functions, so that consistent representations can be deduced from an inconsistent network by *constraint network relaxation*. These distance functions between two constraint networks are based on:

- the number of constraints that differ in the constraint networks,

- the maximum distance between corresponding constraints, and

- the overall sum of distances between corresponding constraints.

In some cases it is reasonable to combine these distance functions. The minimal consistent relaxation of a network is not necessarily unique, because several networks with the same number of relaxation steps might be consistent. Additionally, a minimal consistent relaxation may not correspond to the real world situation. If a small sensor error is assumed, the number of differing constraints is a good choice for detecting the inconsistency. But if a complete sensor failure, e.g. an arbitrary value, is given, a consistent network might be regarded minimal which is not compliant with the situation in the world. To find these kinds of errors the maximum distance between constraints seems to be the better choice.

Finally, we have demonstrated the applicability of qualitative reasoning techniques for agent control in the domain of collision regulations in vessel navigation. In our implementation *SailAway* we have illustrated that these techniques provide effective means for agent control. The underlying representation $\mathcal{OPRA}_m^\star$ supplies a single means for syntax, semantics, and reasoning to link between different components in our application. For effectively controlling agents in a rule-compliant manner we need to combine different reasoning techniques. On the one hand, constraint-based reasoning is valuable for integrating local knowledge into survey knowledge. On the other hand, the action-augmented view on conceptual neighborhood facilitates dealing with prototypical effects of coarse action primitives. We have formalized the restrictions implied by the collision regulations in so-called *rule transition systems*. We have derived these transition systems in a stepwise manner. In the first step an idealized transition sequence is modeled (*idealized thread*), which is expanded in a second step by means of the action-augmented neighborhood. If complex situations with more than two vessels are given, we integrate the admissible actions for each pair of vessels, defined by the rule transition systems, in a global constraint network. If a consistent scenario exists, globally admissible actions are available. If no consistent scenario is given, at least one rule for a pair of vessels must be violated to prevent a collision. Empirical evaluation has revealed that vessels navigate in accordance to the rules, if a globally consistent scenario is available. In addition to the $\mathcal{OPRA}_m^\star$ formalizations, $\mathcal{OPRA}_m$ formalizations have been derived and tested. The $\mathcal{OPRA}_m^\star$ variant is evaluated superior, because less collisions of vessels have been observed in SailAway. With $\mathcal{OPRA}_m^\star$ relations situations are much better differentiated regarding whether rules should be applied and which actions should be executed. Collisions may still occur, because we operate on a point-based abstractions of spatially extended objects. Granularity level 4 turned out to be a good compromise between smooth vessel behavior and complexity of model building.

In this thesis we have shown how representations and reasoning techniques from QSR can be applied to generate actions for controlling agents. We have shown that no explicit metric knowledge is necessary. Currently, the tendency integrating qualitative techniques in robot systems predominates. With this work, we pave the way for a general utilization of QSR methods for agent control, even for developers unfamiliar with the QSR domain.

7.2 Future Work

Based on the work presented there are several possible directions for future work.

Regarding the composition algorithm for $\mathcal{OPRA}_m$ relations, further investigations are useful. By constructing all valid triangle configurations covered by the two relations that are to be composed, completeness of the algorithm can be regarded as given, although it is not proven formally. Whether the algorithm can also be proven to be sound is an interesting question. Whether inconsistent configurations can be detected by constraint-based reasoning and the constructive operations 'rotation' and 'projection' regarding an arbitrary number of points must be examined in further detail. In conjunction, it would be possible to clarify the question whether a mapping of an arbitrary orientation calculus to a set of $\mathcal{OPRA}_m$ relations can be utilized in general to determine composition. We have shown that the construction of all potential o-points in a configuration is not necessary in all cases. The method proposed does not distinguish these cases and all $O(n^2)$ o-points are generated. Empirical observation suggests that in general only three additional o-points need to be generated for some specific four-point configurations to detect an inconsistency. In contrast, in the naive case 24 o-points must be generated. We are confident that we are able to decrease the run-time properties of the algorithm.

We have determined the number of neighborhood relations regarding $\mathcal{OPRA}_m^\star$ relations. For the case of non-'same' relations being neighbored to 'same' relations further investigation is necessary. First considerations revealed that a general formula for calculating these relations for arbitrary m is not easy to determine. Problems arise in case of odd granularities, e.g. $m = 5$, because no perpendicular to the reference direction is defined.

Sometimes objects in the world do not have an intrinsic front and do not move. Regarding $\mathcal{OPRA}_m$ or $\mathcal{OPRA}_m^\star$ some orientation must be assigned to these objects, because o-points have an orientation by definition. Currently, we need to deal with "assigning some direction that is not further specified". Integrating ordinary points as primitives in $\mathcal{OPRA}_m$ is desirable from an application perspective. The integration is not trivial. From a reasoning perspective it is necessary to provide a unique identity relation, which is somehow counter-intuitive regarding two different spatial primitives. Otherwise, some impractical reasoning properties may arise.

In this thesis we considered the derivation of undifferentiated neighborhood structures for an orientation calculus based on mappings to $\mathcal{OPRA}_m$ relations. The next interesting step to be examined is the derivation of action-augmented neighborhoods. Problems arise with respect to the action primitives if complex objects need to be represented by at least two $\mathcal{OPRA}_m$ relations, e.g. in the case of a Dipole Relation Algebra with a dipole representing a single object. Additionally, problems arise if ordinary points are contained in the calculus. To allow for this, we need to incorporate auxiliary orientations that are not trivial to choose.

Considering relaxation of inconsistent qualitative world models the action-augmented neighborhood structure may be utilized. It is an interesting question whether a weighted neighborhood distance function based on the actions necessary to gain a change between neighbored relations is able to improve the relaxation results. In this context we should also analyze what kind of errors arise assuming qualitative sensors, and how they compare to errors in quantitative sensor systems.

Regarding the application of QSR techniques for agent control a multitude of further investigations are worth taking into account. The next reasonable step in our current SailAway implementation is the integration of *wind* and its implications on the formalizations due to additional navigation constraints regarding sailing vessels. Considering the representation layer, experiments with formalizations based on orientation calculi other than $\mathcal{OPRA}_m$ or $\mathcal{OPRA}_m^{\star}$, or formalizations based on finer granularities are possible. Also finer distinctions regarding the available action primitives, e.g. a variety of turning commands with different angular velocity, or the incorporation of speed changes in the rule formalizations is interesting.

If no consistent scenario for a configuration is available, no actions can be inferred to navigate the agents in accordance to the rules. We see three possible approaches to overcome this problem: (a) a variant of minimal constraint network relaxation, (b) the hierarchization of parameters and objects, e.g. objects nearby are preferred to objects further away, or (c) a refinement of granularity, i.e. formalizations with increasing granularity must be available.

Furthermore, SailAway derives actions from a bird's eye perspective. In general, this perspective is not available and each agent must make decisions based on its individual world model. Experiments with individual agents will reveal additional problems and questions. Within this context an integration of our results in GOLOG, a logic-based high-level agent control language based on the Situation Calculus, is worthwhile. In the end, the transfer from simulation to real robot systems is a challenging task to be addressed in future work.

Appendix A

Collision Regulations by the International Maritime Organization

We present parts of the international regulations for preventing collisions at sea (Col-Regs) of the International Maritime Organization here (IMO, 1972). We give these rules here to give an impression of the natural language formalization of such rules. For inland waters some additional types of vessels and thus, some additional rules are defined. We present these in the second part, where we introduce avoidance patterns for pairs of vessels as given in textbooks on piloting vessels.

A.1 The Collision Regulations (ColRegs)

The basic version of the current Collision Regulations was released in 1972 to replace the regulations from 1960. Since then several slight enhancements and modifications were made. The ColRegs in its current version consist of five main parts and four annexes.

- Part A (Rules 1-3): General Rules for responsibilities of people, scope, and definitions

- Part B (Rules 4-19): Steering and Sailing

  - Section I (Rules 4-10): Conduct of vessels in any condition of visibility
  - Section II (Rules 11-18): Conduct of Vessels in Sight of One Another
  - Section III (Rule 19): Conduct of vessels in restricted visibility

- Part C (Rules 20-31): Light and Shapes

- Part D (Rules 32-37): Sound and Light Signals

- Part E (Rule 38): Technical exemptions for vessels built before 1972

- Annexes I-IV: Technical details, e.g. on lights, shapes, and signals

In Part A it is defined to which people and vessels the rules apply to and which responsibilities these people carry. In this part several types of vessels are distinguished: power driven vessels, sailing vessels, vessels powered by muscular strength, and vessels with restricted maneuverability. Additionally, for inshore waters another type, sport vessels larger than 20 meters, is distinguished. In Part B it is defined how different types of vessels have to behave under different conditions of visibility. Part C deals with lights which have to be shown under certain conditions and their visibility ranges. Part D defines which sound and light signals have to be carried by different types of vessels, and under which conditions they have to be used, e.g. to attract attention. Part E gives exceptions for older vessels such that they do not need to be compliant with all requirements as defined in the version of 1972. The Annexes deal with technical details of e.g. lights, shapes, and sound signals.

As we are only concerned with vessels in sight of one another in our example domain, we give a resume of the important parts of Part B Section I, and reproduce Section II. For the complete regulations we refer to the IMO website: `http://www. imo.org/Conventions/contents.asp?doc_id=649&topic_id=257`

Section II, Part A – Conduct of vessels in any condition of visibility

In the Rules 4 to 10 some general behavior on water is defined. For preventing collisions it is necessary to *maintain a proper look-out* (by sight and all available means) so to be able to appraise the situation and risk of collision. Under all circumstances vessels must be operated under *safe speed* and actions for preventing collisions should be taken as early as possible.

The rest of the rules deal with behavior of vessels in narrow channels, in or near traffic separation schemes, and in traffic lanes. For example, traffic lanes should be crossed perpendicular to flow of traffic if possible.

Section II, Part B – Conduct of Vessels in Sight of One Another

We now give a short list of the contents of Rules 11 to 18 as presented by the International Maritime Organisation.

Rule 11 – Application   Rules in Part B apply to vessels in sight of one another.

Rule 12 – Sailing Vessels

(a) When two sailing vessels are approaching one another, so as to involve risk of collision, one of them shall keep out of the way of the other as follows:

    (i)   when each has the wind on a different side, the vessel which has the wind on the port side shall keep out of the way of the other,

   (ii)   when both have the wind on the same side, the vessel which is to windward shall keep out of the way of the vessel which is to leeward,

  (iii)   if a vessel with the wind on the port side sees a vessel to windward and cannot determine with certainty whether the other vessel has the wind on the port or on the starboard side, she shall keep out of the way of the other.

(b) For the purposes of this Rule the windward side shall be deemed to be the side opposite to that on which the mainsail is carried or, in the case of a square-rigged vessel, the side opposite to that on which the largest fore-and-aft sail is carried.

Rule 13 – Overtaking–International

(a) Notwithstanding anything contained in the Rules of Part B, Sections I and II, any vessel overtaking any other vessel shall keep out of the way of the vessel being overtaken.

(b) A vessel shall be deemed to be overtaking when coming up with another vessel from a direction more than 22.5 degrees abaft her beam, that is, in such a position with reference to the vessel she is overtaking, that at night she would be able to see only the sternlight of that vessel but neither of her sidelights.

(c) When a vessel is in any doubt as to whether she is overtaking another, she shall assume that this is the case and act accordingly.

(d) Any subsequent alteration of the bearing between the two vessels shall not make the overtaking vessel a crossing vessel within the meaning of these Rules or relieve her of the duty of keeping clear of the overtaken vessel until she is finally past and clear.

Rule 14 – Head-on Situation

(a) When two power-driven vessels are meeting on reciprocal or nearly reciprocal courses so as to involve risk of collision each shall alter her course to starboard so that each shall pass on the port side of the other.

(b) Such a situation shall be deemed to exist when a vessel sees the other ahead or nearly ahead and by night she could see the masthead lights of the other in a line or nearly in a line and/or both sidelights and by day she observes the corresponding aspect of the other vessel.

(c) When a vessel is in any doubt as to whether such a situation exists she shall assume that it does exist and act accordingly.

Rule 15 – Crossing Situation–International   When two power-driven vessels are crossing so as to involve risk of collision, the vessel which has the other on her own starboard side shall keep out of the way and shall, if the circumstances of the case admit, avoid crossing ahead of the other vessel.

Rule 16 – Action by Give-way Vessel   Every vessel which is directed to keep out of the way of another vessel shall, so far as possible, take early and substantial action to keep well clear.

Rule 17 – Action by Stand-on Vessel

(a)   (i) Where one of two vessels is to keep out of the way the other shall keep her course and speed.

    (ii) The latter vessel may however take action to avoid collision by her maneuver alone, as soon as it becomes apparent to her that the vessel required to keep out of the way is not taking appropriate action in compliance with these Rules.

(b) When, from any cause, the vessel required to keep her course and speed finds herself so close that collision cannot be avoided by the action of the give-way vessel alone, she shall take such action as will best aid to avoid collision.

(c) A power-driven vessel which takes action in a crossing situation in accordance with subparagraph (a)(ii) of this Rule to avoid collision with another power-driven vessel shall, if the circumstances of the case admit, not alter course to port for a vessel on her own port side.

(d) This Rule does not relieve the give-way vessel of her obligation to keep out of the way.

Rule 18 – Responsibilities between Vessels
Except where Rules 9, 10 and 13 otherwise require:

(a) A power-driven vessel underway shall keep out of the way of:

    (i) a vessel not under command,

    (ii) a vessel restricted in her ability to maneuver,

    (iii) a vessel engaged in fishing,

    (iv) a sailing vessel.

(b) A sailing vessel underway shall keep out of the way of:

    (i) a vessel not under command,

    (ii) a vessel restricted in her ability to maneuver,

    (iii) a vessel engaged in fishing.

(c) A vessel engaged in fishing when underway shall, so far as possible, keep out of the way of:

    (i) a vessel not under command,

    (ii) a vessel restricted in her ability to maneuver.

(d)   (i) Any vessel other than a vessel not under command or a vessel restricted in her ability to maneuver shall, if the circumstances of the case admit, avoid impeding the safe passage of a vessel constrained by her draught, exhibiting the signals in Rule 28.

    (ii) A vessel constrained by her draught shall navigate with particular caution having full regard to her special condition.

(e) A seaplane on the water shall, in general, keep well clear of all vessels and avoid impeding their navigation. In circumstances, however, where risk of collision exists, she shall comply with the Rules of this Part.

(f)   (i) A WIG craft shall, when taking off, landing and in flight near the surface, keep well clear of all other vessels and avoid impeding their navigation.

    (ii) A WIG craft operating on the water surface shall comply with the Rules of this Part as a power-driven vessel.

A.2   Collision Avoidance Patterns

Here we present collision avoidance patterns as presented in text books for student sailors, e.g. Overschmidt & Gliewe (2006) or Bark (2006). The patterns are presented in Table A.2 and Table A.3 and the associated legend in Table A.1.

Icon	Declaration	Abbreviation
	Sports vessel of 20m or more in length	S20
	Power driven vessel (motor vessel)	MV
	Sailing vessel with wind from starbord	SVs
	Sailing vessel with wind from port	SVp
	Sailing vessel with additional engine	SVm
	Vessel empowered by muscular strength (rowing vessel)	RV
	Wind direction	
	Stand-on vessel	
	Give-way vessel	

Table A.1: The legend for Table A.2 and Table A.3.

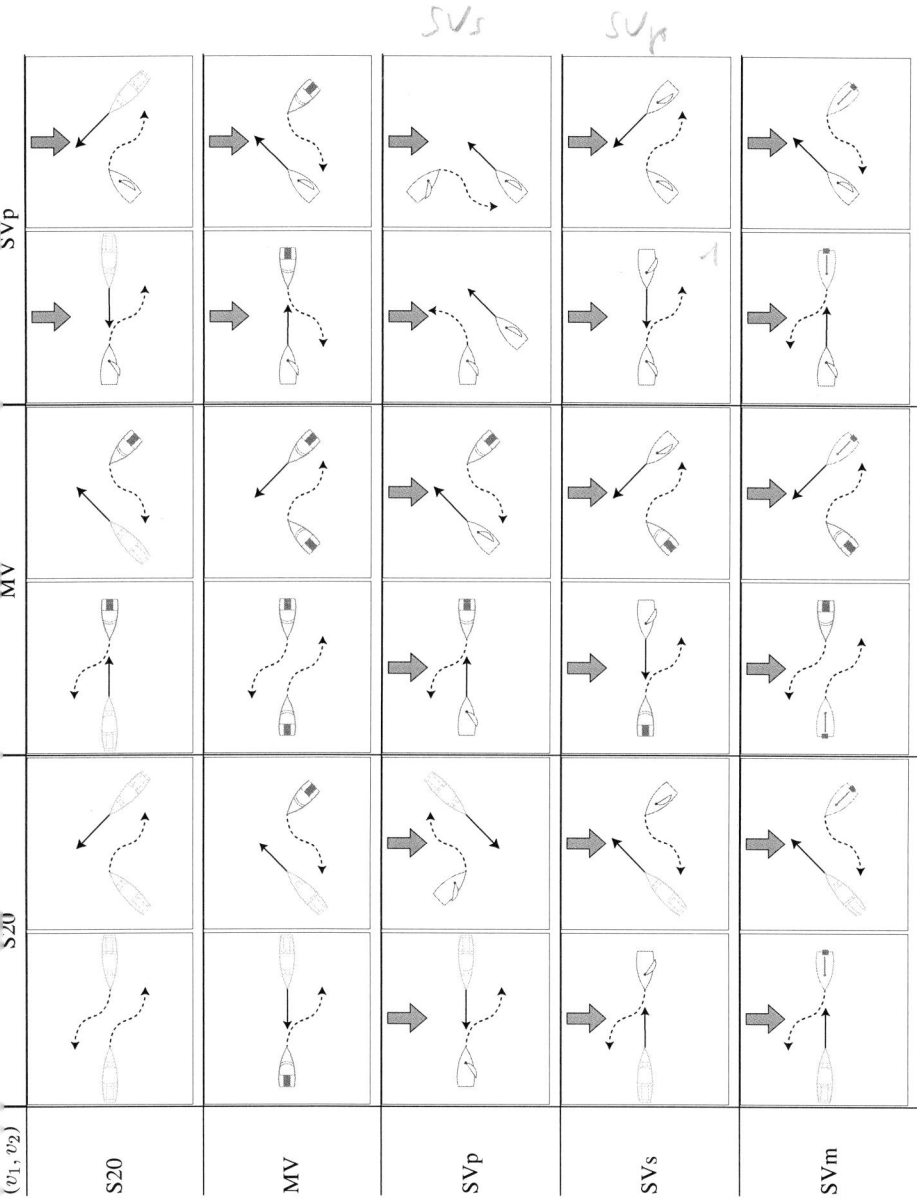

Table A.2: Part I: An iconic representation of right-of-way rules for pairs of vessels regarding the types of the vessels (v_1, v_2). For abbreviations of types confer Table A.1.

Table A.3: Part II: An iconic representation of right-of-way rules for pairs of vessels regarding the types of the vessels (v_1, v_2). For abbreviations of types confer Table A.1.

Bibliography

Adams, J. A. (1961). Human tracking behavior. *Psychological Bulletin*, 58(1):55–79.

Allen, J. F. (1983). Maintaining knowledge about temporal intervals. *Communications of the ACM*, (pp. 832–843).

Balbiani, P. & Condotta, J.-F. (2002). Spatial reasoning about points in a multidimensional setting. *Applied Intelligence*, 17(3):221–238.

Balbiani, P. & Osmani, A. (2000). A model for reasoning about topologic relations between cyclic intervals. In A. G. Cohn, F. Giunchiglia, & B. Selman (eds.), *KR2000: Principles of Knowledge Representation and Reasoning*, (pp. 378–385). San Francisco: Morgan Kaufmann.

Balbiani, P., Condotta, J.-F., & del Cerro, L. F. (1998). A model for reasoning about bidimensional temporal relations. In A. G. Cohn, L. Schubert, & S. C. Shapiro (eds.), *KR'98: Principles of Knowledge Representation and Reasoning*, (pp. 124–130). San Francisco, California: Morgan Kaufmann.

Balbiani, P., Condotta, J.-F., & del Cerro, L. F. (1999a). A new tractable subclass of the rectangle algebra. In *16th International Joint Conference on Articial Intelligence*, (pp. 442–447).

Balbiani, P., Condotta, J.-F., & del Cerro, L. F. (1999b). A tractable subclass of the block algebra: Constraint propagation and preconvex relations. In *Portuguese Conference on Artificial Intelligence*, (pp. 75–89).

Bark, A. (2006). *Sportküstenschifferschein + Sportbootführerschein See*. Delius Klasing. (in German) ISBN: 3-7688-1136-0.

van Beek, P. (1992). Reasoning about qualitative temporal information. *Artificial Intelligence*, 58(1-3):297–321.

Beetz, M., Kirchlechner, B., & Lames, M. (2005). Computerized real-time analysis of football games. *IEEE Pervasive Computing*, 4(3):33–39.

Bennett, B. (1997). *Logical Representations for Automated Reasoning about Spatial Relationships*. Ph.D. thesis, School of Computer Studies, The University of Leeds.

Bennett, B. & Galton, A. P. (2004). A unifying semantics for time and events. *Artificial Intelligence*, 153(1-2):13–48.

Bik, A. & Wijshoff, H. (1995). Implementation of Fourier-Motzkin elimination. In *Proceedings of the first annual conference of the ASCI*, (pp. 377–386). Netherlands.

Billen, R. & Clementini, E. (2004). *Advances in Database Technology - EDBT 2004*, vol. 2992 of *LNCS*, chap. A Model for Ternary Projective Relations between Regions, (pp. 310–328). Springer Berlin / Heidelberg.

Clementini, E. & Billen, R. (2006). Modeling and computing ternary projective relations between regions. *IEEE Transactions on Knowledge and Data Engineering*, 18(6):799–814.

Clementini, E., Felice, P. D., & Hernandez, D. (1997). Qualitative representation of positional information. *Artificial Intelligence*, 95(2):317–356.

Cohn, A. G. (1997). Qualitative spatial representation and reasoning techniques. In G. Brewka, C. Habel, & B. Nebel (eds.), *KI-97: 21st Annual German Conference on Artificial Intelligence*, vol. 1303 of *Lecture Notes in Computer Science*, (pp. 1–30). Berlin: Springer.

Cohn, A. G. & Hazarika, S. M. (2001a). Continuous transitions in mereotopology. In *Commonsense-2001: 5th Symposium on Logical Formalizations of Commonsense Reasoning*.

Cohn, A. G. & Hazarika, S. M. (2001b). Qualitative spatial representation and reasoning: An overview. *Fundamenta Informaticae*, 46(1-2):1–29.

Condotta, J.-F., Saade, M., & Ligozat, G. (2006). A generic toolkit for n-ary qualitative temporal and spatial calculi. In *TIME '06: Proceedings of the Thirteenth International Symposium on Temporal Representation and Reasoning (TIME'06)*, (pp. 78–86). Washington, DC, USA: IEEE Computer Society.

Davis, E. (2001). Continuous shape transformation and metrics of shape. In *Fundamenta Informaticae*, vol. 46, (pp. 31–54). Amsterdam, The Netherlands, The Netherlands: IOS Press.

Dechter, R., Meiri, I., & Pearl, J. (1991). Temporal constraint networks. *Artificial Intelligence*, 49(1-3):61–95.

Dylla, F. & Moratz, R. (2004). Empirical complexity issues of practical qualitative spatial reasoning about relative position. In *Workshop on Spatial and Temporal Reasoning at ECAI 2004*, (pp. 37–46). Valencia, Spain.

Dylla, F. & Moratz, R. (2005). Exploiting qualitative spatial neighborhoods in the situation calculus. In C. Freksa, M. Knauff, B. Krieg-Brückner, B. Nebel, & T. Barkowsky (eds.), *Spatial Cognition IV. Reasoning, Action, Interaction: International Conference Spatial Cognition 2004*, vol. 3343 of *Lecture Notes in Artificial Intelligence*, (pp. 304–322). Berlin, Heidelberg: Springer.

Dylla, F., Ferrein, A., Lakemeyer, G., Murray, J., Obst, O., Röfer, T., Stolzenburg, F., Visser, U., & Wagner, T. (2005). Towards a league-independent qualitative soccer theory for RoboCup. In D. Nardi, M. Riedmiller, C. Sammut, & J. Santos-Victor (eds.), *RoboCup 2004: Robot Soccer World Cup VIII*, vol. 3276 of *Lecture Notes in Artificial Intelligence*, (pp. 611–618). Berlin, Heidelberg, New York: Springer.

Dylla, F., Frommberger, L., Wallgrün, J. O., & Wolter, D. (2006). SparQ: A toolbox for qualitative spatial representation and reasoning. In *Proceedings of the Workshop on Qualitative Constraint Calculi: Application and Integration at KI 2006*, (pp. 79–90). Bremen, Germany.

Egenhofer, M. J. & Sharma, J. (1993). Topological relations between regions in r^2 and z^2. In *SSD '93: Proceedings of the Third International Symposium on Advances in Spatial Databases*, (pp. 316–336). London, UK: Springer-Verlag.

Eschenbach, C., Habel, C., & Kulik, L. (1999). Representing simple trajectories as oriented curves. In A. Kumar & I. Russell (eds.), *Proceedings of the 12th International FLAIRS Conference*, (pp. 431–436). Orlando, Florida: AAAI Press.

Escrig, M. T. & Toledo, F. (1998). A framework based on CLP extended with CHRs for reasoning with qualitative orientation and positional information. *Journal of Visual Languages and Computing*, 9(1):881–101.

Fajen, B. R. & Warren, W. H. (2004). Visual guidance of intercepting a moving target on foot. *Perception*, 33(6):689–715.

Ferrein, A., Fritz, C., & Lakemeyer, G. (2005). Using Golog for deliberation and team coordination in robotic soccer. *KI Künstliche Intelligenz*, 19(1):24–43.

Forbus, K. D. (1980). Spatial and qualitative aspects of reasoning about motion. In *First Annual National Conference on Artificial Intelligence (AAAI-80)*, (pp. 170–173). Stanford, California.

Forbus, K. D. (1981). Qualitative reasoning about physical processes. In P. J. Hayes (ed.), *Proceedings of the 7th International Joint Conference on Artificial Intelligence (IJCAI '81), Vancouver, BC, Canada, August 1981*, (pp. 326–330). William Kaufmann.

Forbus, K. D. (1984). Qualitative process theory. *Artificial Intelligence*, 24(1-3):85–168.

Forbus, K. D. (1990). Qualitative physics: Past, present, and future. *Readings in qualitative reasoning about physical systems*, (pp. 11–39).

Forbus, K. D., Nielsen, P., & Faltings, B. (1990). Qualitative kinematics: A framework. *Readings in qualitative reasoning about physical systems*, (pp. 559–567).

Fox, D., Thrun, S., Burgard, W., & Dellaert, F. (2001). Particle filters for mobile robot localization. In *Sequential Monte Carlo Methods in Practice*, (pp. 401–428). New York: Springer.

Frank, A. (1991). Qualitative spatial reasoning about cardinal directions. In *Proceedings of the American Congress on Surveying and Mapping (ACSM-ASPRS)*, (pp. 148–167). Baltimore, Maryland, USA.

Frank, A. U. (1992). Qualitative spatial reasoning about distances and directions in geographic space. *Journal of Visual Languages and Computing*, 3:343–371.

Fraser, G., Steinbauer, G., & Wotawa, F. (2004). Application of qualitative reasoning to robotic soccer. In *18th International Workshop on Qualitative Reasoning*, (pp. 173–178). Illinois, USA.

Freksa, C. (1991). Conceptual neighborhood and its role in temporal and spatial reasoning. In M. G. Singh & L. Travé-Massuyès (eds.), *Proceedings of the IMACS Workshop on Decision Support Systems and Qualitative Reasoning*, (pp. 181–187). North-Holland, Amsterdam: Elsevier.

Freksa, C. (1992a). Temporal reasoning based on semi-intervals. *Artificial Intelligence*, 1(54):199–227.

Freksa, C. (1992b). Using orientation information for qualitative spatial reasoning. In A. U. Frank, I. Campari, & U. Formentini (eds.), *Theories and methods of spatio-temporal reasoning in geographic space*, (pp. 162–178). Berlin: Springer.

Freksa, C. (2004). Spatial cognition – An AI perspective. In *Proceedings of 16th European Conference on AI (ECAI 2004)*.

Freksa, C. & Röhrig, R. (1993). Dimensions of qualitative spatial reasoning. In N. P. Carreté & M. G. Singh (eds.), *Proceedings of the III IMACS International Workshop on Qualitative Reasoning and Decision Technologies – QUARDET'93*, (pp. 483–492). CIMNE Barcelona.

Freksa, C. & Zimmermann, K. (1993). On the utilization of spatial structures for cognitively plausible and efficient reasoning. In F. A. H. Güsgen & J. v.Benthem (eds.), *Proc. of the Workshop on Spatial and Temporal Reasoning*, IJCAI 93, (pp. 61–66). Chambery.

Frommberger, L., Lee, J. H., Wallgrün, J. O., & Dylla, F. (2007). Composition in $\mathcal{OPRA}_m$. *Tech. Rep. 013-02/2007*, SFB/TR 8 Spatial Cognition; http://www.sfbtr8.uni-bremen.de/.

Galton, A. (1999). The mereotopology of discrete space. In *COSIT '99: Proceedings of the International Conference on Spatial Information Theory: Cognitive and Computational Foundations of Geographic Information Science*, (pp. 251–266). London, UK: Springer-Verlag.

Galton, A. (2000a). Continuous motion in discrete space. In A. Cohn, F. Giunchiglia, & B. Selman (eds.), *Proc. 7th Internat. Conf. on Principles of Knowledge Representation and Reasoning (KR2000)*, (pp. 26–37). San Francisco, CA: Morgan Kaufmann.

Galton, A. (2000b). *Qualitative Spatial Change*. Oxford University Press.

Ghose, K., Horiuchi, T. K., Krishnaprasad, P. S., & Moss, C. F. (2006). Echolocating bats use a nearly time-optimal strategy to intercept prey. *PLoS Computational Biology*, 4(5). E108 doi:10.1371/journal.pbio.0040108.

Goyal, R. K. & Egenhofer, M. J. (2001). Similarity of cardinal directions. In *7th Int. Symposium on Spatial and Temporal Databases (SSTD01)*, vol. 2121 of *Lecture Notes in Computer Science*, (pp. 36–55).

Guesgen, H. W. (1989). Spatial reasoning based on allen's temporal logic. *Tech. rep.*, International Computer Science Institute.

Hayes, P. J. (1978). The naive physics manifesto. In D. Michie (ed.), *Expert Systems in the Micro-Electronic Age*, (pp. 242–270). Edinburgh: Edinburgh University Press.

Hayes, P. J. (1985a). Naive physics i: Ontology for liquids. In J. R. Hobbs & R. C. Moore (eds.), *Formal Theories of the Commonsense World*, (pp. 71–107). Norwood, NJ: Ablex.

Hayes, P. J. (1985b). The second naive physics manifesto. In J. R. Hobbs & R. C. Moore (eds.), *Formal Theories of the Commonsense World*, (pp. 1–36). Norwood, NJ: Ablex.

Hornsby, K. & Egenhofer, M. J. (2000). Identity-based change: A foundation for spatio-temporal knowledge representation. *International Journal of Geographical Information Science*, 14(3):207–224.

Hornsby, K. & Egenhofer, M. J. (2002). Modeling moving objects over multiple granularities. *Annals of Mathematics and Artificial Intelligence*, 36(1-2):177–194.

IMO (1972). International regulations for preventing collisions at sea 1972 (ColRegs). International Maritime Organization (IMO). Adopted 2001.

Isli, A. & Cohn, A. G. (1998). An algebra for cyclic ordering of 2d orientations. In *AAAI/IAAI*, (pp. 643–649). Madison, WI.

Isli, A. & Cohn, A. G. (2000). A new approach to cyclic ordering of 2d orientations using ternary relation algebras. *Artificial Intelligence*, 122(1-2):137–187.

Isli, A. & Moratz, R. (1999). Qualitative spatial representation and reasoning: Algebraic models for relative position. *Tech. Rep. FBI-HH-M-284/99*, Fachbereich Informatik, Universität Hamburg.

Isli, A., Haarslev, V., & Möller, R. (2001). Combining cardinal direction relations and relative orientation relations in qualitative spatial reasoning. *Tech. Rep. FBI-HH-M-304/01*, Fachbereich Informatik, Universität Hamburg.

Israel, D. (1985). A short companion to the naive physics manifesto. In J. R. Hobbs & R. C. Moore (eds.), *Formal Theories of the Commonsense World*, (pp. 427–447). Norwood, NJ: Ablex.

Johnson, M. (1987). *The Body in the Mind*. Chicago, USA: University of Chicago Press.

Kessler, C. W. (1996). Parallel Fourier-Motzkin elimination. In *Proc. of Euro-Par'96*, (pp. 66–71). Lyon, France.

Klatzky, R. L. (1998). Allocentric and egocentric spatial representations: Definitions, distinctions, and interconnections. In *Spatial Cognition, An Interdisciplinary Approach to Representing and Processing Spatial Knowledge*, (pp. 1–18). London, UK: Springer-Verlag.

Krieg-Brückner, B. & Shi, H. (2006). Orientation calculi and route graphs: Towards semantic representations for route descriptions. In *Proceedings of GIScience 2006*. To appear.

Kuipers, B. (1994). *Qualitative Reasoning: Modeling and simulation with incomplete knowledge*. Cambridge, Massachusetts, USA: MIT Press.

Kuipers, B. (2000). The spatial semantic hierarchy. *Artificial Intelligence*, 119:191–233.

Kuipers, B. & Byun, Y. (1991). A robot exploration and mapping strategy based on a semantic hierarchy of spatial representations. *Journal of Robotics and Autonomous Systems*, 8:47–63.

Kuipers, B. J. (1977). Representing knowledge of large-scale space. *Tech. Rep. 418*, Massachusetts Institute of Technology, Cambridge, MA, USA.

Ladkin, P. & Reinefeld, A. (1992). Effective solution of qualitative constraint problems. *Artificial Intelligence*, 57:105–124.

Levinson, S. C. (1996). Frames of reference and Molyneux's question. In P. Bloom, M. A. Peterson, L. Nadel, & M. F. Garrett (eds.), *Language and Space*, (pp. 109–169). Cambridge, MA: MIT Press.

Levinson, S. C. (2003). *Space in language and cognition: explorations in cognitive diversity*. Cambridge, MA: Cambridge University Press.

Ligozat, G. (1991). On generalized interval calculi. In *AAAI-91*, (pp. 234–240).

Ligozat, G. (1993). Qualitative triangulation for spatial reasoning. In A. U. Frank & I. Campari (eds.), *Spatial Information Theory: A Theoretical Basis for GIS, (COSIT'93), Marciana Marina, Elba Island, Italy*, vol. 716 of *Lecture Notes in Computer Science*, (pp. 54–68). Springer.

Ligozat, G. (1998). Reasoning about cardinal directions. *Journal of Visual Languages and Computing*, 9:23–44.

Ligozat, G. (2005). Categorical methods in qualitative reasoning: The case for weak representations. In A. G. Cohn & D. M. Mark (eds.), *COSIT*, vol. 3693 of *Lecture Notes in Computer Science*, (pp. 265–282). Springer.

Ligozat, G. & Renz, J. (2004). What is a qualitative calculus? A general framework. In C. Zhang, H. W. Guesgen, & W.-K. Yeap (eds.), *PRICAI 2004: Trends in Artificial Intelligence, 8th Pacific RimInternational Conference on Artificial Intelligence, Auckland, New Zealand, Proceedings*, vol. 3157 of *Lecture Notes in Computer Science*, (pp. 53–64). Springer.

Liu, J. (1998). A method of spatial reasoning based on qualitative trigonometry. *Artificial Intelligence*, 98(1-2):137–168.

McCarthy, J. & Hayes, P. J. (1969). Some philosophical problems from the standpoint of artificial intelligence. *Meltzer and Michie, Machine Intelligence 4*, (pp. 463–502).

Miene, A. & Visser, U. (2002). Interpretation of spatio-temporal relations in real-time and dynamic environments. In *RoboCup 2001: Robot Soccer World Cup V*, (pp. 441–447). London, UK: Springer-Verlag.

Miene, A., Visser, U., & Herzog, O. (2003). Recognition and prediction of motion situations based on a qualitative motion description. In D. Polani, B. Browning, A. Bonarini, & K. Yoshida (eds.), *RoboCup 2003: Robot Soccer World Cup VII*, vol. 3020 of *Lecture Notes in Computer Science*. Springer Verlag.

Montemerlo, M., Thrun, S., Koller, D., & Wegbreit, B. (2003). FastSLAM 2.0: An improved particle filtering algorithm for simultaneous localization and mapping that provably converges. In *International Joint Conference on AI*, (pp. 1151–1156).

Moratz, R. (2006). Representing relative direction as a binary relation of oriented points. In G. Brewka, S. Coradeschi, A. Perini, & P. Traverso (eds.), *ECAI*, (pp. 407–411). Riva del Garda, Italy: IOS Press.

Moratz, R. (2007). A granular point position calculus for solving ambiguous landmark problems in cognitive robotics. In *Proceedings of the AISB'07 Artificial and Ambient Intelligence Symposium on Spatial Reasoning and Communication*.

Moratz, R. & Freksa, C. (1998). Spatial reasoning with uncertain data using stochastic relaxation. In W. Brauer (ed.), *Fuzzy-Neuro Systems 98*, (pp. 106–112). Infix; Sankt Augustin.

Moratz, R. & Ragni, M. (2008). Qualitative spatial reasoning about relative point position. *Journal of Visual Languages and Computing*. To appear.

Moratz, R., Renz, J., & Wolter, D. (2000). Qualitative spatial reasoning about line segments. In W. Horn (ed.), *Proceedings of the 14th European Conference on Artificial Intelligence (ECAI)*. Berlin, Germany: IOS Press.

Moratz, R., Tenbrink, T., Bateman, J., & Fischer, K. (2002). Spatial knowledge representation for human-robot interaction. In C. Freksa, W. Brauer, C. Habel, & K. F. Wender (eds.), *Spatial Cognition III*, (pp. 263–286). Berlin, Heidelberg: Springer.

Moratz, R., Nebel, B., & Freksa, C. (2003). Qualitative spatial reasoning about relative position: The tradeoff between strong formal properties and successful reasoning about route graphs. In C. Freksa, W. Brauer, C. Habel, & K. F. Wender (eds.), *Spatial Cognition III*, vol. 2685 of *Lecture Notes in Artificial Intelligence*, (pp. 385–400). Berlin, Heidelberg: Springer.

Moratz, R., Dylla, F., & Frommberger, L. (2005). A relative orientation algebra with adjustable granularity. In *Proceedings of the Workshop on Agents in Real-Time and Dynamic Environments (IJCAI 05)*, (pp. 61–70). Edinburgh, Scotland.

Moreira, J., Ribeiro, C., & Saglio, J. (1999). Representation and manipulation of moving points: An extended data model for location estimation. *Cartography and Geographical Information Systems*, 26(2):109–123.

Muller, P. (1998a). A qualitative theory of motion based on spatio-temporal primitives. In A. G. Cohn, L. Schubert, & S. C. Shapiro (eds.), *KR'98: Principles of Knowledge Representation and Reasoning*, (pp. 131–141). San Francisco, California: Morgan Kaufmann.

Muller, P. (1998b). Space-time as a primitive for space and motion. In N. Guarino (ed.), *1st Int. Conf. (FOIS-98), Frontiers in AI and Applications*, vol. 46, (pp. 63–76). IOS Press.

Murphy, R. R. (2000). *Introduction to AI Robotics*. Cambridge, MA, USA: MIT Press.

Olberg, R. M., Worthington, A. H., & Venator, K. R. (2000). Prey pursuit and interception in dragonflies. *Journal of Comparative Physiology A: Neuroethology, Sensory,
Neural, and Behavioral Physiology*, 186(2):155–162.

Overschmidt, H. & Gliewe, R. (2006). *Sportbootführerschein Binnen (Segel, Motor)*.
Bielefeld, Germany: Delius Klasing Verlag GmbH. (in German) ISBN: 978-3-7688-
0657-2.

Papadias, D. & Theodoridis, Y. (1997). Spatial relations, minimum bounding rectangles, and spatial data structures. *International Journal of Geographical Information
Science*, 11(2):111–138.

Pinto, J. (1998). Integrating discrete and continuous change in a logical framework.
Computational Intelligence, 14:39–88.

Pujari, A. K. & Sattar, A. (1999). A new framework for reasoning about points, inter-
vals and durations. In *IJCAI '99: Proceedings of the Sixteenth International Joint
Conference on Artificial Intelligence*, (pp. 1259–1267). San Francisco, CA, USA:
Morgan Kaufmann Publishers Inc.

Rajagopalan, R. (1994). A model for integrated qualitative spatial and dynamic reasoning about physical systems. In *National Conference on Artificial Intelligence*,
(pp. 1411–1417).

Randell, D. A., Cui, Z., & Cohn, A. (1992). A spatial logic based on regions and
connection. In B. Nebel, C. Rich, & W. Swartout (eds.), *Principles of Knowledge
Representation and Reasoning: Proceedings of the Third International Conference
(KR'92)*, (pp. 165–176). San Mateo, CA: Morgan Kaufmann.

Renz, J. (2001). A spatial odyssey of the interval algebra: 1. Directed intervals. In
B. Nebel (ed.), *IJCAI*, (pp. 51–56). Morgan Kaufmann.

Renz, J. (2002). *Qualitative Spatial Reasoning with Topological Information*. No.
2293 in Lecture Notes in Computer Science. New York, NY, USA: Springer-Verlag
New York, Inc.

Renz, J. & Ligozat, G. (2005). Weak composition for qualitative spatial and temporal
reasoning. In *Proceedings of the 11th International Conference on Principles and
Practice of Constraint Programming (CP 2005)*, (pp. 534–548). Sitges (Barcelona),
Spain.

Renz, J. & Mitra, D. (2004). Qualitative direction calculi with arbitrary granularity.
In C. Zhang, H. W. Guesgen, & W.-K. Yeap (eds.), *PRICAI 2004: Trends in Artificial Intelligence, 8th Pacific RimInternational Conference on Artificial Intelligence,
Auckland, New Zealand, Proceedings*, vol. 3157 of *Lecture Notes in Computer Science*, (pp. 65–74). Springer.

Retz-Schmidt, G. (1988). Various views on spatial prepositions. *AI Mag.*, 9(2):95–105.

Riedel, B. (2003). *Die Entwicklung von Ähnlichkeitsmaßen für den Vergleich von Spielsituationen im RoboCup (in german)*. Master's thesis, Knowledge-based Systems Group, RWTH Aachen, Germany.

Röfer, T. (1999). Route navigation using motion analysis. In C. Freksa & D. M. Mark (eds.), *Spatial Information Theory: Foundations of Geographic Information Science. Conference on Spatial Information Theory (COSIT)*, (pp. 21–36). Springer, Berlin.

Röhrig, R. (1994). A theory for qualitative spatial reasoning based on order relations. In *AAAI'94: Proceedings of the twelfth national conference on Artificial intelligence (vol. 2)*, (pp. 1418–1423). Menlo Park, CA, USA: American Association for Artificial Intelligence.

Russell, B. (1903). *Principles of Mathematics*. Cambridge University Press. Second edition, published by Norton, New York.

Schiffer, S. (2005). *ReadyWorld - A Qualitative Worldmodel for Autonomous Soccer Agents in the ReadyLog Framework*. Master's thesis, Knowledge-based Systems Group, RWTH Aachen, Germany.

Schiffer, S., Ferrein, A., & Lakemeyer, G. (2006). Qualitative world models for soccer robots. In S. Wölfl & T. Mossakowski (eds.), *Qualitative Constraint Calculi, Workshop at KI 2006*, (pp. 3–14). Bremen, Germany.

Schlieder, C. (1993). Representing visible locations for qualitative navigation. In N. Piera-Carrete & M. Singh (eds.), *Qualitative reasoning and decision technologies*, (pp. 523–532). Barcelona: CIMNE.

Schlieder, C. (1995). Reasoning about ordering. In *Proc. of COSIT'95*, vol. 988 of *Lecture Notes in Computer Science*, (pp. 341–349). Berlin, Heidelberg: Springer.

Schrijver, A. (1989). *Theory of Linear and Integer Programming*. John Wiley & Sons.

Scivos, A. & Nebel, B. (2001). Double-crossing: Decidability and computational complexity of a qualitative calculus for navigation. In *Spatial Information Theory: Foundations of Geographic Information Science (COSIT-2001)*, (pp. 431–446). Morro Bay, CA: Springer, Berlin.

Scivos, A. & Nebel, B. (2005). The finest of its class: The practical natural point-based ternary calculus $\mathcal{LR}$ for qualitative spatial reasoning. In C. Freksa, M. Knauff, B. Krieg-Brückner, B. Nebel, & T. Barkowsky (eds.), *Spatial Cognition IV. Reasoning, Action, Interaction: International Conference Spatial Cognition 2004*, vol. 3343 of *Lecture Notes in Artificial Intelligence*, (pp. 283–303). Berlin, Heidelberg: Springer.

Steinbauer, G., Weber, J., & Wotawa, F. (2005). From the real-world to its qualitative representation – practical lessons learned. In R. B., H. M., & W. F. (eds.), *International Workshop on Qualitative Reasoning*, (pp. 186–191). Graz, Austria.

Stolzenburg, F., Obst, O., & Murray, J. (2002). Qualitative velocity and ball interception. In M. Jarke, J. Koehler, & G. Lakemeyer (eds.), *KI-2002: Advances in Artificial Intelligence – Proceedings of the 25th Annual German Conference on Artificial Intelligence*, vol. 2479 of *Lecture Notes in Artificial Intelligence*, (pp. 95–99). Aachen: Springer, Berlin, Heidelberg, New York.

Vilain, M., Kautz, H., & van Beek, P. (1990). Constraint propagation algorithms for temporal reasoning: A revised report. In D. S. Weld & J. de Kleer (eds.), *Readings in qualitative reasoning about physical systems*, (pp. 373–381). San Francisco, CA, USA: Morgan Kaufmann, San Mateo, CA.

Vilain, M. B. & Kautz, H. A. (1986). Constraint propagation algorithms for temporal reasoning. In *AAAI*, (pp. 377–382).

Wallgrün, J. O., Frommberger, L., Wolter, D., Dylla, F., & Freksa, C. (2006). A toolbox for qualitative spatial representation and reasoning. In *Spatial Cognition V: Reasoning, Action, Interaction: International Conference Spatial Cognition*, (pp. 79–90). Bremen, Germany.

van de Weghe, N. (2004). *Representing and Reasoning about Moving Objects: A Qualitative Approach*. Ph.D. thesis, Ghent University, Belgium.

van de Weghe, N., Kuijpers, B., Bogaert, P., & Maeyer, P. (2005). A qualitative trajectory calculus and the composition of its relations. In *First International Conference on GeoSpatial Semantics (GeoS 2005)*, vol. 3799, (pp. 181–211). Springer.

Weld, D. S. & de Kleer, J. (eds.) (1990). *Readings in qualitative reasoning about physical systems*. San Francisco, CA, USA: Morgan Kaufmann Publishers Inc.

Worboys, M. (2001). Modelling changes and events in dynamic spatial systems with reference to socio-economic units. In A. Frank, J. Raper, & J.-P. Cheylan (eds.), *Life and Motion of Socio-Economic Units*, no. 8 in ESF GISDATA, (pp. 129–138). Taylor and Francis.

Worboys, M. F. (2005). Event-oriented approaches to geographic phenomena. *International Journal of Geographical Information Science*, 19:1–28.

Zimbardo, P. G. (1988). *Psychology and Life*. Scott, Foresman and Company, Glenview, Illinois.

Zimmermann, K. (1993). Enhancing qualitative spatial reasoning – combining orientation and distance. In *Spatial Information Theory: a theoretical basis for GIS*, no. 716 in Lecture Notes in Computer Science, (pp. 69–76). Springer Verlag.

Zimmermann, K. (1995). Measuring without measures: The delta-calculus. In A. U. Frank & W. Kuhn (eds.), *Spatial Information Theory: A Theoretical Basis for GIS, International Conference COSIT '95, Semmering, Austria*, vol. 988 of *Lecture Notes in Computer Science*, (pp. 59–67). Springer.

Zimmermann, K. & Freksa, C. (1993). Enhancing spatial reasoning by the concept of motion. In A. Sloman (ed.), *Prospects for Articial Intelligence*, (pp. 140–147). IOS Press.

Zimmermann, K. & Freksa, C. (1996). Qualitative spatial reasoning using orientation, distance, and path knowledge. *Applied Intelligence*, 6:49–58.

Dissertationen zur Künstlichen Intelligenz

Weitere Titel aus dieser Reihe / Available in the same series

Gesamtverzeichnis und Autoren-Info www.aka-verlag.com oder info@aka-verlag.de